PENGUIN BOOKS

THE VOYAGE OF THE ARMADA

David Howarth, historian of Waterloo, the Norman Conquest, and other turning points in history, lives and writes in Sussex, England. His other books are *1066: The Year of the Conquest* (also published by Penguin Books); *The Greek Adventure; Sovereign of the Seas; Trafalgar; A Near Run Thing; The Golden Isthmus; The Desert King: A Life of Ibn Saud; The Shadow of the Dam; Dawn of D-Day; The Sledge Patrol; We Die Alone (Escape Alone);* and *The Shetland Bus.*

The Chanell of Bristol

HONI SOIT MAL Y PENSE

The lands ende of En
& openeth when you
Spanish

According to this manner Ap
North West & by Wes

St Iust

Lezard.

PENSANCE

The landes ende
S Burien
Newlyn
Mousbay.
Boskenna
Lamorley point
S. Michaels
mount.

Seuen stones

THE SORLINGES

The gulfe

THE CHANELL

THE SEA COASTES
of England, from the Sor=
linges by the landes end to
Plymouth with the hauens
and harbroughes

pening of the *Iles* called the *Sorlinges*
North East from you two leagues

The saide *Iles*, when they lye South East from you
aboutes two leagues

The Easterne Coast of
Englands ende when it
lyeth East North East
from you three leagues

The Lizard or Cape of Cornewall
as it appeareth when the West ende
therof lyeth North West from you
aleague, and the East ende North
two leagues

Falemouth, when the Castell lyeth North West
& by West from you; And Dudmans poynt
North from you, three leagues

the lande or Coaste of Lizard, Falemouth, & Dudmans poynt when the Castel is South East
two leagues, and likewise Dudmans poynt three leagues from you Northewardes

Falemouth,

Dudman poynt.

Pendennis castell

Treuro

Limehouse

GLIÆ   PARS

Plymmouth

Milbrooke

Edgcome

Mylles

Mylles pool

Maker

S. Nicholas

Foye

Haule

Bank

Low

Ramhead

Talyn

Tallant poynt.

Ide stone

Mewstone

Dudman poynt

SEPTENTRIO

Kanaden
poynt

30 ENGLAND AND FRAVNCE 30

ORIENS

Theodore de Bry fecit

Englishe leagues 20 in a degree
Spanishe leagues 17½ in a degree
Dutche leagues 15 in a degree

The Ile of Wight as it appeareth when you sayle there alongst two leagues of

The needles.   Welburton

A N G L

Peele
Ely
Eling
Hamp
ton
Vpham
Titchfeld
Porcheslee
Southwork
Falley
Lemington
Portesmouth
Stansted
Arrundel
Amus
Shingle
Southsea
cast
Codlow
Standerest
Bayes
Hurst cast
Chilfey
Terry
The needles.
Cosbrok
Ryde
Newport
Sinun
Elong
poinet
Shorum
WIGHT
Welburton
Culuer Clif
Donnose

THE CHANELL BETWEENE

35

English leagues 20 in a degree
Spanish leagues 17½ in a degree
Dutch leagues 15 in a degree

of the land or Coast of Beache
seuen Cliffes or hilles

The land & Coast of Hastinges when you sayle there
alongst

Æ · P A R S

Lewes

Cattespret · Rhoterbrudg

Arlington

Battel · Hastinges

Offerle
Cukemere hauen
Pemsey

Faierlighte

Winchelsey

Rhother flumen

Aylestowre

Rye

Rumney

lyd

The nesse poynt

Hyde Cas

Lymninge

Dover

ENGLAND · AND · FRAVNCE

THE SEA COASTES OF ENGLAND
betweene the Ile of Wight & Douer, with
the principal hauens thereof according
to their situation and Appearing

THE VOYAGE
OF THE ARMADA

The Spanish Story

DAVID HOWARTH

PENGUIN BOOKS

Penguin Books Ltd, Harmondsworth,
Middlesex, England
Penguin Books, 625 Madison Avenue,
New York, New York 10022, U.S.A.
Penguin Books Australia Ltd, Ringwood,
Victoria, Australia
Penguin Books Canada Limited, 2801 John Street,
Markham, Ontario, Canada L3R 1B4
Penguin Books (N.Z.) Ltd, 182–190 Wairau Road,
Auckland 10, New Zealand

First published in the United States of America by
The Viking Press 1981
Published in Penguin Books 1982

LIBRARY OF CONGRESS CATALOGING IN PUBLICATION DATA
Howarth, David Armine, 1912–
    The voyage of the Armada.
    Reprint. Originally published: New York: Viking
Press, 1981.
    Bibliography: p.
    Includes index.
    1. Armada, 1588.   2. Spain—History—Philip II,
1556–1598.   I. Title.
DA360.H68   1982   946'.04   82-9123
ISBN 0 14 00.6315 3   AACR2

Printed in the United States of America by
R. R. Donnelley & Sons Company, Harrisonburg, Virginia
Set in Garamond

Contents

Illustrations

Preface

In 1884 a Spanish naval captain, Cesareo Fernandez Duro, published one hundred and ninety-nine letters and documents of the sixteenth century which he had discovered in the royal archives. Between them they told a story of how and why the Spanish armada made its voyage, which had been unknown before. A selection of them was published in English in 1899, in Volume IV of the Calendar of Letters and State Papers. In 1892, the British historian James Anthony Froude used them to write a long essay, in which he said, 'When the asperities of theology shall have mellowed down at last, Spanish and English authorities together will furnish materials for a great epic poem.'

After nearly a century, that time has surely come, although the taste for epic poems has gone. There cannot be many people who still take sides, either patriotic or theological, in the quarrels of the sixteenth century, although sadly similar quarrels still happen today. Yet Duro's discoveries have been only sparsely used in English history, and never used, so far as I know, to make a thorough narrative of the Spanish voyage. Most of what we are taught about the armada comes from English sources. Those were meagre, but were embellished by nineteenth-century historians, who wrote at the peak of British imperial pride and made the armada story into a national heroic tale which was far from true. For many years I have wanted to do what I could to put the balance right, and give whatever credit was due to the Spanish soldiers and sailors. After all, it was they who needed most courage in 1588: the English fought to defend their own shores, but the Spaniards ventured into unknown seas.

I have set deliberate limits to the story. It simply tells what happened on the voyage that began in May and ended in September, and the little that the soldiers and sailors knew of the reasons why they went. Mainly it comes from Duro's and later discoveries in the Spanish archives, and I have used contemporary English documents only to complete the picture. So it is a Spanish story; but I cannot entirely avoid judging things as a twentieth-century Englishman, and Spaniards might not agree with all my judgements, especially perhaps of King Philip. This is a perennial difficulty: one honestly tries to discard all personal prejudice and to respect all honest opinion; but in the end one is left with certain people one cannot admire – people who were themselves extremely prejudiced and had no respect for anyone else's opinion. King Philip was one of those.

I have tried, as I always do, to live up to a sentence from Robert Louis Stevenson's essay on The Morality of the Profession of Letters, which I read when I was a teenager and never quite forgot. 'In all narration,' he wrote, 'there is only one way to be clever, and that is to be exact.'

I

Exurge Domine

On Monday, 25th April 1588, before the sun was up, the squares of Lisbon were lined by seven companies of soldiers, armed with arquebus and musket, who had landed from a fleet of ships that lay at anchor in the river. There were tens of thousands of men in the fleet, and the landing party had been chosen as the best equipped and smartest of them all. But they had been standing around for most of the night. Unless they differed from all other soldiers they were grumbling as they stamped their feet in the chilly dew of dawn, and were asking each other what they were waiting for.

Before six o'clock they were called to attention. The palace gates were opened and a noble procession emerged. It was led on horseback by the Cardinal Archduke, the Viceroy in Portugal of King Philip of Spain. On his right hand rode the Duke of Medina Sidonia, Captain General of the High Seas and commander-in-chief of the fleet. Behind them were commanders whose names, within that year, were to enter not only Spanish history but English history too: Don Juan Martinez de Recalde, a veteran of many fights at sea; Don Pedro and Don Diego de Valdes, who were cousins but bitter enemies; Don Miguel de Oquendo, another revered sea-fighter; and Don Alonzo de Leyva, a cavalry soldier of Milan, appointed by the king to take command if any misfortune befell the duke. Behind them again, most if not all of the captains of the one hundred and thirty ships; and, far outnumbering the sea-captains and outmatching them in elegance, the senior officers of the army that was aboard. Somewhere towards the rear were a hundred or so young gentlemen-adventurers, valiantly dressed, who had joined in the hope of glory; and by contrast in their sombre habits, a hundred and eighty priests and friars appointed to the voyage that was ready to begin. One man was very conspicuously absent: King Philip, who had ordered the creation of the fleet, had not come to Lisbon to see it.

They marched to the cathedral, where the Archbishop of Portugal received them. The cardinal archduke accepted a royal standard from its bearer and placed it on the altar. Mass was sung, and the standard was consecrated. The archduke presented it to the Duke of Medina Sidonia, who took it with reverence; and at that moment a signal was given, the troops outside shot off their weapons and the ships in the river fired their guns in salute – only three guns from each ship, it was noted. They were saving their powder for battle.

The procession re-formed, headed now by the archbishop and the cathedral choir, and the standard was paraded through the streets by a bearer on a white horse. The duke symbolically held a fringe of it. Everyone saw it was embroidered with the royal arms of Spain. The figure of the Virgin Mother was on one side of the arms, and on the other the figure of Christ on the Cross; and below on a scroll were the words *Exurge Domine et Vindica Causam Tuam* – Arise O Lord and Vindicate Thy Cause.

When it had passed, the soldiers were marched back to the quays and taken in boats and shut up in their ships again. They were the only people who were supposed not to know what the fleet was for. A few weeks earlier the king himself had sent instructions that the soldiers and sailors had better be told they were going to the Indies. But for once his instructions were ignored; it was too late for deception. Everyone in Lisbon knew the truth. All over Europe, indeed, everyone of any consequence knew it: the fleet was bound for the conquest of England. The men who manned it had not been told a lie, as the king proposed. Officially, they had not been told anything at all. But even the most dim-witted of them had been discussing it for months. Without any information, their ideas of England, and of what they were in for, can only have been the vaguest: a cold, wet, windy and altogether unpleasant island far to the north – barbaric and said to be guilty of devilish heresies. Rumour said the conquest would be easy.

'The officers and officials,' one witness of this occasion wrote, 'were all very happy that the ceremony had gone well.' There are several accounts of it and all of them have these hints of uncertainty. Perhaps the hints were not intentional, but officials may have been worried that things might not go well. It was not because of the soldiers – they were well disciplined – though it certainly crossed people's minds that this might be a last chance for anyone who was thinking of deserting. It was the people of Lisbon who might have spoiled the show. No account of the procession mentions cheering crowds; for the fleet was Spanish, yet Lisbon was the capital of Portugal. The Archbishop of Portugal might ask God's blessing on the standard and the fleet's endeavours: both countries were united in the Catholic Church. But the boundaries of religion were not the same as the boundaries of politics and power, and the Portuguese were far from being Spanish in outlook or sympathy. It was only seven years since the King of Spain had seized the throne of Portugal and added the country to his vast dominions; and many of the people of Lisbon still looked on the Spanish Viceroy, holding his court in the palace of their kings, as a foreign usurper.

Their pride was especially shocked because this was a seafaring matter. The Portuguese tradition of seamanship and exploration was longer and grander than Spain's. All of them knew that their own Prince Henry had founded the system of navigation that every seafarer used, and that Vasco Da Gama had sailed from this same river to round the Cape of Good Hope and discover India before the Spaniards had any reputation at sea. Now Philip was using their harbour for his own armada (a word that simply means a fighting fleet). He had taken the galleons that had been the core of Portugal's fleet, the finest fighting ships in the world as they believed, and without any gratitude had added them to his own. Even the flagship *San Martin*, which was to wear the royal standard, was a Portuguese ship. It was an insult that was hard to bear. The aristocrats and gentlemen of Lisbon were therefore absent from the cathedral. The Spaniards had not invited them on the ground that there was not enough room; but the Spaniards probably knew that if they had been invited they would not have come.

In these surroundings of suppressed hostility, some of the Spanish officers may have needed the reassurance of the church's blessing. The most senior of them, the viceroy and the duke, had been told time and again, in letters from the king, that the expedition he had planned was exclusively in the service of God: it was God's will that he should rescue the people of England from their heretic queen and bring them back to the true and only church. Whether the officers believed it depended on their temperament: they were brave men anyway, and professionals, perfectly willing to face a long voyage into unknown seas and fight the enemies of their king, whoever they might be. But the enmity of the Portuguese was insidious and depressing. After the dreary winter they had spent in Lisbon, the blessing of the standard may have been a comfort to them.

But the soldiers might have been forgiven if they were bewildered by the whole performance, and the Portuguese certainly watched from their windows with doubt. *Exurge Domine!* Why should the cause of God be always the aggrandisement of Spain? Why should the figure of Mary and Jesus be shown on the standard as mere supporters of the royal arms? It seemed to the Portuguese that Philip was up to his tricks again: he was hoping to do to England what he had done to Portugal. And the Portuguese were not alone. However much the king protested his holy purpose, every head of state in Europe, including the pope, had the same suspicion. This doubt hung over the armada throughout its years of preparation and its months of voyaging: was it really a crusade to extend the kingdom of God on earth, or was it really a political adventure, to extend the kingdom of Spain?

However, the people of Lisbon had one good reason to welcome the ceremony: it meant the armada was going. It had been lying there in the river far too long, slowly growing as ships came to join it – royal ships, ships that were chartered or requisitioned, ships from the ports of Spain and Italy, from the Indies and even from the Baltic. Their crews came with them, and they and increasing numbers of soldiers had been living on board all winter. Every time the soldiers and sailors were counted the sums came out differently, but at the final reckoning there were nearly thirty thousand. The city had been teeming with foreigners, grand and humble, on duty or shore leave; and naturally, when they set foot on land, a good many of them behaved badly. Feeding them, and fitting out the ships with all the things they needed, had made havoc of the city's normal life. Traders profited, of course, but the markets were empty and prices were going up and up. To feed the armada the poor of the city went hungry and everyone wanted to see the last of it.

In fact it was not quite ready. No fleet of such a size could ever be perfectly ready. For one thing, the men ate up the stores as fast as they could possibly be replenished. And, inevitably, gear went wrong, defects were discovered, things got broken, men fell sick or had accidents or deserted and had to be replaced by new recruits, and boatswains and pursers checking their lists yet again found things that had been forgotten. Ships had to be careened to have their bottoms scraped, and when the last was finished the first was needing it again. At the last moment, on the king's express orders, every man was required to confess and receive absolution, and to be given a ticket to confirm that he had done so. At the last moment, also, the fleet had to be searched for hidden women: twenty were discovered – not very many really – and bundled ashore. But everything was ready in the sense that the commander-in-chief was prepared to give the signal to weigh as soon as the wind came fair.

They had to wait another fortnight. On 11th May, a light easterly breeze coincided with a falling tide to take the fleet downriver. The duke ordered a gun to be fired from his flagship, the galleon *San Martin*, and then on a bugle-call each of the ships in turn hauled in its cables, made sail and broke out its anchors from the river mud.

The watchers on shore that morning, seeing the fleet for the first time under way, must have marvelled at the stupendous size and strength of it. So must the men on board, feeling their own ship free at last of the land. Downstream in stately order came sixty-five galleons and other major ships of war, with towering fore and aftercastles freshly painted, and flying every flag and pennant they possessed – including specially big flags that had been painted with images of the Virgin 'so that the soldiers could see them'. Here also were twenty-five urcas, which were Baltic merchantmen or freighters, smaller on average than the galleons; and thirty-two of the much smaller ships and despatch boats called pataches and zabras (the English would have called them pinnaces); and four galleasses from Naples, large ships propelled by sail and oars, expected to be the most useful of all in battle; and finally four small Portuguese galleys, also oared, which had been chosen for some reason that nobody seemed to remember.

There were probably not many nautical critics who saw the scene from the shore. If there were any, they might have noticed that only twenty-five of the big ships – twenty-one galleons and four galleasses – were really ships of war, designed and built for the purpose of carrying soldiers and fighting other ships. Nearly double that number were what the Spaniards called naos, which simply means ships in general. They were converted Mediterranean cargo carriers, mainly used for grain, from Genoa, Venice and Ragusa, which is now called Dubrovnik. They looked impressive, because they were large and fighting castles of extra height had been built on them fore and aft. Some of them were carrying the biggest naval guns of all, fifty-pounder cannon. Experts would have known they were much more lightly built than fighting galleons, and were slower and less handy under sail because they were much broader in the beam. But if those experts had doubts about using naos as fighting ships, they would only have shrugged their shoulders and supposed the king knew what he was doing.

Every statistic of the fleet was listed and reported to the king – and not only to the king. The lists were also printed and published: there were copies of them in England before the armada sailed. The Spaniards were well aware they had assembled the largest fleet in all the history of the sea: so it was better not to keep the figures secret, but to use them to awe the English and impress the rest of Europe. The fleet was armed, for example, with 2431 guns, apart from the weapons of the soldiers, and stocked with 123,790 shot of iron or stone. It carried (though the estimates varied almost from day to day) about 11,000 pipes or barrels of water and 14,000 of wine; 11 million pounds of ship's biscuit; 600,000 pounds of salt pork, 800,000 of cheese and the same of rice; 18,000 bushels of beans and chick peas; 40,000 gallons of olive oil and 80,000 of vinegar: according to calculations, enough food and drink for six months.

Also, somewhere stowed away in its holds, it had masses of miscellaneous stores for the army that was to land in England: among them 5000 pairs of shoes, 11,000 pairs of sandals, 8000 leather bottles, 10,000 pikes, 7000 spare arquebuses and 1000 muskets, 20 gun carriages for the land artillery and 40 mules to draw them.

Above all, the statistics of men. Every deck and every corner was crammed and packed with men. A ship of say five hundred tons, which was about the average, was large in that era, but still not very large, not more then one hundred feet in length. Such a ship – though again the figures varied – was carrying about one hundred sailors, which was the normal sort of complement for a long voyage; but also she had about three hundred soldiers as passengers. Overall, the landsmen outnumbered the sailors by nearly three to one. At a more or less final count, there were 8052 sailors, 18,973 soldiers and 2088 oarsmen – who were not sailors but convicts sentenced to the galleys and galleasses instead of prison.

In addition, among the landsmen were 146 gentlemen (who demanded cots and even cabins of their own) and 238 'officers unattached'; and between them they had 728 servants. There were also the officers of justice and the paymaster and their staffs, and 167 men listed only as gunners. There were the 180 priests and friars and – the most remarkable statistic of all – there were precisely six surgeons and six physicians, who between them had sixty-two medical orderlies.

The majority of these people were Spaniards, but not by any means all, especially among the sailors. They were never listed by race, but probably there were round about 4000 Portuguese, Italians, Germans and Flemings, and there were certainly several hundred Irish and English.

Whenever a ship leaves port for an ocean voyage, the men in it re-adjust their minds, saying goodbye to wives and lovers and all the other comforts and complications of the shore, and settling down to the simple masculine life ahead of them. With luck, their regret is balanced by pride in their ship and her company, and pleasant anticipation of adventure.

That pleasure was justified on the day the armada sailed. Every man could see himself as a member of a noble enterprise; everyone accepted that his cause was just; everyone had confessed his sins and received absolution – whether the voyage led him to death or glory, his conscience was at rest. He could be proud as the fleet slipped slowly down the river, and the fortresses ashore saluted it with guns, and the peasants in the vineyards paused in their work to wave and watch it pass. The duke himself was proud that he had succeeded in getting the fleet away, as well he might have been, and in a letter he wrote that day he discreetly drew the king's attention to the achievement, ascribing it to the work of the Lord, and His Majesty's holy zeal.

But in that same letter to the king he told a revealing story. 'In the monastery of San Benito at Loyos,' he wrote, 'there is a holy friar called Antonio de la Concepcion, with whom I have had discussions lately in my leisure time. He is certain our Lord will give a great victory to Your Majesty. He told me to tell you so, and to beseech you not to undertake this enterprise out of vengeance for the injuries that infidels have done to you, or to extend your dominions; but only for the honour and glory of God Almighty, and to reclaim to His church the heretics who have strayed from it.'

Even the commander-in-chief himself was still in doubt about the purpose of the voyage, and suspected that the king's intentions were selfish and less than holy.

The moment of pride and pleasure was short. Before the flagship reached the river mouth the easterly wind dropped and then backed to the north west, where it had lain for months, and began to blow more strongly. The tide turned, and the duke perforce had to anchor again inside the bar and signal the rest to do the same. They had made only seven miles.

'God ordains all things,' he wrote to the king, 'and He has not seen fit to send us weather for the sailing of the armada. It is as boisterous and bad as if it were December; but He knows best.'

There, in sight of the open sea, another fortnight passed. Everyone now could see the white horses beyond the bar. A heavy swell was breaking on the southern shore of the estuary; and on the northern shore they were in sight of the bay of Cascais, where the English captain Drake, of whom some Spanish sailors spoke in superstitious awe, had lain with his fleet the summer before and challenged the armada to come out. Lying alternately to the tide and the wind, ships rolled unpleasantly in the echoes of the swell, and men began to be seasick. All in all, the ocean looked very uninviting. After the exhilarating start the delay was depressing and pride began to falter. They wondered where Drake was lurking now. It is a fair guess that many of the thousands wished they were ashore again; and it is perfectly certain the duke wished he was. One of the many remarkable things about the armada was that its commander-in-chief, the Captain General of the High Seas, had scarcely ever been to sea and did not want to go.

2

Duke and King

The name of the seventh Duke of Medina Sidonia was Don Alonzo Perez de Guzman el Bueno. He was master of the most ancient duchy in Spain and one of the greatest private estates in Europe, and was a man misjudged by many later generations. The only surviving portraits of him show an old man, small, grey-bearded and sombrely dressed, with an unmistakable air of melancholy. But the portraits were painted long after the events of 1588 had wrecked his health and reputation. When he commanded the armada he was only thirty-seven.

The town of Medina Sidonia which gave him his title is far in the south of Spain, a few miles inland from Cadiz. It stands high on a hill with a beautiful prospect across the plains of Andalusia. It is surrounded by ranches where they breed fighting bulls; and right on top of the hill a few broken walls remain of the medieval ducal fortress.

But ever since the year 1297 the dukes had lived in a modest palace forty miles away, close to another fortress at San Lucar de Barrameda. The palace is still there, surrounded by the houses of the town. It has been altered and extended by generations of dukes, but the present duchess still lives in it, with several of her grown-up children. It has been the family's home for nearly seven hundred years.

Naturally, the dukes have felt a strong attachment to the house and estate they have lived in so long; and none more than the seventh duke. San Lucar is on the estuary of the River Guadalquivir, which runs down from the city of Seville. It was a busy harbour in the sixteenth century, the port of shipment for the famous wines of Jerez. All through the war against Spain, English drinkers continued to demand their sherry wine, and by devious routes they got it; and most of it was grown and blended on the duke's estate. From his windows and terraces, he could gaze out across the wide river mouth, across the marshes beyond and across the fertile plain, a prolific, sun-blessed, placid and prosperous countryside of wheatfields, olive trees, vineyards, orange and lemon groves and untidy little whitewashed towns, each with a monumental church as its centre. He loved it, and every yard of it was his.

Among the aristocracy of Spain, or indeed of anywhere in Europe, the duke was a most unusual man. He was peaceful and gentle by nature, polite, considerate and not often angry. He disliked violence and high intrigue and military life, and so far he had always succeeded in avoiding them – except in his hereditary duty as Captain General of Andalusia, which was seldom much of a burden. There was nothing in his ancestry to explain this strangely pacific taste. The Guzmans had always been fighters. Family tradition said they had come from England six hundred years before; they may have been among the Norse marauders who reached the northern coast of Spain in the tenth century. They had won their way to power by fighting, mainly against the Moors. The suffix to their name, el Bueno, the Good, dated back to the thirteenth century, and had always meant good in the military sense – reliable, loyal and ruthless. It was given first to a Guzman who was besieged in a town. The enemy had captured his son, and threatened to kill him unless the town surrendered. Guzman earned his name by refusing, and letting the boy be murdered. Ever since, the Guzmans had produced generals and colonial governors for the Spanish empire. There is every reason to think the seventh duke was also good, but not in the same way: a good family man, a good churchgoer, not a bad scholar, and even a good landlord by the standards of his time – in short, a charitable man. But he had never pretended to be a good soldier, nor ever wanted to be; and much less a sailor.

No doubt there was something in his upbringing that gave him this unusual character. It was certainly out of the ordinary: his father died when he was five, and he was still a boy when he inherited the title and the vast estates from his grandfather. When he was fifteen, he was betrothed to a girl named Ana, who was four. She was the daughter of the Princess of Eboli, a notoriously turbulent and scheming lady. Most betrothals of children, made to cement the power of great families, were quietly forgotten before the children came to marrying age. But when the duke was twenty-one and Ana was ten, the pope gave a special dispensation for the marriage to be solemnized. It was, and by the beginning of 1588 the duke and duchess had four sons. Later, they had twelve more children.

It was a popular rumour in Spain that King Philip himself had had an affair with the Princess of Eboli, and that he showed special favour to the duke because he took a paternal interest in the duchess. It could never be proved, and people who compared the king and the princess in their later years could hardly believe it – the king had grown into a solemn recluse, while the princess was still such an active political menace that he had ordered her to be kept under house arrest. But twenty-five years before, the king had been a different man and was known to have made the most of his kingly opportunities. On the wrong side of the blanket, the duke could have been his son-in-law.

Rumour also had something else to say about the marriage: that the duchess took after her mother and had grown up a termagant. It was said the duke was hen-pecked, and perhaps he was. He behaved like the sort of man who prefers to be domineered, rather than domineering. Perhaps he even loved the duchess better for her masterful ways.

At all events, he certainly loved his home and – for a duke – his pleasures were blameless. He liked to ride round the Andalusian countryside, where the peasant girls curtseyed and the men took off their caps, and people received his benevolence with gratitude. Possibly power sometimes corrupted his judgement, but at least he valued justice. Running the great estate had plenty of worries, especially financial: the Guzmans were enormously rich, yet always in debt. But this was the life he understood. He was born to it, it was his vocation, and he had never wanted anything except to be left alone to enjoy it in peace and do his duty as well as he was able.

It was the middle of February, two months before the ceremony in Lisbon, when the calm of San Lucar was suddenly shattered by a royal courier, who rode into the courtyard bringing an urgent letter from the king's secretary, Don Juan de Idiaquez. It told the duke that the commander-in-chief of the great armada that was being assembled in Lisbon, the Marquis of Santa Cruz, was dying. It did not offer the post to the duke; it merely informed him that the king had appointed him Captain General of the High Seas. It ordered him to ride at once to Lisbon, take over command of the fleet and lead it in the name of God and the king to the conquest of England.

Almost any other Spaniard would have been overwhelmed with pride. The duke was horrified. He wrote at once in agonized protest. The words poured out with frantic repetition as he searched for the phrase that would make the king understand that he would not and could not do any such thing: 'I first humbly thank His Majesty for having thought of me for such a great task, and I wish I had the talents and strength it requires. But, Sir, I have no health for the sea, I know from the small experience I have had afloat that I am always seasick and catch cold. Beside this, I am in such need that when I had to go to Madrid I had to borrow money for the journey. My house owes 900,000 ducats, and I am therefore quite unable to accept the command. I have not a penny I can spend on the expedition.

'Apart from this, neither my conscience nor my duty will allow me to take this service. The fleet is so great, and the undertaking so important, that it would be wrong for a person like myself, with no experience of seafaring or war, to take charge of it. So, Sir, in the interest of His Majesty's service, and for the love I bear him, I submit to you, for communication to him, that I possess neither aptitude, ability, health nor fortune, for the expedition. The lack of any of these qualities would be enough to excuse me, and much more the lack of them all, which is the case with me at present.'

It is possible to read the long letter as the excuses of a coward scared out of his wits by the prospect of danger, and since it was re-discovered in the royal archives a century ago many people have judged it that way. But it deserves more careful thought. A man needed moral courage to write in this way to King Philip, and in the battles to come the duke proved he had plenty of physical courage too. Besides, every word in the letter was true. The king's order really was impossible: there was no reasonable hope he would succeed in the task. By a fairer judgement it was not the letter of a coward – it was the letter of a man who had the wisdom and sensibility to know his own limitations and to foresee exactly what would happen, yet was so appalled he could hardly express himself.

No doubt he guessed why the king had chosen him: it was simply because he was a duke. A great royal fleet could only be commanded by an eminent aristocrat, because admirals and generals were jealous, difficult men who would not serve together under any lesser mortal. (For exactly the same reason, Queen Elizabeth had appointed Lord Howard of Effingham to command her fleet.) The dying commander, Santa Cruz, was the most famous fighting seaman Spain possessed: but also – which was just as important – he was a marquis. There was nobody else like him. The duke would therefore start with the respect that was due to his birth, but how could he possibly hope to keep it?

'Beside all this,' he went on, 'for me to take charge of the armada afresh, without the slightest knowledge of it, of the men who are taking part in it, of the objects in view, of the intelligence from England, without any acquaintance with the ports there, or with the arrangements the marquis has been making for years past, would be simply groping in the dark, even if I had the experience. Suddenly and without preparation I would have to begin a new career. So, Sir, you will see that my reasons for declining are so strong and convincing, in His Majesty's own interests, that I cannot attempt a task of which I am sure I should give a bad account. I would be travelling in the dark, and would have to be guided by the opinions of others, knowing nothing of their good or bad qualities or which of them might seek to deceive and ruin me.'

This perhaps was a clue to what the duke dreaded most: not danger, battle or death – not even failure – but simply making a fool of himself. The armada was the greatest fleet the world had seen: how could a man like himself conceivably be its commander? – a man who was seasick, who hardly knew a ship from a haystack, who would always have to ask his subordinates what to do and take the blame if it was wrong, who would have to pretend not to listen when he knew they were laughing at him. This is a kind of fear that most people have some time in their lives, and it merits sympathy, not scorn. He ended his letter with all the emphasis that any man would dare to use to his king: 'This is all I can reply. I write with all frankness and truth, which is my duty; and I have no doubt that His Majesty in his magnanimity will do me the favour which I humbly beg, and will not entrust to me a task in which I could certainly not succeed; for I do not understand it, know nothing about it, have no health for the sea and no money to spend on it.'

Of course there were plenty of other aristocrats in Spain, and many of them would have been delighted to take command. But the king had made his choice, and he was not used to having his high appointments rejected: probably it had never happened before. Also, he was a man who could not admit he was wrong. All the duke got in return for his passionate plea was a repetition of the order to go to Lisbon at once. This was despatched from the king's secretariat on 18th February and probably reached the duke by the 21st. It added that the armada was to sail, under his command, by 1st March at the latest. Just over a week – no time to ride to Madrid and plead with the king in person. There was nothing he could do but obey the adamant order and hope for the best. He wrote back that he had salved his conscience by confessing his inability.

With that submission, the king wrote again in a rather more gracious mood, not merely a secretary's letter but one signed with his own subscription, 'I, the King'. It had a postscript in his spidery hand. He said he wished he could lead the armada himself, but he was too busy at home. He reminded the duke, inappropriately, of the great deeds of his ancestors, and was confident he would succeed. The duke need not worry, because the enterprise was entirely devoted to the service of God. God would uphold him, and therefore he could not fail.

Before he read that pious attempt to reassure him, the duke had said goodbye to his family, and to San Lucar, and ridden for Lisbon. Of course he knew that long weary road was leading him to a place in history. Also, with his gift of introspection, he must have known that history would not judge him for the virtues he valued, it would judge him by military standards which were foreign to his nature, and its judgement would be harsh.

At least it was not a solitary journey. He took with him to Lisbon, and aboard his flagship when he got there, a retinue of twenty-two gentlemen and forty servants.

*

It was typical of King Philip that the duke received all his orders by letter. For years past, the king had ruled his empire by writing letters, and had seldom emerged from a small suite of rooms in the huge monastic palace he had built in the mountains north west of Madrid, San Lorenzo del Escorial. In those rooms the armada was conceived in his solitary mind and planned in the utmost detail; and it was brought into physical existence by the letters he dictated to his secretaries, or the letters they wrote on his behalf.

The king left two memorials to posterity. One is the austere nobility of the Escorial; the planning and building of it occupied him in his happiest moments through most of his adult life. The other is the royal archive he established in the medieval castle of Simancas, eighty miles farther north. Within that castle are thirty-three million documents, stored in forty-six rooms. There are thousands upon thousands of the letters King Philip wrote four centuries ago and the despatches he studiously read, scribbling his comments in the margins; and among them, the documents that created the armada and sent it to its doom.

In spite of this mass of original letters, the most difficult thing to understand about the armada is the mind of the king. It was difficult enough for the duke, who knew him well; and indeed, it may be a hopeless quest for a twentieth-century mind to probe the mind of a sixteenth-century bigot. But one has to try – and not only try, but try with sympathy. Without some comprehension of King Philip's mind, the story of what happened makes no sense; the mere facts of the armada do not explain why it was launched, or what it was meant to win, or why it failed.

In 1583 Philip was sixty-one and had been king for over thirty years. From the Escorial he ruled, or hoped to rule, a world of almost infinite complexity. Geographically his empire was the biggest any king in history had controlled: in Europe there was Spain and Portugal, Sicily, Naples and Milan, and parts of the Netherlands and France; and overseas the Spanish and Portuguese dominions in America, Africa, India and the East. Right on the other side of the world the Philippine Islands were named after him. And for two years in his youth his marriage to Mary Tudor had also made him titular King of England.

Only the Spanish possessions overseas had come to him purely by conquest; those in Europe had fallen into his hands by tricks of inheritance, through the tangled branches of royal family trees. Royal marriages, like the duke's, were always political. Babies could be betrothed before they were born, laws against incest could be cast aside, doddering palsied old men could be married to teenage girls in last-minute hope of producing an heir to combine the power of two royal houses. All princes and princesses had to expect this calculated, unromantic mating: Queen Elizabeth alone refused it, and played the inheritance game by keeping her suitors guessing.* Philip himself had been married four times, to heiresses of Portugal, England, France and Austria, and had not seen any of his brides before the ceremonies started. All of them had died. One way and another he could prove he was related to almost everyone with royal blood, and could lay some kind of a claim to every throne. Sometimes he had supported a shaky claim with the threat of the Spanish army.

But it was not only a political empire; it was also a religious entity, and that was what made it so complex. King Philip was His Most Catholic Majesty. He believed he was appointed by God to defend the truth against infidels and heretics. The pope was Vicar of Christ: Philip, in his own eyes, was Champion of God, the equal of the pope in God's designs. In this sense, his boundaries were vague. There were people all over Europe, caught in the ebb and flow of Reformation and Counter-Reformation, whose loyalties were divided between their country and their church. In almost all of Philip's Catholic domains, Protestants had been exterminated, or pushed far under ground, by the Inquisition. The only exception was the Netherlands. All through his reign they had been in revolt, partly against the shame of foreign rule and partly to protect their Protestant creed: he had to keep an immensely expensive army there, and it had never succeeded in putting the rebels down. But he was not only concerned with his own domains. It was his personal duty, divinely imposed as he

*One of the graceful verses attributed to her is this:
   'When I was fair and young, and favour graced me,
   Of many was I sought, their mistress for to be;
   But I did scorn them all, and answered them therefore,
   Go, go, go seek some otherwhere,
   Importune me no more.'

believed, to punish Protestants everywhere and rescue Catholics who lived under Protestant rule.

He was a strange crusader. By inclination, he was not a man of action: he had never been any good at the martial arts, and had never tried to inspire or lead an army. He had only once in his life been present at a battle and then, although his own side won, the whole thing had disgusted him. Luckily, there were excellent generals in Spain, among them his own much younger illegitimate brother Don Juan, his nephew Alexander Farnese, Duke of Parma, the ageing Duke of Alba, and at sea the Marquis of Santa Cruz. These men directed his battles – God's battles, he would have said – while he stayed at home and decided whom they should fight against.

But neither was he a man of much intellect. The brain he applied to God's problems and his own was quite remarkably slow. He dreaded quick decisions; it always took him days, and sometimes years, to make up his mind about anything. His people called him Philip the Prudent, and he made rather a virtue of his chronic hesitation. 'Time and I are one,' he would say while he procrastinated, expecting – and sometimes rightly – that problems would disappear if he waited long enough. He was also extremely slow to learn, either from his own experience or from the much more brilliant men of his court. The mixture of mediocrity and power made him immovably self-righteous and obstinate.

He must at least have learned that he was not quick-witted, and that was probably why he insisted, as he grew older, on shutting himself away and ruling his realm by writing. It insulated him from face-to-face meetings and oral discussions, which only confused him. Sometimes, of course, he had to give audience to ambassadors or men of exalted rank who had some special plea. He evolved a way of dealing with them: they had to speak Spanish, or use an interpreter, because that was the only language he had ever mastered – except enough Latin to follow the prayers of his priests. He would listen, silent and perfectly expressionless, while they made the eloquent impassioned speeches they had prepared; and when they had quite finished and could not think of anything more to say, he would rise and dismiss them politely with the words, 'These matters will receive the attention they deserve.' It was totally crushing. They bowed themselves out wondering whether he had even begun to understand what they had been talking about. But to do him justice, he usually had. He would ponder their questions alone, taking all the time he wanted, consulting God in prayer; and long afterwards a letter would emerge from his cabinet expressing his answers in carefully measured phrases. Not that these letters always made his judgement crystal clear; when it suited him he was a master of the art of hiding meaning with complicated prose.

He led an unhealthy life, immured in the Escorial. It was said he spent three or four hours of every day at his prayers. No doubt that was a solace, but it was also a penance: he suffered from very painful and swollen knees. His physicians said it was gout, and perhaps they were right; but perhaps it was an early symptom of the disease which led him at last, ten years after the armada, to a death of slow disgusting agony, when his body decomposed while there was still life in it. Whatever it was, those hours of kneeling on marble floors must have made it worse; so must the physicians, who treated it by frequent bleeding, drawing off the blood from his feet. By the age when he had to apply his mind to planning the armada his knees were so grossly swollen that he could hardly hobble the yards from his bed to the desk where he worked, and he lived in such pain that he could never sleep soundly. Instead, he often sat at his desk until dawn, working his ponderous, industrious way through the mountains of papers that never grew any less. The armada was created, an act of immense will-power, by a man distracted by insomnia and pain.

King Philip loved his children, except Don Carlos the eldest, who was too warped in mind and body for anyone to love. His letters to them were gentle and even mildly humorous in a paternal way. He had also loved at least one of his wives, and was said to be kind to his servants. But outside that little circle he was seldom moved by pity – and he once said, to a man condemned to the stake for heresy, that he would carry the wood to burn his own son for such an awful crime. He was far from being alone in this lack of pity; it was an era when churches, especially the Spanish Church, disregarded the virtues of charity and mercy. The God that Philip served was all-powerful, all-knowing and unforgiving. He could and did take part by miracles in men's affairs. Yet paradoxically He depended on His servants to do His will. He demanded worship absolutely exactly in the forms the Catholic Church proclaimed, and not in any other. He also demanded the most cruel and terrible punishments men could devise for anyone who deviated in the least degree. Especially, He demanded this service from the man to whom He had given the highest earthly power: King Philip. It was truly an awful burden for a man to carry.

It was also a burden for a human empire. Saddled with that primitive belief, the Spanish empire was doomed to fall to pieces, and during Philip's reign the cracks had begun. In an age when reports and orders were carried by horsemen and sailing ships, the empire was too big for any kind of central control – and far too big for the clerkly bureaucratic control he tried to impose on it. He hated to delegate an atom of his power: among the heaps of papers momentous questions waited his decisions while he struggled with trivialities. The empire was choking to death on paper.

Also it was bankrupt. Vast treasures flowed into it from dominions in east and west, but nobody understood that continually creating new money only led to inflation. Philip had mortgaged all the empire's revenues for years ahead, mainly to foreign bankers. He always hoped some windfall would pay off his debts; but the bankers knew he would never be solvent again, and he began to find he could not even borrow. Trite though it might seem, the designs of God cost an awful lot of money.

It would be quite absurd to say that Philip, or the Spanish people or anyone else, were to blame for having this difficult concept of the Christian God. It had grown through generations, and they had inherited it. For a century past the Inquisition had very strictly imposed on them the Catholic forms of worship, and they wore their conformity as a soldier wears a uniform. Few Spaniards ever met a heretic, and those who did, in the Netherlands for example, met them only as political and warlike enemies. Inevitably, military and religious affairs were mixed in their minds. The mixture was made more profound by St Ignatius of Loyola, a Spanish soldier himself, who founded the Society of Jesus in 1540. The Jesuits became an international organization with a frankly military structure, which demanded, like an army, unquestioning obedience to its senior officers, and oaths which overrode mere national loyalty. This kind of religious institution had an immense appeal for Spaniards, especially soldiers; in them, religious and national loyalty coincided.

But in Philip's simple mind the mixture of military and religious thought became an insoluble muddle. The God he conceived had the vices and ambitions of an earthly tyrant, which has always been a philosophical impossibility, suited only to primitive people in elementary societies. Yet the society Philip ruled was highly complex. In all his problems as a ruler, how could he ever distinguish his own will from the will of a God who was so much like himself? He never could and never did. In all his projects he explained to everyone that he was pursuing God's design, as if it were just a happy coincidence that God's purpose happened to add to Philip's power. Foreigners, fearful or envious of the dominance of Spain, thought this was hypocrisy, but it was not. Reading Philip's letters in the twentieth century and judging him by twentieth-century standards – which of course has the inherent unfairness of history – one has to say he was bigoted, dogmatic, self-righteous, illogical, ruthless and hopelessly confused; but also, he was appallingly sincere.

This then was the man whose orders had brought the armada to its awkward anchorage in the river mouth. But what did he hope to gain from the fleet he had created? With God's help, as he saw things, it would defeat the English at sea, and his armies would land and beat the English army and capture or kill the queen; but what then? Looking back, it seems obvious now that Elizabethan England would never have accepted Spanish rule whatever happened. Philip might have conquered England, but he could never have held it without enormous permanent garrisons which he could not conceivably afford. This should have been obvious then – if he had learned anything from the thirty years' struggle to put down revolt in the Netherlands. That had crippled his finances and cost uncounted lives, and was still nowhere near success. England would only have been another endless burden – and a far worse one, because it was equally Protestant, equally patriotic and far more powerful.

This is the first enigma of the armada: what did Philip mean to do if it won? The Simancas archives reveal exactly the answer one would expect of such a man: after half a lifetime of thinking about it, after spending a mortgaged fortune on it and organizing it all, he had still not made up his mind what to do if it won. To rescue the people of England from their heretical queen – in secular terms, this might have meant anything. Most people assumed it meant he would try to rule England himself, probably by giving the crown to one of his children. Undoubtedly that is what the men who were going to fight for him thought. But at the last minute, while the armada was waiting for its wind, he wrote another letter which would have astonished and horrified his commanders, not to mention his soldiers and sailors, if they had known what it said. But they did not. The letter was carried by the armada to the shores of England and back to Spain, but nobody read it. It lay unopened for three hundred years.

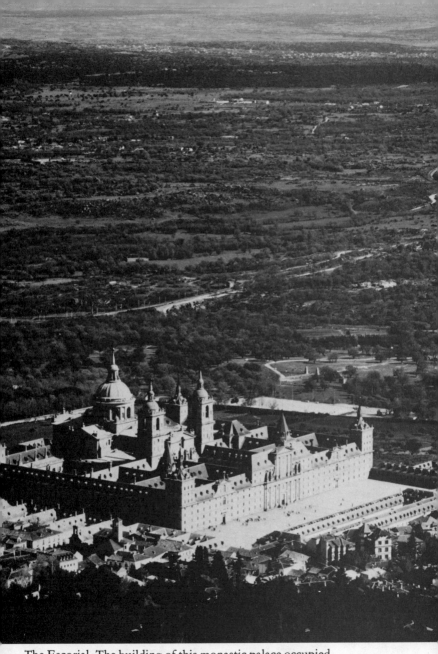

The Escorial. The building of this monastic palace occupied
King Philip in his happiest moments through most of his reign.

The fortress of San Lucar de Barrameda. In a modest palace beside it the family of the Dukes of Medina Sidonia have lived for nearly seven hundred years.

Opposite : King Philip II, circa 1580.

The Duke of Medina Sidonia. The few surviving portraits show him as an old man, but when he commanded the armada he was only thirty-seven.

Don Juan Martinez de Recalde. At sixty-two he was the oldest of the Spanish commanders, and perhaps the most heroic figure on either side.

3

Evolution of an Idea

t may be true that men who fight in wars never really know what they are fighting for, unless there is an obvious threat to their own homes and families: more often they are told whatever seems likely to make them fight most fiercely. This was certainly true of the men of every rank who sailed in the armada. Not even the duke had a clear idea of the reasons for the voyage. The rest of them, when they were clear of the shore and were waiting in the river mouth, were told a bewildering mixture of untruths and half truths. To get anywhere near the whole truth – and to put the king's final secret letter in its context – one has to delve back, however briefly, for thirty-four years in the past. That was when the armada had its roots.

In 1554, before he was king, Philip married Mary Tudor, the Catholic Queen of England who was remembered by her people, for her persecution of Protestants, as Bloody Mary. The marriage had been arranged by his father, the Emperor Charles V, and the Emperor's object had been political, to form an alliance of England, Spain and the Netherlands against the power of France. Philip accepted the filial duty but his interest in it, so far as he had any, was religious: to father a Catholic heir who would keep England safely within the Church when Mary died. 'I am going to a crusade, not a marriage feast,' he said to one of the entourage he took to England.

For the queen it was a most pathetic marriage. Philip was a dapper young man of twenty-seven, Mary a spinster of thirty-eight. He had already been a widower for nine years, and had a devoted mistress who entered a nunnery when he left her to sail to England. He had never seen Mary, and his father had explained very clearly that this was a matter of dignity: 'No prince of equal rank to hers would undertake the adventure of going to England with the possibility of being refused. This is the reason why princes, noblemen and private gentlemen too, marry without the contracting parties seeing each other.'

Philip met his bride at Winchester, and found her desperately unattractive. But his father had instructed him to 'demonstrate much love and joy to her'; it was only by charming her that he could rule England. So he set to work with charm, and succeeded so well that the poor woman fell in love with him. She soon believed she was pregnant, and carried her belief to the stage when the bells of London were rung for the birth of an heir. But it was a tumour from which she never recovered; and Philip, knowing he could not achieve his object, left her in England and went to his father in the Netherlands. His father abdicated, because his health was failing, Philip received his kingdoms, and Mary died grieving for the man she thought was her lover.

Afterwards it was said that Philip had had a moderating influence on Mary and her English advisers, and had not encouraged the burnings and tortures of Protestants that distinguished her reign. Whether he was responsible or not, these Catholic excesses made England more firmly Protestant after Mary's death and sowed more seeds of Philip's future troubles.

Within a month of her death, he decided it was his duty to marry her sister and successor, Elizabeth, whom he had briefly met when he was in England and rather liked. He wrote to his ambassador explaining 'the enormous importance of such a match to Christianity and the preservation of religion which has been restored in England by the Grace of God. Seeing also,' he went on, 'the importance that the country should not fall back into its former errors, which would cause serious dangers and difficulties in our neighbouring dominions, I have decided to set aside all other considerations and am resolved to render this service to God and offer to marry the queen.' And he added a list of strict conditions. The first, of course, was that she should declare herself a Catholic; the second that she, not he, should ask the pope for dispensation from the law that forbade a man to marry his deceased wife's sister.

This was not the way to charm Elizabeth. She had many meetings with the ambassador, and contrived to keep him and Philip waiting a long time before the ambassador had to report,

'She says she cannot marry Your Majesty because she is a heretic.'

Jilted, Philip's thoughts turned to Mary, Queen of Scots, whom Catholics considered the legitimate heiress of England. Philip mistrusted her because of her French connections – he was said to have said he would rather have England heretic than French – and he did not propose to marry her himself. He proposed that she should marry his son Don Carlos: the most enchanting of princesses, whom dozens of men were in love with, was to accept the most repulsive of princes – who was then seventeen, and not only deformed but already hovering in and out of madness. Philip instructed his ambassador again: 'This marriage,' he wrote, 'may be the beginning of a reformation in England, and I have therefore decided to make the negotiations. You will be serving God as well as myself.' Of course it came to nothing; and in this particular plan Philip was suspected in later years of a motive that was human, but neither political nor religious: Don Carlos was already betrothed to a girl of fourteen, Isabel of Valois. Philip had her portrait, which was beautiful, and he wanted to marry her himself. And so he did. Elizabeth sent him mocking congratulations; but Don Carlos, seeing the girl every day at court, became murderously jealous of his father, and his subsequent imprisonment and death were one of the unsolved mysteries of Philip's reign.

Some years later, when Mary had been forced out of Scotland and was confined in England, another of Philip's family set his hopes on her. This was his illegitimate brother Don Juan. Don Juan was at least a desirable husband, indeed the most eligible bachelor in Europe: extremely handsome, young and dashing, and the hero of the victory over the Turks in the Battle of Lepanto, the last great battle fought in galleys propelled by oars. After that famous success, Don Juan thought Philip ought to reward him with one of the many kingdoms in his gift. Instead, Philip appointed him general of his army in the Netherlands, with the thankless and endless task of trying to suppress the rebels of Holland and Zeeland. While he was there Don Juan thought of a more ambitious plan: to take the army across in boats to England, depose Elizabeth and set Mary free from her confinement. It was not unthinkable that Mary would marry her liberator, who would thus become King John II of England. She was thirty-five: there was still time to hope for a Catholic heir; and her young son James, who had succeeded her in Scotland, could somehow be disinherited. Philip cautiously approved the plan; but before it could be tested Don Juan caught a fever and died.

That was in October 1578. At that same moment Francis Drake was sailing through the Straits of Magellan into the Pacific Ocean, which Philip claimed as his own. English seamen were growing more and more audacious in capturing and robbing Spanish ships, and in the last few years had made really serious inroads on Spanish wealth. Queen Elizabeth was growing more audacious too, in helping the Protestant rebels in the Netherlands. The defeat of England was becoming a pressing financial and political need, besides remaining a crusade; and having failed four times to conquer the country by marriage, Philip was turning his thoughts to force.

The use of force became feasible after his capture of Portugal in 1581. That put in his hands new harbours and dockyards, and a new fleet as powerful as his own. In the elation of that success his Captain General of the High Seas, the Marquis of Santa Cruz, offered to clear the English pirates off the oceans and seize their country. Philip told him to estimate the forces he would need, and the marquis submitted the kind of report that Philip loved, listing not only the ships and troops and armament, but all the quantities of every kind of stores. But his needs were enormous, a fleet about twice as large in all respects as the armada that Philip finally assembled. The cost of it was out of the question. 'The time has not yet come to discuss this,' he wrote on the document, and put it away in his files.

Anyhow, the conquest of England by force, as opposed to marriage, could only have one result: to give the crown to Mary, Queen of Scots. All Catholics would expect it. Philip still mistrusted her, and even more mistrusted her heir apparent James, a vacillating young man who seemed to care very little about religion but said he was a Protestant. 'I cannot undertake a war in England,' Philip wrote at the end of 1586, 'merely to put a young heretic like the King of Scotland on the throne.'

What was in the back of his mind all the time, and slowly coming to the forefront, was his own hereditary claim to the kingdom of England. On his mother's side he could trace his descent to two forebears who had both married daughters of John of Gaunt, the son of Edward III of England – who had died two centuries before, in 1377. As a claim of right, this was fantasy. It passed over all the twelve kings and queens of England who had reigned since Edward, and all their descendants. On that basis, scores if not hundreds of people could have claimed the throne. But Philip persuaded himself that everyone else was disqualified, either by heresy or bastardy or both. What was more, he persuaded Mary to disinherit her son and bequeath her claim to himself.

He began in 1584 to assemble the ships which, after four years' labour, formed his armada. He himself had had the idea that seemed to make invasion possible: to combine the plan of Santa Cruz with the plan Don Juan had made before he died. The fleet would sail from Lisbon; most of the troops for the landing would come from the Netherlands. So the fleet could be smaller and more economical. It would beat the English fleet, or drive it away from the Narrow Seas between the Netherlands and England; and then when the seas were clear the Netherlands army would cross to England in boats. This army, since the death of Don Juan, was commanded by Philip's nephew the Duke of Parma. The Marquis of Santa Cruz would lead the fleet and Parma would lead the invasion.

Preparing the fleet was a slow job. In the meantime Philip was tempted time and again to support the plots that extremist Catholics made to assassinate Queen Elizabeth. Two of his ambassadors in succession were expelled from England when they were caught red-handed in these affairs. Assassination was a common weapon in matters of state, and Philip cannot be specially blamed for trying to use it. But he or his confederates can be blamed for trying over and over again and always failing. In England, the odium for these repeated plots fell on Mary, who was the obvious beneficiary. The plotting only added to the affection English people had for their queen – a loyal affection felt not only by Protestants but by many Catholics too. They came to believe, correctly, that the queen's life would never be safe while Mary was alive, and the execution of Mary inevitably followed.

Philip heard of her execution from his ambassador in Paris, Don Bernardino de Mendoza. Mendoza wrote to him on 28th February 1587, ten days after the event, and he sent his letter by special courier; but no reaction came from the Escorial until 31st March. Perhaps the letter had been put at the bottom of the pile on Philip's desk: such things could happen, even to him. But perhaps he spent the second half of March in making up his mind what to do.

For the death of Mary changed everything. There was no obvious claimant left between him and the throne of England, except King James of Scotland – and he had a letter, signed by Mary, declaring she had disinherited her son. Mendoza had written, 'As God has so willed, for His ends, that these accursed people should against all reason commit such an act as this, it is evidently His design to deliver these two kingdoms (England and Scotland) into Your Majesty's hands.' The king echoed this obscure piece of reasoning in a letter to his ambassador at the Vatican, Count de Olivares: 'I am extremely grieved . . . She would have been such an appropriate instrument for converting those countries to our Holy Catholic faith. But since God in His inscrutable judgement has ordered otherwise, He will provide other ways for the success of His cause.' It was perfectly clear to the king and to his ambassadors that the only way God ought to choose was to put Philip on the throne of England and Scotland.

It was also clear, at least to the king, that most of the other rulers of Europe would oppose this design of God, because they were jealous of the power of Spain. The French in particular would favour James to succeed Elizabeth, and try to persuade him to declare himself a Catholic; and it seemed likely the bait of the inheritance of England would make him agree. This was an answer to the problem that should have satisfied Philip's religious scruples. But it defied his worldly ambition. By this time he not only wanted the throne of England for a Catholic, he wanted it for himself. God's wishes and his own had become finally and inextricably mixed in his mind.

That April, exactly a year before the armada sailed, a spate of letters poured out of the Escorial. After the first weeks of hesitation Philip changed: he became a different man, no longer prudent but desperately impatient. He pestered the Marquis of Santa Cruz to get the armada ready, and ordered ships and guns and stores from Cartagena, Malaga, Naples, Genoa, the Adriatic and the Biscay ports, all to be hurried to Lisbon. He instructed Mendoza in Paris to condole with the Scottish ambassador on the death of Mary, and added that Mendoza was not to discuss his own claim with anyone – 'in order not to arouse the evil action the French would take if they thought I was going to claim the succession'. He agreed to give Scottish Catholics a large sum of money to enable them to take up arms, to 'release' their king from his Protestant advisers and convert the country to the Catholic faith: in other words, to bring James into his power, alive or dead. And he sent fresh orders to the Count de Olivares.

The count was in a delicate position in the Vatican, because he despised the pope: a garrulous old man, he said, mean about money, who could never be trusted to keep his mouth shut and had such fits of bad temper that he often threw the crockery about at his dinner table. The pope had rather vaguely promised a million ducats towards the cost of the armada. Philip's orders were now that Olivares should get this offer confirmed, and should also persuade the pope to give his blessing to Philip's claim.

At the end of July Olivares wrote that he had succeeded. He had drawn up a very long and complicated document about the money, and the pope had signed it, committing himself to pay the million ducats – but not before the Spanish army had actually landed in England. In the middle of the document, Olivares had put a clause which gave Philip the right to choose the next king or queen of England. Intent on the money, the pope's eye skimmed over this clause. 'The matter of the succession,' Olivares wrote, 'was so wrapped up that he passed it over without objection or difficulty.'

After that, it was clearly understood by Philip's senior officials that the object of the armada was to win the crown of England for himself. But he would not exercise the claim in person. He was too busy, and also too old and sick, to go to England himself. Nor would he give the kingdom to his son Philip, who was needed in Spain as heir to the empire and, moreover, was only nine. Instead, he would award it to his eldest daughter, the Infanta Isabella, who was twenty-one. Under his control, she would be nominal Queen of England.

That summer of 1587 a strange and quite unexpected hitch occurred in these plans. An English youth called Arthur Dudley turned up in Spain, saying confidently that he was a Catholic and that he was the son of Queen Elizabeth and the Earl of Leicester. He was interviewed many times by Sir Francis Englefield, who was King Philip's English secretary, and he told a very detailed and circumstantial story. He had been brought up by a man called Robert Southern, who had been a servant at court, but he had been given the costly education of a gentleman. On his deathbed Southern had told him that he was not his father: he had been given him, as a new-born baby, in a corridor outside the queen's private chamber at Hampton Court, and his education had been paid for by a courtier.

Perhaps the idea that the queen had a bastard son seemed less unlikely then than it does now. But reading Arthur's story – he wrote it all down for Englefield – one has to believe he was the son of some lady of the court, and that he and Southern sincerely believed his mother was the queen. He had contrived to meet the earl, who had treated him with great affection and said, 'You are like a ship under full sail at sea, pretty to look at but dangerous to deal with' – such a strangely chosen simile that it has the ring of truth. He also believed the queen had arranged with the earl to raise him to the throne of England when she died; and he asked Philip, as one Catholic to another, to protect him from English intrigue until that time came.

Englefield evidently liked the boy and was convinced his story was true – though he thought the queen might be using Arthur for some nefarious purpose that Arthur did not understand. But he put his own loyalty to Philip first. 'It is true,' he reported, 'that his claim at present amounts to nothing, but France or the English heretics, or some other party, might make it a pretext for obstructing the inheritance of the crown by its legitimate master. In my opinion, he should not be allowed to get away, but should be kept very secure to prevent his escape.'

On the face of it Arthur should have been an acceptable answer to Philip's religious qualms. A son of Queen Elizabeth, even a bastard, had a stronger claim to the throne than anyone else, and he was a Catholic. But Arthur must have been a naïve and trusting boy. In fact he had put his head in the lion's mouth, for Philip saw him as nothing but a rather ludicrous rival. On Englefield's report the king wrote, in his own hand, 'It will certainly be safest to make sure of his person until we know more about the matter.' And one may imagine a grim smile on that humourless face as he wrote the words; for Arthur Dudley disappeared at that moment from history and was never heard of again.

With that small interruption adroitly put out of the way, the plans of the armada were pushed ahead with ever-increasing urgency. In this final year of preparation Philip had three principal lieutenants: there was the Marquis of Santa Cruz, who was in Lisbon, and the Duke of Parma, who was in the Netherlands; and the third was Don Bernardino de Mendoza, who was in Paris. Santa Cruz commanded the fleet until he died in February; Parma commanded the army; and Mendoza was the spider at the heart of the web of spying on which it all depended. Each of them sent frequent long despatches to the king, and received from him equally long and frequent orders. But throughout all the preparations the four of them never met. There was never a conference, never a council of war. The king, immovable in the Escorial, never saw his armada, or his army, or his commanders, and the commanders never saw each other.

This was the intrinsic reason why the armada failed: the king's belief that he could organize a huge operation of war without leaving his study, without consulting anyone, without any human advice, without allowing his commanders to discuss it. It was true he inspired it all. But when it came to details he did not always understand what he was doing. Especially, he did not understand seafaring or navigation – he had never embarked in a ship except as a passenger. When a misunderstanding was firmly rooted in his mind, almost nothing could dig it out again. Mistaken decisions emerged from the Escorial with all the force of royal commands, backed by the assumption that his guidance was divine. Sometimes his commanders humbly tried to tell him he was wrong. But they could only do it by letter; and by the time his erroneous orders reached them and their written replies had come back – a week from Lisbon and a month from the Netherlands – his mind was occupied by other problems and he seldom took any notice of what they said.

Nor did he take any notice of their private wishes or difficulties, or their personalities. The Marquis of Santa Cruz was an elderly man with a life-long experience of the sea. Philip bullied him, sneered at him, treated him as though he were creating difficulties through incompetence or obstinacy. When the armada was not ready in the autumn of 1587, Philip insisted it must sail, ready or not, in the middle of winter. The marquis had to try to explain that the voyage could not be made in winter gales, much less the rendezvous with Parma, and least of all the crossing from the Netherlands in boats – facts so obvious to him or to any seaman that they could hardly be put into words. He got his way, by perpetually promising to be ready in a week or two and then, when the time came, producing a new explanation of why he was not. He was said to have died of a broken heart at the king's reproaches, and it is possible to believe that sheer exasperation hastened his end. Philip's expression of regret was no more than formality demanded, and probably he was relieved to appoint the Duke of Medina Sidonia, who did not pretend to know about the sea and might be expected to do as he was told.

The Duke of Parma, on the other hand, was only forty-two, young enough to be ambitious. He had commanded Philip's Netherlands armies for the past ten years, and won a reputation as the greatest general of the age. But his ambition went far beyond generalship. He was always conscious that he was of royal blood. His father was the head of the house of Farnese, which for generations had been among the most illustrious families of Italy. His mother was Margaret of Austria, the bastard daughter of Philip's father, the Emperor Charles V. His wife was a royal princess of Portugal. He had been a loyal servant of Philip all his life, and had good reason to think he had earned some tangible reward, or at least some sign of gratitude. Yet he had never been rewarded: the dukedom of Parma was not a gift of Philip, it was his own Italian inheritance; and when he succeeded to it in 1587, and asked Philip's permission to visit the estate, which he had never seen, he had been refused. As for gratitude, Philip's letters seldom revealed anything except a niggardly mistrust.

All through the story of the armada, the Duke of Parma's smouldering resentment can be seen. He never believed it could succeed and did a minimum to help it, carrying out the letter of his orders but nothing more. Throughout the last months of its preparation, he was negotiating a peace treaty with Queen Elizabeth's emissaries. Philip had instructed him that these negotiations were not on any account to succeed, they were only to give the English a false feeling of security, and to waste time until the armada was ready. But Parma knew the queen was hoping to detach him from his allegiance, and would even consider supporting him as King of the Netherlands. And more than that: his own two sons and daughter, with their Portuguese mother, had the same forebears as Philip and a claim at least as good as his to the throne of England. Philip was ordering Parma to do the work and take the risks of leading the invasion, but it never appeared to cross his mind that Parma might hope for a share of the spoils of victory, much less that his dutiful nephew might see himself as a king.

Don Bernardino de Mendoza was the only one of these three men who was happy in his work and perfectly content to be Philip's servant. What sustained him was a passionate hatred of England. He had been Philip's ambassador to the English court, and was one of the two who had been expelled for planning to assassinate the queen. That was in 1583, when he was caught in the plot for which Edward Throgmorton was hanged. His own head had been saved by his diplomatic status, but he had been hustled ignominiously out of the country, and he had never forgiven the English, or the queen in particular, for his own failure and the affront to his dignity.

So his loyalty to Philip was perfectly secure; but he lived in the twilit world of men whose loyalties were divided between their churches and their states. No period of history has been richer in potential spies. Every country had men who were exiled for their religion, or for crimes their religion had impelled them to commit.

As for England, thousands of English Catholics were living abroad, not merely because they were Catholic, but because they were under suspicion, rightly or wrongly, of all degrees of treason and had had to flee the country to escape imprisonment or even execution. Most of them were hard up, and happy to accept a 'pension' from Mendoza, and to tell him what they knew in exchange. But they did not know much, and their pensions were therefore small – just enough to keep them from starving. More useful, and much better paid, were people playing a double game, who still held official positions under the queen but were willing to sell information to a Catholic power. Most useful of all was probably Sir Edward Stafford, the English ambassador in Paris, who brought the contents of his diplomatic pouches to Mendoza's house and accepted ten thousand golden ducats from time to time. (He was once arrested by the French, crossing a bridge of the Seine on foot in the middle of the night on his way back from one of these clandestine visits. It took a lot of explaining.) His code name in Mendoza's letters to the king was Lucio, and sheaf after sheaf of paper reached the Escorial relating what Lucio had told.

Mendoza had correspondents in England too, brave men undoubtedly, risking their lives every day, who smuggled coded despatches across the Channel in boats. Among them was at least one, whom he never named, who visited Plymouth from time to time and wandered round the waterfront observing what Drake was doing, and listening to the gossip in the taverns.

Yet he could never trust anybody. His letters are full of hints of a cloak-and-dagger world with all the elements of a modern spy romance. There were horsemen waylaid on the roads, despatches mysteriously stolen, and nobody knew by whom, knives slipped between ribs in the dark alleys of cities, shaded torches on the coasts at night and men put ashore in rowing boats. There were successful double agents, and men who unaccountably changed sides; and there was also false information, deliberately 'planted' on him and his men by rivals in English pay. Infinite care and cunning were needed not to press people too far and provoke an adverse reaction. Mendoza could never be sure; but labouring day and night, he manipulated his puppets with sinister unrelenting patience, and despatched his couriers, sometimes three and four in a week, to ride the eight hundred miles from Paris to the Escorial with packets of coded letters to the king. He seldom used pious expressions, and probably cared very little for spreading the faith. What he wanted was revenge, to play his part in humbling the English and overthrowing Queen Elizabeth: 'the Englishwoman', he called her in all his letters, as if he could not bear to write her name.

But in spite of all his skill as a master spy, Mendoza had one disastrous fault: he was much too ready to believe what he wanted to hear. And of course what he wanted to hear was precisely what his paid informants tried to tell him. All the Englishmen he knew were Catholics whose religious zeal had led them to be traitors. They only lived for the day when they could go home again, not as criminals but as heroes of the faith. They had all persuaded themselves that day was coming. Consequently the picture of England that Mendoza gave to Philip was one-sided, misleading and untrue.

Philip himself had no means of checking what Mendoza told him. On the contrary, the very few Englishmen he met, and the larger number who wrote to him, were all equally outcasts from their country, men with private axes to grind, men with a consuming personal grudge against England. Philip never met an ordinary Englishman. He never met one of the vast majority, and never had any conception of their patriotism, their pride in being English, or their immense affection for their queen. Nor would he ever have believed that a heretic might cherish his creed as dearly as a Catholic cherished his.

Perhaps no monarch about to launch a war was ever so mistaken about his enemies. Philip was led to believe the Protestants of England were a small minority of oppressors; that the majority were Catholics who would gladly rise in revolt when they sighted his armada; and finally, the most tragic misapprehension of all, that England would welcome him as king or his daughter as queen.

4

Orders

The men in the armada ships, rolling unhappily in the swell at the river mouth, knew very little if any of this history, which would have given them some clue to the reasons why they were there. Instead, on or soon after the day they sailed from Lisbon, a kind of sermon was read aloud in every ship. It was not strictly official, in so far as it was certainly not written by the duke – it was nothing like his style – but it must have had official approval. Probably it was the work of one of the bevy of priests. It was a ranting, violent, passionate recital of all the sins and crimes of England, and especially of Queen Elizabeth. The main factual point of it all, perhaps, was the statement that the heretics of England were really few in number, and the great majority of the people were Catholics eagerly waiting to welcome the armada – which of course was the king's belief and was totally untrue.

'Onward, gentlemen, onward!' it continued. 'Onward with joy and gladness, onward to our glorious, honourable, necessary, profitable and not difficult undertaking. Glorious to God, to His Church, to His saints, and to our country. Glorious to God, who for the punishment of England has allowed Himself to be banished from the land, and the holy sacrifice of the Mass to be abolished. Glorious to His Church, now oppressed and downtrodden by the English heretics. Glorious to the saints, who have there been persecuted, maltreated, insulted and burned. Glorious for our country, because God has deigned to make it His instrument for such great ends. Necessary for the prestige of our king, necessary for the preservation of the Indies, and the fleets and treasures that come from them. Profitable because of the plunder and endless riches we shall gather in England and, by the favour of God, bring gloriously and victoriously back to our homes. We go on a task which offers no great difficulty, because God, in whose sacred cause we go, will lead us. With such a Captain we need have no fear . . .'

The saints of heaven, it promised, would go in the company of the fleet, and the martyrs of England would come out to meet it. 'There also will await us the groans of countless imprisoned Catholics, the tears of widows who lost their husbands for the faith, the sobs of maidens who were forced to sacrifice their lives rather than destroy their souls, the tender children who, suckled on the poison of heresy, are doomed to perdition unless deliverance reaches them in time; and finally myriads of workers, citizens, knights, nobles and clergymen, and all ranks of Catholics, who are oppressed and downtrodden by the heretics and are anxiously looking to us for their liberation . . .

'Let us live Christian lives,' it ended, 'without offence towards our God, in brotherhood with our fellow soldiers and in obedience to our Captains. Courage! Steadfastness! And Spanish bravery! With these the victory is ours, and we have nothing to fear.'

It is impossible to guess what effect all this can have had on the minds of men of that era. A modern propagandist would have said it was far too long and verbose, and grossly overstated its case; and perhaps there were some cynics among the crews who said the same. But it offered, among its fantasies, a well-tried formula for urging men to fight, the incitement of a war both holy and profitable. Plunder if they succeed, and heaven if they fail: all through history, this dual promise has been used to drive men into battle.

One thing they certainly believed was that half of England would rise to welcome them: this came out clearly in the interrogation of prisoners afterwards. Only one man's letters from Lisbon have survived. He was an army captain, and the letters he sent to his home in Andalusia mysteriously found their way into English archives. It was perfectly clear what he hoped for. 'Pray to God for me,' he wrote, 'that He will grant me in England the house of some very rich merchant. I shall raise my standard on it, and he will ransom it from me for thirty thousand ducats, so that I shall be able to repair my own house at home and live at ease.' But he was afraid the Duke of Parma's men would get the lion's share.

At the same time as the sermon, two rather more sober documents were issued to every ship. The first was addressed to the ships' masters: and the second contained a strict instruction that it was to be read out to the crews, not only once but three times a week as long as the voyage lasted. Both of them repeated, in different words, the orders the king had given to the duke; for the king had made use of the duke's inexperience to take the utmost details into his own hands, and had given him elementary directions that not even he would have dared to offer to an old hand like the Marquis of Santa Cruz.

The first of these documents dealt with rations. Each man was to have $1\frac{1}{2}$ pounds of biscuit every day, or 2 pounds of fresh bread. On Sundays and Thursdays he got 6 ounces of salt port and 2 ounces of rice; on Mondays and Thursdays 6 ounces of cheese and 3 ounces of beans or chick peas; and on Wednesdays, Fridays and Saturdays 6 ounces of dried tunny, cod or squid, or 5 sardines, with 3 ounces of beans or chick peas, an ounce and a half of oil and a quarter of a pint of vinegar.

Very detailed orders were given about the wine. The daily ration was roughly equal to a modern bottle, except of Candia wine, which was stronger and 'would bear a double quantity of water'. When that was issued, it would only be a pint. Condado and Lisbon wines were to be used first, and then Lemego and Monzon. Sherry and Candia would be kept until last, because they bore a sea voyage better. Of water, the ration was 3 pints a day for all purposes, cooking, drinking and washing – if anybody thought of washing. Ships' masters were warned against drawing rations for men who were dead or had otherwise left the ship (somebody must have told the king about this common practice). And the ration was apparently the same for everyone: 'You must not serve out more than the ordinary ration to any captain, ensign, sergeant, corporal or other official; nor to any drummer, fifer or other without my order.' But it is hard to believe the officers and gentlemen adventurers were content with such a humble diet. Perhaps, in addition to their hundreds of servants, they brought their own delicacies with them.*

---

*The Spanish ration was much less filling than the standard ration of an English ship at the time. An English sailor got, or was supposed to get, a gallon of beer and a pound of biscuit every day; on Sunday, Tuesday and Thursday 2 pounds of salt beef; on Wednesday, Friday and Saturday 'one quarter of a stockfish or one eighth part of a ling', plus cheese and butter; and on Monday a pound of salt pork with pease. Both diets, of course, were bound to lead to scurvy in the long run.

The second document was the duke's General Order to the Fleet. It was issued as soon as the fleet was clear of the land and was lying at the river mouth, and it showed the king's influence at the very beginning.

The king had sent the duke the first of several letters of instructions in early April, and the very first of all his instructions was as follows: 'In the first place, as all victories are the gift of God Almighty, and the cause we champion is so exclusively His, we may fairly look for His aid and favour, unless by our sins we render ourselves unworthy. You must therefore exercise special care that such cause of offence shall be avoided in the armada, and especially that there shall be no sort of blasphemy. This must be severely enforced, with heavy penalties.'

People since then have said that the orders of the king were more suited to a Sunday School picnic than a fighting fleet. But this was the way his mind worked. He was confident God was on his side, that the whole great project had divine approval; yet he believed God might change his mind if sailors were heard to swear. This injunction therefore reappeared as the first of the duke's written orders. All ranks were to be confessed and absolved before they sailed. 'I also enjoin you to take particular care that no soldier, sailor or other person in the armada shall blaspheme, or deny Our Lord, Our Lady or the Saints, under very severe punishment to be inflicted at our discretion. With regard to other less serious oaths, the officers of the ships will do their best to repress their use, and will punish offenders by docking their wine rations, or in some other way at their discretion. As these disorders usually arise from gambling, you will endeavour to repress this as much as possible, especially the prohibited games, and allow no play at night on any account.'

Next the duke proclaimed a truce in all existing quarrels or disputes, to last the whole time of the expedition and a month afterwards. For violation of it the penalty was death on the ground of treason. And he went straight on: 'As it is an evident inconvenience, as well as an offence to God, that public or other women should be permitted to accompany such an armada, I order that none shall be taken on board. If any attempt be made to embark women, I authorize the captains and masters of ships to prevent it, and if it is done surreptitiously the offenders must be severely punished. Every morning at daybreak the ships' boys shall, as usual, say their "Good morrow" at the foot of the mainmast, and at sunset the Ave Maria. Some days, and at least every Saturday, they shall say the Salve with the Litany.'

Finally among the moral injunctions, the duke asked for 'perfect good feeling and friendship between soldiers and sailors', and decreed that nobody should carry a dagger. This was a wise precaution. Whenever sailors took large crowds of soldiers to sea, there was likely to be friction between them. Sailors regarded soldiers as a nuisance because they got in the way of the working of the ship; and soldiers, at a disadvantage in unfamiliar surroundings, resented the sailors' air of superior knowledge. At all ranks, both sides were touchy and ready to take offence.

The rest of the duke's orders were more or less standard practice in any large fleet under sail, though the king left none of them unsaid. The fleet was to keep well together. No ship was to leave it without the duke's permission. The squadron of urcas or merchantmen was always to be in the middle, and no ship was to get ahead of the flagship, or enter port or drop anchor unless the flagship had done so. Signals by guns, flags and lights, or by taking in one or more topsails, were laid down for alterations of course and for sighting strange ships or land. Men of quick sight were to be stationed at mastheads, particularly at sunrise and sunset, and they were to count the sail of the armada to ensure that no intruders had joined it. All ships, or at least the leaders of squadrons, were to come up into the lee of the flagship every day for orders and to receive the watchword, saluting as they did so with bugles if they had any, or fifes if they had not, and two cheers from the crew. But in case the weather made this impossible, a watchword was provided for every day of the week: Sunday, Jesus; Monday, Holy Ghost; Tuesday, Most Holy Trinity; Wednesday, Santiago; Thursday, The Angels; Friday, All Saints; and Saturday, Our Lady.

Then rendezvous were established – one of the many obvious precautions the king had thought he must mention to the duke: 'If any ship be forced off course by storms before reaching Cape Finisterre, they will make direct for that point, where they will find orders from me; but if no such orders await them, they will make for Corunna. Any infraction of this order will be punished by death and forfeiture. On leaving Cape Finisterre the course will be to the Scilly Islands, and ships must try to sight the islands from the south, taking great care to look to their soundings. Ships are not to return to Spain on any account. If on their arrival at the Scillies the armada is behind them, they will cruise off the place, keeping up to windward, until the armada appears, or until they have satisfied themselves that it has passed them, in which case they will make for Mounts Bay, between Lands End and the Lizard, where instructions will await them if the armada is not there.'

The duke then went on to more individual orders, on points one would suppose were obvious to any well-trained soldier. He wrote them in no particular sequence and sometimes repeated himself, as if he had simply noted them down as they came into his head, or as they were suggested to him by officers who knew about such things. The soldiers' arms, for example, must be kept clean and ready for use. So must the guns, with plenty of shot made ready, with the necessary powder and match, and 'the usual buckets and tubs full of vinegar and water, and all the customary preparations of old sails and wet blankets, to protect the ships against fire thrown upon them.' (Was he right about this? Surely vinegar and water was used as a sort of antiseptic, not for putting out fires.) 'Let great care be taken with the cartridges of each piece, to avoid their taking fire, and let the ramrods and sponges be close at hand . . . Great care must be taken to extinguish the galley fires before sunset . . . The soldiers must allow the rations to be distributed by those responsible for the duty, and must not themselves go down and take or choose them by force as they have sometimes done . . . As the mariners have to attend to the working of the ship, their quarters should be in the fore and after castles, out of the way of the soldiers who might embarrass them . . . I also order that the soldiers' quarters be kept clear of boxes and other things, and that truckle beds are not to be allowed in any ship. If any such exist, they are to be demolished immediately, and I order the sailors not to allow them. If the infantry possess them let the sailors inform me, and I will have them removed . . .'

The whole document ended abruptly, without any valediction or prayer, or the rousing words that most commanders put in their battle orders, but merely with a final comprehensive threat: 'In the interests of His Majesty's service, no infraction whatever is to be allowed of any portion of these orders, otherwise the offenders shall be well punished at our discretion.'

It was a long way short of inspiring. It all had the unmistakable air of being put together in a hurry. The duke could have done much better – he wrote forcefully and logically when he had time. But, after all, he could not have given orders from his own experience because he had none, and at the time he was certainly harassed by too many people too eager to offer advice. At least, the orders provided for all the eventualities the king or the duke, or the advisers, had been able to think of – everything, that is, except disaster.

The General Orders, however, stopped short at the coast of Cornwall. What was to happen after that was included in separate secret letters from the king; and it seems the duke made use of the delay in the river mouth to call a council of war and pass on these secrets orally to his senior officers – for it was only after that interlude that the sea-officers made any protest against what the king expected them to do.

It is a pity, but one can hardly discover anything authentic about the characters of these senior men, whose names are so well known: Recalde, Oquendo, Bovadillo, Bertendona, de Leyva and the two cousins de Valdes. One can read of their martial achievements, which were considerable, but those give no clue to what sort of people they were. Pedro and Diego Flores de Valdes were known as quarrelsome men, apart from the permanent quarrel they had with each other. De Leyva was the glamorous man among them, distinguished by flaxen hair and beard, a well-known courtier and a favourite of the king; but he was not a mere playboy, he was also a brilliant and popular commander. Recalde was much the oldest of them (he was sixty-two, an old man in those days) and he seems in retrospect the most admirable, always calm and wise and friendly. But the others are shadowy figures, and so they must remain.

They were divided, of course, into soldiers and sailors, with the soldiers claiming the most importance; but it was not a perfectly sharp division because many of them in the past had fought both on land and sea. Sometimes there were angry words among them, but surprisingly few considering the awful experience they went through together. On the whole, they seem to have liked and respected the duke, though Pedro de Valdes was sometimes furious with him, as he was with almost everyone; for the duke never pretended to have any expert knowledge and was always ready to accept advice – but also, when any knotty problem arose, was prepared to cut through it by innate common sense.

In general, however, there are two things one can say with certainty about these men: they were no fools, and their courage was beyond question. Stupid mistakes were made in preparing the armada and in its strategic plan. But once it was at sea its commanders made no mistakes at all.

No report has survived of that meeting in the river mouth – perhaps through its highly secret nature none was ever written. One must imagine a glittering cavalcade of rowing boats or barges which brought the senior officers from their ships, splendidly cloaked and armed, to be saluted according to their rank by the crew of the flagship *San Martin* and greeted in the waist of the ship by their diffident commander-in-chief. And perhaps one may also imagine, at this particular meeting, long silences, raised eyebrows, as he unfolded to them, round the table in his cabin, the scheme the king had proposed – a scheme which he himself had been unqualified to query.

In essence the scheme was simple, although the king's letters were long. 'You will sail with the whole of the armada,' he had written, 'and go straight to the English Channel, which you will ascend as far as Cape Margate, where you will join hands with the Duke of Parma, my nephew, and hold the passage for his crossing.' The success of the business, he pointed out, depended on striking at the root, and therefore the armada was not to seek battle on the way, even if Drake (as some reports suggested) had sailed to Spanish waters. Nor was it to attempt any landing. If Drake followed and approached it, it could attack; but nothing was to divert it from reaching Margate and carrying out the plan.

Simple it was, but the more the old sea-officers mulled over it the less they liked it. It defied a basic principal of generalship: never attempt a rendezvous in the presence of the enemy. It was only in later centuries that this was accepted as a dictum, but it was always a matter of common sense; and men like Recalde were not lacking in military common sense. What if Parma was not there? Indeed, how could he be there if he was depending on the armada to protect him? Margate was nearly fifty miles from Parma's nearest port, Dunkirk. By what means of communication could the two dukes arrange to arrive at the same moment? How could two sailing fleets in narrow seas reach the same place from opposite directions? And, incidentally, what did the king mean by Cape Margate? Margate, on the eastern point of Kent, had no sort of anchorage or shelter. Did he perhaps mean the Downs, the anchorage farther south between the coast and the Goodwin sands, where English ships habitually waited for a change of wind when they were turning from the Channel to the Thames, or the Thames to the Channel? If so, that anchorage above all other was sure to be held in strength by the English fleet, and not by Parma. This last point, in fact, the king had admitted as a possibility. 'If you do not come across the enemy before you arrive off Cape Margate, and find there only the Lord Admiral of England with his fleet, or even if you find the united fleets of the Lord Admiral and Drake, yours should be superior to both of them in quality, and you may, in God's name and cause, give battle to them, trying to gain the wind and every other advantage, in the hope that Our Lord may give you the victory.'

This raised the point that distressed them most of all. Not the prospect of a major battle, they were perfectly willing for that; but the prospect of having to fight it without any harbour behind them. The English would have their own harbours close at hand for repairs and supplies: the Spaniards would have none except in Spain. There was no harbour big enough for the armada between the Thames and the Isle of Wight. The Isle of Wight, somebody said, was very strongly guarded. In that case, they all agreed, they ought to take one of the harbours farther west; Falmouth, Plymouth or Dartmouth.

But the king had clearly said they were not to go ashore. About the Isle of Wight he had been especially vehement. They might take it on their way back to the westward, after Parma's army was safely landed, or if the main design had failed, but they were not on any account to enter harbour there on the way up the Channel. (Coming back, he added, they might also consider taking Ireland.) He made only one concession about harbours on the voyage east.

If they were caught out in a storm, they might shelter in a defenceless port or refuge on the English coast. But that was not much help, because there was no such thing as a port or refuge that was undefended.

The duke knew of one particular reason, apart from the king's impatience, why he had been forbidden to go ashore and take a harbour. The king had promised Parma that the armada would give him six thousand veteran Spanish soldiers to add to his landing force. The duke had always had doubts about this and had refused to commit himself; it was the only point in the plan that he had queried. He had told the king he would hand over the soldiers if he had not had to fight on the way; but if there had been a battle, the number of men he could spare would have to depend on the casualties. The king, as usual, had not taken the slightest notice of this reservation and had not changed his promise to Parma. He had left Parma to believe he would certainly get the men, and had left the duke to believe it was understood that he would do it if he could. Consequently, this was one of the points on which the two dukes were at cross-purposes throughout the whole affair.

But clearly, if the duke were to capture a port, he would have to fight for it and leave a garrison in it too. In that case, he certainly could not supply the whole of the six thousand men, and on that ground alone, he knew the king would not hear of such a change of plan.

This was just the sort of situation the duke had dreaded. He perfectly understood his officers' worries when he heard them discussed. No doubt he regretted very much that he had not understood them earlier. But he could not promise to make the king change his mind. He did not even promise to try. Instead, the idea arose in the course of discussion that Recalde should be the one to write to the king.

This the old admiral did, and despatched his letter as soon as he had a chance. It was a marvellous letter, neither sycophantic nor critical, but tactful and ingenious. It never appeared to tell the king what he ought to do, but it gently provided facts on which the king, had he been an intelligent man, must have reached the correct decision. The duke, it said, was working with great energy as usual. Lately, the admiral had not been able to help him much

because he had had an attack of sciatica; but, thank God, the
remedies he applied had been effective and he had risen that
morning without any pain.

'So far as I understand,' he went on with sailorly bluntness,
'the object of the armada is to meet and vanquish the enemy by
main force, which I hope to God we shall do if he will fight us, as
doubtless he will. If he will not, we have to proceed to the Downs,
and join hands with the Duke of Parma's forces in Dunkirk, whose
passage across we are to protect to the most convenient point
which may be agreed upon. This point should be the nearest
possible one on either side of the Thames. This will take some
time, as I understand there will be a cavalry force, which cannot be
carried over in one passage and we shall be lucky if it can be done
in two.'

This was not what the king had said, but it may have been
what he meant. At any rate, when it was put like this it made sense.
They would not meet Parma off Margate, but would first give
battle to any enemy forces they found in the Downs, and then go
across to Dunkirk to collect Parma's forces there.

Then the admiral went on to mention harbours, looking at it
from the point of view of the 'highly necessary reinforcements of
men and stores'. The Netherlands, he supposed, would be 'much
exhausted', and therefore reinforcements would have to come
from Spain. 'In the case of our encountering and defeating the
enemy, I feel sure he will not suffer so much damage that he cannot
repair it, at least enough to be able to impede our reinforcements
high up the Channel. But it will be difficult for him to do this if our
armada is stationed in one of the [English] ports lying closest to
Spain. If it is possible for the reinforcement to be sent in sufficient
strength to attack those ports while the conquest is being effected
higher up, that will be the best course. The armada might then
return to the western ports and push a force in towards the Bristol
Channel, or make a junction by land with Parma's army. As the
Turk is not troubling us,' he added, 'a dozen galleys might be sent
with the supplies and men, the latter being as much needed as the
former, for they dwindle in the same way.'

This is the first recorded reference to any reinforcements for
the armada. Certainly the king had made no provision for them in
his plans. But Recalde wrote as if he took it for granted that the

king had thought of everything and expected to send reinforcements. In fact, Recalde knew better than anyone how much
the resources of Spain had been stretched already. More men
might be collected, and more supplies in a few merchant ships, and
even the galleys he suggested; but a fighting force, able to capture
ports on its own account – this was entirely out of the question. To
keep the Channel open, to hold a line of supply between the
armada and home, a port in the west of England was essential: the
only force that could take one was the armada itself, and the
obvious time to do it was when it passed those ports on its voyage
east. But Recalde, with his admirable tact, did not propose this to
the king: he merely provided the facts, and left it to the king to
propose the one feasible solution.

But so far as the archives show, the king never even
acknowledged the admiral's letter. Certainly he made no change
whatever in his plan.

On board the *San Martin* during that council meeting in the river
mouth, probably filed away in the very cabin where they met, was
the sealed letter from the king that none of them had read. It was
directed to the Duke of Parma, to be delivered by the Duke of
Medina Sidonia only after Parma had landed in England. In any
other event, it was to be returned to His Majesty. In a covering
letter the king had given slightly different orders to the duke: he
was to deliver it only after Parma had landed, or had shown
uncertainty of being able to do so.

Why had the king chosen to send the letter in this unusual
way? It can only have been that he was afraid, if he sent it straight
to Parma, that Parma would be tempted to open it too soon. If he
had, the resentment he carefully repressed would certainly have
exploded.

The letter revealed that at the last moment the king had got
cold feet. It told Parma what he was to do if the expedition 'should
not be so prosperous that our arms can settle matters, nor, on the
other hand, so contrary that the enemy shall be relieved of anxiety
on our account (which God surely will not permit), and affairs be
so counterbalanced that peace may not be altogether undesirable'.
Parma must then seek a treaty with three conditions: 'The first is
that in England the free use and exercise of our holy Catholic faith

shall be permitted to all Catholics, native and foreign, and that those who are in exile shall be allowed to return. The second is that all the places in my Netherlands which the English hold shall be restored to me; and the third that the English shall compensate me for the injury they have done to me, my dominions and subjects; which will amount to a very great sum.

'These points stand in importance in the order they are here given, and although the first is the one I especially demand, you will use your own discretion as to whether you should press it first, or propose them all together, or begin with the two last. The question of returning the Netherlands fortresses is also very important, especially that of Flushing; but on the third point, after you have discussed it thoroughly and proved that the recompense due to me would be more than their Treasury could meet, you may drop it in favour of the free exercise of the Catholic faith. This point may be used as a lever to obtain the other two.

'With regard to the free exercise of Catholicism, you may point out to them that since freedom of worship is allowed to the Huguenots in France, there will be no loss of dignity in allowing the same privilege to Catholics in England. If they reply that I do not allow the same toleration in the Netherlands, you may tell them that their country is in a different position, [he did not say how it was different] and point out how conducive to their tranquillity it would be to satisfy the Catholics in this way, and how much it would increase the trade of England and their profits . . .

'However much they may promise, you must not assume they will fulfil it unless they have given very good security. For this reason, you should try to obtain as hostages some men of rank, with large followings and many friends, or perhaps some English fortresses to hold, even for a limited time. During that time, we would see how they carried out the conditions. To disregard this point would be to build on sand . . .'

The more one looks at this letter, the more outrageous it seems. The king could never have dreamed that if it was not read by Parma his own filing system at Simancas would preserve it to be read by posterity. After all his protestations he was now prepared to agree, if he had to, that Elizabeth should remain Queen of England; he was prepared to leave the heretics to their own belief. Of his three demands, the money recompense was only a bargaining point. So they were reduced to two.

The places in the Netherlands were under negotiation between Parma and the emissaries of the queen at that very moment. It was not unlikely that the queen, to save trouble, would surrender Flushing, and it was more than likely she would withdraw from the Netherlands altogether if Philip would offer the Netherlands Protestants anything like the same tolerance he was demanding for the English Catholics.

As for the Catholics, the queen would have answered that they were already free to exercise their faith and she was quite willing to let them continue, provided they behaved as good citizens. That left the exiles as the only difficult, and indeed impossible demand. In English eyes, these people were not in exile because they were Catholics but because they were on the run from the law, accused or suspected of treason, of trying to overthrow the government or assassinate the queen. Many of them admitted and even boasted of their crimes. Philip, of course, had never seen them in that light: he had heard only their side of the story. If he could have heard and listened to the other side, he would have had to admit, as a ruler himself, that the amnesty he was proposing was a demand no civilized state could accept. It would have made chaos of the law.

If Parma had known the king was prepared to settle on such simple terms, he would have said there was nothing worth fighting for: excepting the return of the exiles, the terms could be won by negotiation without an invasion at all – or at least it was well worth trying. And if he had known the king was tricking him, by deliberately keeping him in the dark until it was too late to stop, he would have rebelled, and perhaps tried to make a bargain with the queen in his own name.

This secret letter shows Philip in a true light. He could not have proposed to compromise with the purpose of God. Therefore, he must have believed these terms fulfilled it. He also believed they could be won by negotiation. What more then could the armada win? In the end, not even he could define in any reasonable words the motive for which the armada was sent to sea and the whole immense tragedy was endured.

5

The Armada at Sea

The armada came out of the river in the evening and night of 30th May with a very light offshore breeze. Some of the ships were towed across the bar by the galleys. The duke, who watched anxiously as best he could in the darkness, thanked God when dawn showed all of them safely out.

But during the day the weather broke again. The first leg of their voyage, up to Cape Finisterre, was north, and the wind came in from the north north west, as foul as it could have been. The fleet stood out to sea close-hauled on the starboard tack. Somebody told the duke that farther offshore, in the open sea, the wind was sure to be southerly.

But it was not. They held the same course for thirty-six hours. Then the wind backed to the west north west – usually an omen of bad weather – and the duke gave the order to put about. It was a laborious business and took a lot of time, but at length the fleet was on the other tack. In the next dawn, after three days at sea, they sighted land again and found they had only progressed five miles from where they had started. In that dawn the wind fell calm, and the ships were left without steerage way, drifting helplessly and rolling abominably in the Atlantic swell. The duke sent a pinnace back to the river to tell the king that when the wind got up he proposed to change tack again and hoped to weather the Berlengas Islands, fifty miles north of Lisbon, on the following day.

Far from it. Within the next week they were beating to and fro in a storm and the pilots told him they were near Cape St Vincent, over a hundred miles from Lisbon but in the wrong direction. One of the urcas, the 440-ton *David Chico*, lost her mainmast. A galleon took her in tow but that delayed everybody, and the duke had to put some expert Basque sailors on board and leave her to make her own way to land. Among other things, she was carrying twenty of the mules or horses for the invasion force.

It was not until 10th June that the duke could report a ray of hope. 'It seems,' he wrote guardedly, 'that the wind has begun to blow from the west south west, so I hope to God I can begin to sail this armada on a straight course.' The pilots said they were ninety leagues from land in latitude 40° north. If so, after eleven days' hard sailing, they were still a hundred miles farther from Finisterre than they had been when they left the river at Lisbon.

They had made the all-important discovery that the armada, as a coherent fleet, could not make any progress at all to windward. On the contrary, however hard the sailors tried, it lost ground on every tack. Its first three days of sailing give a measurement of the course made good when it was as close-hauled as it could go. Between the seaward and the landward tacks, the wind backed by four points, and the armada finished up almost where it had started. Therefore, doing its best to sail to windward, it actually progressed two points to leeward.

The causes of this crippling disability make rather a long story. The main physical cause was that the Spanish ships had high fighting castles, and the fundamental reason why they had them was that the Spaniards were not seafaring people by nature; they had no innate respect, as the English had, for the art of seamanship. Their sailors were skilful but their aristocrats and their national heroes were soldiers; so their concept of sea-fighting was soldierly. In a Spanish galleon the soldiers regarded themselves as the most important people. They were commanded by their own land officers, not by the captain of the ship, and they looked on the sailors somewhat as their servants, men not far removed from galley slaves, whose only job was to carry them to the scene of battle and put them in an advantageous position to win it.

This idea went back to the early years of chivalry, when kings requisitioned merchant ships to transport their armies. The regular captains and crews continued to sail these requisitioned ships, but seamen had a lowly social status, and the men in charge were the knights who commanded the army. They avoided fighting at sea if they could, but if they had to do it their only method was to tell the sailors to lay the ship alongside the enemy's, and then board it and fight hand to hand with the weapons they used on shore. To help them, they built little castles at either end of the medieval ships, the fore- and aftercastles, and decorated them with model wooden battlements; some even had Gothic windows, and brickwork painted on. These looked imposing and gave the advantage of height for throwing missiles, and also perhaps gave the soldiers an illusion of protection – no more than an illusion, because they had to be lightly built, to avoid upsetting the stability of the ship.

In Spain that ancient outlook had survived the invention of sea artillery. The soldiers did not despise the guns the armada carried, but the use of them, as they saw things, was to slow down an enemy ship by cutting up its masts and rigging, so that they could overhaul it and get alongside it. They still expected to win their battles by grappling and boarding the enemy and fighting hand to hand; and so they still insisted on castles.

In the course of time, as ships grew bigger, the castles had also grown to such a size that the area of the hull of a fighting ship was almost as much as the area of her sails. That did not matter much with the wind astern, and the Spaniards made their ocean voyages, across the Atlantic and Pacific, by choosing the routes and seasons so that the wind was almost always astern. But to windward the castles destroyed the sailing ability of the ships. The forecastle blew the heads of them off the wind, and the size and windage of both the castles blew them bodily down to leeward.

A single galleon might have made a point or so to windward, and the small pinnaces, which had a fore-and-aft rig, could do much better still; while the galleasses and galleys, of course, could move dead into the wind if the sea was not too rough for their oars. But the progress of a fleet was limited by the worst of its sailers. In the armada, the worst were not the galleons but the merchant ships, the Baltic urcas and the Mediterranean naos. These were very broad in the beam, probably only twice as long as they were wide. They were built for carrying cargo round the coasts of Europe, and designed without any thought of sailing to windward; for in their everyday work if the wind was against them they simply anchored, with the patience of the ages of sail, and waited for it to change. With castles built on them, their sailing performance was laughable.

On top of all this, it was always more difficult to tack a whole fleet than to tack a single ship, unless all the crews were equally and impeccably trained. Coming about from one tack to the next, somebody in the crowd was sure to make a mess of things, to miss stays, fall off on the wrong tack and lose his steerage way; and then all the rest would have to give ground to keep their formation.

Being a mixed fleet, with ships that ranged from very good to very bad, the armada had every possible disadvantage. It was extremely difficult to keep them all together. Even sailing downwind the urcas were slow and the galleons had to shorten sail to avoid leaving them astern. The fleet could make some progress with the wind abeam, but only at the cost of a lot of leeway. To windward it was hopeless. Even at this early stage of the voyage it must have been evident to anyone who looked ahead that the English Channel would be a one-way ride. The fleet could not sail up it except with a westerly wind, and unless the wind changed it could not sail out again. Nor could it stop and anchor. If it did, it would not be able to defend itself.

No doubt the sailors in the armada had foreseen these troubles, but with the soldiers in charge there was nothing they could do about them. Some of the armada ships, waiting in Lisbon, had had new castles built on them, or had the old ones heightened by a deck or two. Besides, nobody had ever tried before to manage a fleet of a hundred and thirty ships, and it may have been worse than any of them expected. At any rate nobody had warned the duke how difficult it would be, and if they had warned the king he had not taken any notice but had trusted, as he always did, that God would solve any problem he could not solve himself.

Yet while the Spaniards, at the last moment, were building up their castles to even greater heights, they knew the English were building ships without any castles at all, or with only vestigial remains of them. Even the king had warned the duke that the English would use novel tactics, and the sea-officers had been discussing them for months, if not for years. 'You must remember,' the king had written in his secret instructions, 'that the enemy's object will be to fight at long range, because of his advantage in artillery. The aim of our men, on the contrary, must be to bring him to close quarters and grapple with him, and you will have to be very careful to have this carried out. For your information, a statement is sent to you describing the way the enemy uses his artillery, in order to deliver his fire low and sink his opponents' ships; and you will take such precautions as you think necessary in this respect.'

The words suggest self-satisfied conservatism, but may only have meant the king knew when he wrote them that it was too late to change the Spanish ships and tactics, whether the threatened English method was better or not.

Some of the Spaniards, even perhaps the king, must have suspected their soldiers' ideas of sea-fighting were out of date. Some of the sailors must have suspected the English ships would sail much better than their own. What they did not yet know, but were soon to learn, was that the castle-less English ships were an outward sign of an epochal revolution in fighting at sea.

The king had told the duke to keep him well informed of everything he did, and during this early part of the voyage he dutifully sent a pinnace to carry a letter back to Lisbon every two or three days. He also wrote to the Duke of Parma. Just before they left port, a messenger from Parma named Captain Moresin had sailed into the river in a pinnace. The message he brought was the first communication the duke had had from Parma; and as things turned out, it was the last.

Not that Moresin had much to tell, except that Parma's army was smaller than the duke expected, seventeen thousand men and one thousand horse. He had really come to see how the armada was getting on, and Parma had told him to come back at once. But for three weeks the duke would not let him go, for fear of what would happen if he was captured sailing back up the Channel. On 10th June, however, he changed his mind.

In a letter he sent with the captain, the duke showed he had taken Recalde's point about capturing a port, but not the point about picking up Parma in Dunkirk. He still expected to meet him at sea, as the king had ordered. 'The king has instructed me not to turn aside,' he wrote, 'and even if I am impeded simply to clear the way and proceed to join hands with you, advising you when I reach the English coast, so that knowing my whereabouts Your Excellency may bring out your fleet. I very much wish the coast were capable of sheltering so great a fleet as this, so that we might take a safe port to have at our backs; but as this is impossible, we shall have to make the best use we can of what accommodation there may be; and it will be necessary that as soon as Captain Moresin arrives with you (which will depend on the weather) you should come out to meet me, and should send back to me the pinnace which takes the captain, to tell me your position and where we may meet.'

He went on to say that he had called together all the pilots and practical seamen who knew the English coast to advise him about a harbour; but unluckily the names of the two they recommended, as he wrote them in the letter, are unrecognizable: one was Gouchepe and the other Harlage. Possibly he meant Ipswich and Harwich. He had told them the most important thing was to make a junction between the armada and Parma's fleet.

Moresin made wonderful time on his voyage back to Dunkirk. Parma replied to this letter twelve days after it was written. But he did not reply to the duke, he replied to the king – and replied in a fine fit of indignation. 'From what Moresin says, it seems the duke still has doubts about being able to give me the six thousand Spanish troops from the fleet, which Your Majesty always said I should have, and even promised me more, if possible, quite recently. He also seems to have persuaded himself that I may be able to go out and meet him with my boats. These things cannot be.' (The king wrote in the margin here, 'God grant that no embarrassment may arise from this.') Parma insisted he could not depart in the slightest degree from the plan laid down, or the king's express orders: he must have the six thousand troops, or more. 'As for my going out to join him, he must be made to see that with these little, low, flat boats, built for rivers and not for the sea, I cannot diverge from the short direct passage across which has been agreed. Indeed it will be a great mercy of God if we are able to reach land in these boats, even when the passage is protected and free from the enemy's ships. This was one of the principal reasons which moved Your Majesty to lay down the precise and prudent orders you did, that your Spanish fleet should assure us the passage across, as it was perfectly clear that these boats could not contend against ships, much less stand the sea, for they will not weather the slightest storm.'

The fatal misunderstanding was growing. Parma told the king

he would send Moresin back to the duke to tell him all this. But there is no record that he ever did so, and certainly Moresin never arrived. Nor did the king tell the duke what Parma had said, although he had ample opportunity. The duke was left to believe that Parma had a seagoing fleet and even some fighting ships, not merely river boats and barges; that Parma would come out to sea to meet him; and that his own reservations about the troops were agreed.

Inevitably, they must have made another discovery in those first days out of Lisbon: the hellish discomfort of overcrowded sailing ships.

Of course this hit the soldiers more than the sailors. The sailors at least knew what they were in for. Their quarters were in the castles and most of their work was on the upper deck, or indeed up the rigging. So they had fresh air – too much of it perhaps; they could see what was happening; and they had plenty to occupy their minds.

But most of the soldiers had never been to sea. They were quartered below decks, and discouraged from coming up to the daylight, where they got in the way of the sailors. Life on board had not been too bad in Lisbon, where the ships stood still and the gunports were open to let in some light and air. But at sea the ports were shut, the main hatches were battened down. Below, the ships were airless and stinking, and the pitch darkness was only relieved by a few candle lanterns or oil lamps swinging from the beams. Without any kind of heating or ventilation, these lower decks were stifling hot on summer days and bitterly cold at night, and hot or cold they were perpetually wet. There the soldiers slept and ate on the bare boards, crowded elbow to elbow, and sat around with nothing to do except when they were called to drill or clean their arms or eat their dinners – if they could, for all the time, the dark decks reeled and creaked and lurched. Nothing could have been more sickening: the dark, the swinging lamps, the narrow space, the smell, the crowd, the lack of air.

Ever since ocean sailing began, being seasick has been a joke for men who are not afflicted by it. One of the earliest sea ballads tells the comical story of pilgrims on their voyage to a shrine in Spain, who could only eat toast although they had paid for their dinners; and in the armada at first there were probably ribald chuckles when men, or especially officers, abruptly lost their dignity. But before long it was not amusing at all. Indeed, seasickness must have had a far-reaching effect on history. It was weakening and discouraging in itself, and also it began a vicious circle of other ills which always sapped the strength of soldiers who were sent to sea.

No doubt the duke himself was miserably sick, as he had predicted. He probably never got over it, although he had the delicacy not to say so in his letters. But he at least had a cabin in decent seclusion. For the soldiers, the only sanitary arrangements were on the upper deck, either side of the bowsprit, under the open sky and over the open sea. It stood to reason that men in the desperate throes of seasickness were unlikely to struggle up there. Instead, they used a bucket for all their needs, if they could find one that was not already full; and if they could not they used the corners of the decks they lived on. Their living quarters were nauseous with vomit and excreta. The only way to clean up the muck was to swill down the decks with buckets of sea water. That washed most of it down through the holds where their food supply was stored, and into the bilges. They lived on top of a cess pit.

Consequently they infected each other with every intestinal disease they had brought on board, and outbreaks of what the English called the flux or dysentery made matters even worse. Moreover they could never wash their bodies or their clothes or blankets — three pints of water a day, for cooking and drinking too. So they all got fleas and lice, and the first of the deaths on long voyages were usually from typhus. Scurvy from lack of vitamins perhaps killed more in the end, but it took longer.

The armada was the first large fleet sent on a long voyage crammed with soldiers, in the expectation that the soldiers would still be fighting fit at the end of it; and it was the duke who was fated to make this historic experiment. Seafaring nations, especially the English, went on trying to do the same thing for centuries, but in the days of sail it never worked. Starting with the armada, it took them two hundred years to learn that conditions on board, with such a crowd, were worse than the human body or spirit could withstand; so that even soldiers who survived needed weeks of rest ashore before they were able to do their job and face a well-armed enemy.

A third discovery the armada made in those early days was the most alarming of all. Their huge supplies of food were going rotten. The duke first mentioned this in the same letter, on 10th June, which expressed his hope of better weather. He pointed out how many men he had to feed, how many ships there were, how slow their progress was and how long it had taken to load the provisions, so that some had already been on board for months before he sailed. 'Now,' he wrote, 'they have gone bad, rotted and spoiled. I can see it causing the men much difficulty, but there is nothing I can do to improve the situation. We have had to throw a large part of the food overboard because it was only giving men the plague and making them sick. I very much hoped not to worry Your Majesty with this sort of thing, but the success of what we are going to do is so important that I must feed the men properly and satisfy everyone's needs. So I must inform Your Majesty, and humbly beg you to agree to send out to us more provisions to supplement what we have. What we mainly lack is meat and fish, but we need everything else as well.'

Anyhow, the duke was right about the weather. On the 11th the wind settled into the south west, dead astern for the course they now had to make, and in three days they sighted Cape Finisterre. That was an average speed of a good four knots, and it was the highest speed the armada ever made. In that frustrating fortnight, they had made good only two hundred and forty miles, seventeen miles a day, so everyone was delighted to see the Cape at last. The duke wrote again, a cheerful letter without a word about sickness or provisions. 'The men are well, God be praised, and the cool weather is helping to keep us in good health, so I have great hope that His Divine Majesty will bring us in this expedition to a happy and favourable conclusion.' He told the king how he summoned the generals and the most experienced sailors, whenever it was fine enough for boats, to tell them his ideas, weigh up their arguments and reach the wisest decisions. He had ordered the commanders and generals of the squadrons to inspect their men and ships and make sure they had carried out his orders and were ready, so that when they found the enemy everyone would know what to do and go to his station without confusion. And he added: 'As we pass Finisterre I shall give orders for all ships to clear their decks so that no bath, bed, chest or trunk remains there but all are stowed away and everything not needed shall be thrown overboard. Beginning with this galleon, and then with those I can reach, I shall carry out this order myself, and I shall send trustworthy men to do it throughout the armada with no exception. We shall continue from here cleared for action as if we were in the presence of the enemy.'

He seems to have been a little obsessed by these beds and boxes. Of course it was necessary to clear the decks before action, but in later years a well-run ship could do the job in six minutes, so there was really no desperate need to hurry. He had already given the order before they left Lisbon, but clearly nobody had done very much about it; and perhaps indeed, hating the sea as he did, he had some sympathy for the men who were lucky enough to possess these last shreds of comfort.

Anyone would have thought from that letter that everything was going splendidly. But it was an exception, and it was sent un-coded, as if it was meant for other eyes than the king's. The next day, he sent another one, in code, about the mounting disaster of the food. 'Four days ago I sent a ship to Corunna to tell the Marquis de Cerralvo [the governor of Galicia] this armada's position and to ask him to load all the meat, salt meat, salt pork, cheese, fish and tallow which he had there into ships, barges, fishing boats or any other vessels that could be found, and to send them out to look for me, and if the weather forces me to change position to follow me. I also sent a commissar with orders to help in the loading of all these supplies, to check them as they were loaded and to make every effort to reach me. And now I am sending this pinnace for the same purpose, because if the weather permits I intend not to stop but to press on without delaying a moment. Rather than be delayed, I will put up with everything, hoping that Your Majesty will see fit to order fresh supplies to be sent immediately, especially meat, fish and water, for since yesterday several ships have sent asking me for water, and it is this shortage that is causing me most concern.'

Water was a new worry. Broaching fresh barrels, some ships had found that many had leaked and were empty, and those that were full were green and slimy and undrinkable. Some crews had had to try drinking the water, slime and all, because they had nothing else, and it had given them acute diarrhoea – and the effect on the lower decks of hundreds of men with diarrhoea is better not thought about. As the rumour spread from ship to ship, others started to tap their barrels and made the same discovery; and the farther they rummaged into the depths of the holds, trying the oldest casks at the bottom, the less likely it grew that they would find anything fit to drink. The wine was all right, and they could perhaps have drunk their bottle a day and nothing else; but they could not boil their salt meat and fish in it.

To be at sea with contrary winds in command of thirty thousand men with uneatable food and undrinkable water – this was a nightmare not even the duke could have dreamed. He did not lose his head, or his determination to do his unwelcome duty. He had begged the king to send more food, but had not relied on him and had made his own arrangements with the local governor. His advisers had begun to press him to put in to Corunna for fresh supplies, but he was reluctant to do that for fear, he said, that the soldiers and sailors would desert as usual. 'As usual' was the phrase he used, but to enter a Spanish harbour again, now that the soldiers had seen what life at sea could be like, would surely have tempted them far more than usual. Besides, it would have seemed an admission of failure. So he resolved to wait offshore until the boats he had asked for came out, and then to set course for the Channel. Meanwhile, more and more lurid stories of sickness and stinking barrels were brought to him in his flagship. There was nothing fit to eat except biscuit, he was told, and some of that was very bad. All the squid had gone overboard, which no doubt was the best and only place for barrels of decaying squid. Some ships had beans and peas they could use. Others had nothing that was any good, for the simple reason that when the food was served, the men refused to eat it. Nobody yet had died, but uncountable hundreds of men were out of action with symptoms of food poisoning and were lying around the decks in pain and misery.

It is hard to say why this particular disaster should have struck the armada. The Spaniards and Portuguese had plenty of experience in provisioning ships for long voyages, though neither they nor anyone else had ever tried to do it on such an enormous scale. Some English writers have given the credit to Drake. The year before, after his attack on Cadiz, he had captured and burned a number of small coasting ships off Cape St Vincent, and some of them were loaded with barrel staves. The story is that these were the seasoned staves to make the barrels for the armada's food and water, and that the coopers of Lisbon, without them, had to use unseasoned staves – which of course did not swell when the barrels were filled, and so let the air in or the contents out. But this is putting two and two together and making five. There is no evidence whatever of a shortage of seasoned staves in Portugal or Spain – and certainly Drake did not do it with magical foresight. He did not know what was in the ships before he captured them, and he would have burned them whatever their cargoes had been. Moreover, nobody in the armada ever said there was anything wrong with the barrels.

A more plausible guess might be that the food was packed and barrelled in Portugal, not in Spain. The Portuguese contractors, and the coopers who made the barrels, might not have taken all the care they should, or might have swindled their Spanish overlords. But this also is only a guess; and the men in the armada itself, who must have been itching to put the blame on somebody, never mentioned the contractors or the coopers. The duke was prone to take the blame for everything, but he did not blame himself for this. The stores had been ordered and loaded under the regime of the Marquis of Santa Cruz, and the duke had not had a chance, even if he had thought of it, to unload them all again and have the barrels opened to see what state they were in. In fact, the only explanation among the experts in the armada was that the food and water had been on board too long – and that of course, by implication, put the blame on the way the king had organized the assembling of the fleet. Two of the contractors were put in prison by the king. But nobody else was punished, as if – and this, to them, was a real possibility – it had been an act of God.

The duke hovered round Cape Finisterre for four more days, anxiously watching the rugged shore for the fleet of barges and fishing boats he had asked the marquis to send out to his rescue. Nothing happened. Everyone, more or less, was urging him to go in.

He must have longed to go in himself. Nobody who has never

been seasick knows the strength of the longing for sheltered water, for a chance of rest from the endless motion and a good night's sleep. Only the strongest sense of duty, and fear perhaps of what the king would say, can have kept him at sea.

By the fourth day the armada had drifted round the Cape and was off the mouth of Corunna Bay itself. There was no sign of activity inside. That night, the wind got up again from the north, blowing straight into the harbour mouth. The fleet tacked round all night under shortened sail, to give itself enough offing to be safe. Next day, the duke still hesitated. By afternoon the wind was hopeless for continuing the voyage, and it was obvious that small boats and barges would not be able to beat out against it. He capitulated, and sailed into Corunna. About forty ships came in behind him, but it was getting too dark to find an anchorage, and it was agreed the rest should stand off and on outside and wait for daylight. It was 19th June, three weeks out from Lisbon.

As soon as his anchor was down, he sent off a hurried note to the king: 'With the agreement of the generals, because of the bad weather and shortage of water and provisions, I entered Corunna this evening with part of the armada, the rest remaining outside because it was late and they could not make the port. They will come in tomorrow, God willing, and I shall hurry to load as much as possible in two days. I shall stock up with water and put ashore the dangerously sick, and then, weather permitting, put to sea again. The wind that takes me out will be the right one for our voyage. So I hope only to stay here a short time.'

But suddenly in the middle of the night the wind backed again to the south west and the most furious gale of all hit Corunna Bay. Inside, ships dragged their anchors and collided, and through driving rain in the wan light of dawn the northern horizon was seen to be empty. All the ships that had stayed outside had vanished.

6

Corunna

'The local people say such a violent sea and wind, with fog and rainstorms, has never been seen before.' So the duke wrote two days afterwards. It is a common way of describing bad weather, but it was not far from the truth in that stormy summer. English sailors in Plymouth were saying exactly the same.

Corunna is a spacious sheltered bay, and its small walled city still stands on a rocky peninsula inside it. It has a reputation of being wetter than most of Spain, but it has a right to expect warm sunshine and calm seas in June, and its rainfall makes its countryside prolific. It grows indifferent wine but plenty of wheat and vegetables, and supports many cattle. So it was a good place to revictual a fleet. The Governor of Galicia, in response to the letters the duke had sent him, had started to collect food, and the duke began at once to have it ferried out from the town in boats to the ships that were there, and loaded into pinnaces ready to be transhipped to the ones that were missing. The weather was moderating when he wrote, and he managed to put on a show of cautious optimism.

Many men were still falling sick, he reported; he was afraid this trouble might spread and get out of control. He was not in good health himself, though he did not say what was wrong with him: perhaps the aftermath of three weeks of seasickness, or perhaps the prevalent diarrhoea. But he was seeing to everything in person, as carefully as he could, with sorrow, as the king might imagine, for the misfortune that had overcome the armada. Two thirds of it had disappeared, but he was still able to say things might have been worse. 'In spite of all my efforts not to enter port, I find myself here with the best of the armada out at sea. God be praised for all He may ordain. I see that everything has been planned by His mercy, so that we may more readily reunite, as the rest of the ships will know where to find me, which they would not have done if the storm had caught us all together at sea.'

Two days later, on 23rd June, there was a second storm, even worse than the first. But the duke still wrote, on the 24th, about the practical steps he was taking to put things right. Several of the missing ships had come in, and there was news of many more in other ports on the northern coast of Spain. Most were more or less damaged; in fourteen, so far, the damage was serious: one galleon was reported to have lost her mainmast, and one galley had lost her rudder. He had sent out pinnaces in all directions to order the ships to rendezvous at Corunna, and he hoped that eventually all, or nearly all, would come in.

He supposed that if the English did not already know of the armada's misfortune, they very soon would, and their corsairs would sally out in search of the scattered ships. He was doing all he could to prevent this, by sending out pinnaces and rowing boats to reconnoitre. It had also occurred to him that some of the ships might have run on as far as the Scilly Islands, in accordance with the general orders he had issued in Lisbon. So he had sent two very fast oared pinnaces, well armed and with an experienced ensign in each, to tell them to come back. Meanwhile, he was pushing on with the watering and revictualling as best he could in such terrible weather; and he had posted a company of local infantry on the quay of the town to stop anyone landing unless they had his special permit. He thought this would be effective in preventing desertion.

To the first of these letters the king replied on the 28th, making no comment on the misfortune, but approving the measures the duke was taking, and urging him to put to sea again as soon as he possibly could. He had ordered new biscuit, wine, vinegar and fish to be sent from Lisbon. The duke was to take great care of the sick, and serve out all the fresh meat he could get.

But on the same day when the duke wrote the second of his letters, 24th June, he wrote a third to the king. It was quite different. It was evidently very carefully written, and it expressed his inmost belief. It seems that the weather had seriously strained his faith – not in the Almighty, of course, but in the king's interpretation of the Almighty's will. 'I am very anxious about the weather. In any summer, it would be remarkable at the end of June, but at this moment, on such a great occasion in the service of our Lord, it is even more extraordinary, considering how fervently the enterprise has been commended and devoted to Him. We must therefore conclude that what has happened has some good and just reason. I have delayed saying to Your Majesty what I am now about to say, in case it should be thought that any personal interest moved me; but seeing matters in their present state, I feel impelled by my conscientious duty to Your Majesty to submit the following points for consideration.'

He then reminded the king how reluctant he had been to take command of the armada. This, he now said (though he had not said it at the time), was because he recognized they were to attack a kingdom so powerful that they would need a much larger force than the king had collected at Lisbon. 'This was my reason for at first declining the command, seeing that the enterprise was being represented to Your Majesty as easier than it was known to be by those whose only aim was Your Majesty's service.' Like Recalde, he had the tact not to tell the king he was wrong, but only that other people were misleading him. 'Nevertheless, matters reached a point when Your Majesty ordered me to sail, which I did, and we have now arrived at this port so scattered and shaken that we are much inferior in strength to the enemy, in the opinion of all who are competent to judge. Many of our largest ships are still missing, as well as two of the galleasses; while on the ships that are here there are many sick, whose numbers will increase because of bad provisions. These are not only very bad, as I have constantly reported, but are so scanty that they cannot last more than two months.

'By this Your Majesty may judge whether we can continue this voyage, on the success of which so much depends. Your Majesty has embarked in this expedition all your resources both in ships and warlike stores, and I can see no means whatever of recovering from any disaster we may meet. It would take a long time to collect a naval force again, and it could not be done without using merchant ships, which are unsuitable for these seas. Meanwhile, Your Majesty would have no ships on the coasts of Biscay, Portugal and Andalusia; so that both Portugal and the Indies would be in danger, and the States of the Netherlands would take heart and rise again as soon as they heard of any disaster to this armada.

'To undertake such a great task with forces equal to the

enemy's would be inadvisable; to do it with an inferior force, as ours is now, with our men lacking in experience, would be even more unwise. I am bound to confess I see very few men in the armada with any knowledge of, or ability to perform, the duties entrusted to them. I have tested and watched this point very carefully, and Your Majesty may believe me when I assure you we are very weak. Sir, do not let yourself be deceived by anyone who may want to persuade you otherwise. I am supported in my views by knowing what a small force the Duke of Parma has collected. Even our two forces united would still be weak, but if we do not join we shall be feeble indeed. Moreover, we shall not be able to reinforce them, seeing how things stand with us at present.

'I recall the great force Your Majesty collected for the conquest of Portugal, although that country had boundaries with our own and many of its people were in your favour. Well, sir, how do you think we can attack so great a country as England with such a force as ours is now? I have earnestly commended this matter to God, and feel bound to put it before Your Majesty, so that you may choose the best course for your service while the armada is refitting here. This opportunity might be taken, and the difficulties avoided, by making honourable terms with the enemy. All Your Majesty's interests make it desirable that you should deeply ponder beforehand what you are undertaking, with so many envious rivals of your greatness.'

When this letter was published at the end of the nineteenth century, a good many English historians took it as further proof that the duke was a coward and a fool: a poltroon was the nineteenth-century word that some of them used. This was the reputation he had already been given in English legend and to some degree in Spanish legend too. But nobody could have found cowardice or foolishness in the letter unless this preconceived idea had been firmly embedded in his mind. It shows nothing of the sort. As for cowardice, it shows as much moral courage as the letter in which he declined the king's appointment; and as for foolishness, this was the wisest advice that anyone gave to the king.

What it does reveal is the important fact that the armada's

commander-in-chief had not believed, from the very beginning, that it was strong enough to win.

The duke could perhaps be blamed for being changeable — though it is not surprising that he sometimes felt the whole appalling burden was too much for him, or that he was sometimes depressed when he was ill or seasick, or that he never stopped longing for San Lucar. His letters to the king reflected his varying state of mind. When things were going well he was almost chatty; he wrote as a young man might to a rather formidable uncle. When he had something to say of outstanding importance, as he had in this letter, he wrote with all the formality of a diplomat. But when he had to report disasters, he was almost obsequious, and apologized for things that his wildest critics could not have blamed him for. Evidently the storm at Corunna was one of his worst moments. He had first apologized for being forced into harbour. But then, after sleeping on it perhaps, he had pulled himself together and taken a long and honest look at what the storm implied.

Reading between the lines of his letters, it seems that in the early days in Lisbon the duke had found some comfort in the king's assurance of his holy purpose. Even then, he had had his doubts about it; but he had let himself be persuaded that whatever shortcomings the armada had, it could hope for the miraculous help of God. The weather in the past six weeks had slowly shattered that tenuous belief. In the height of summer, it had indeed been almost miraculous; but the miracle had been to delay and finally to damage and scatter the armada, not to help it.

The head winds, the storm, the vanished fleet — in the logic of that era these could not have been merely chance, a bit of prolonged bad luck. They must, as he had written, have had some just and good reason. The king might perhaps have thought some trivial sins like the sailors' swearing had given offence to God. But the duke felt forced to believe the king's premise was fundamentally wrong; God had not accepted the armada's cause as his own. Bereft of that faith, he had to look at the armada in the chilling light of military power, and to admit that if it could not hope for miracles, it had no hope at all.

It seems very unlikely that he was the only man in the fleet who had come to this conclusion. The omen of the storm had been eloquent. One wonders whether there was anyone he could confide in. Obviously, it was a dangerous opinion to discuss; in the wrong company, it could have been made to look like treason. The same writers who called him a coward also said the captains despised him for his cowardice. But there is not the faintest suggestion of this in the documents that have survived. On the contrary, all the evidence is that they liked him and were happy to make allowances for the ignorance he admitted so freely. The only exception perhaps was Don Pedro de Valdes, who had the reputation of a cantankerous, argumentative man. Yet lying alone in his cabin at night, or pacing across the poop as he did by day, the duke must have yearned for somebody who could share his burden and understand his perplexity.

Perhaps he had trusted friends among the twenty-two gentlemen he had brought from San Lucar: their names are listed but they are shadowy people whose characters and thoughts were never recorded. Perhaps he could have confided in his deputy de Leyva, who was a likeable man; but he was in one of the ships that had disappeared. Or perhaps the admiral, Recalde. Recalde agreed with him on one point at least – the incompetence of the armada's men, or some of them. 'I hear great complaints,' he had written to the king, 'about the command of companies being given to young fellows just because they are gentlemen. Very few of them are soldiers or know what to do, and their officers are no better.'

In the same letter, Recalde had told the king how the duke had come to see him when he was laid low with sciatica. They had had a long discussion about the sailing of the expedition. The duke had seemed to be vexed at the need to hurry the departure from Corunna, and was worried that the new provisions might not arrive in time. Recalde had reminded him of the importance of speed – probably because the season was far advanced and the autumn was only a couple of months away. There is something attractive in the scene of the duke going to sympathize with the crippled admiral, who was old enough to be his father, and having a heart-to-heart talk with him alone. But did he dare to tell him he had advised the king to abandon the enterprise entirely?

On 27th June, the duke called a council. Its discussions were very thoroughly minuted, and the minutes still exist. They show how the duke made use of his authority, and also how closely he dared, in general meeting, to approach the central question of whether the armada should be abandoned; for the meeting was held three days after he wrote his letter to the king, and before the king replied.

Present at this meeting, besides the duke and the admiral, were the senior army general, Don Francisco de Bovadillo; four of the squadron commanders, Pedro and Diego Flores de Valdes, Miguel de Oquendo and Martin de Bertondona; Hugo de Moncada who commanded the galleasses; two of the senior captains, and Jorge Manrique, whose title was Inspector General of the Fleet. Presumably one of the duke's secretaries, Jeronimo de Arceo or Andreas de Alva, was also there to write the minutes.

It was a good Spanish custom in councils of war for the commander-in-chief to submit a question, and for everyone else to express his opinion in turn, beginning with the most junior. The duke's first question was whether they should wait in Corunna for the missing ships, or go out to look for them along the coast. That was easy. Nobody wanted to go out. Everyone voted it was better for the missing ships to seek the armada, rather than have the armada seek them.

The duke then asked the council to decide whether the armada should pursue its journey at once, with the ships that were in Corunna and other ports along the coast, and without waiting for those that were still missing.

Don Jorge Manrique was the first to answer. Perhaps he had the most junior rank in that exalted assembly, but he was also the expert who could give statistics. One of his jobs was to keep the musters of men, and another to know the state of the ships' provisions.

He reported that twenty-eight ships were still missing, apart from those whose whereabouts was known in other ports. They had six thousand men on board. Although it was said that 27,884 men had been shipped in the armada (he seems to have been unsure of the total himself), he had to point out that only 24,500 were effectives, after deducting general and field officers, staffs, cabin boys and ships' boys, gentlemen adventurers, officers of justice, hospital staff, artillery officers, ministers of religion and the oarsmen of the galleys and galleasses. If another 6000 men were deducted, there would only be 16,000 effective soldiers and sailors (so he said); and some of them had already 'gone away' or died or fallen sick. Nearly a third of the strength of the armada was therefore missing, and among that third were three maestres de campo, regimental commanders, with the flower of their regiments. His opinion was therefore that the armada should not sail without the missing part, and this view should be expressed emphatically to His Majesty. Everyone present agreed, except Don Pedro de Valdes: the armada should stay in Corunna until the whole force was reunited, as it had been in Lisbon.

Nobody, according to the minutes, actually put into words the obvious conclusion, but it must have been in all their minds: nobody knew what had happened to their missing ships, they might have foundered or been cast ashore, or sunk or captured by the enemy, and they might never return – in which case the armada would never be reunited and would never sail.

Strangely, the minutes repeat the main argument of the duke's letter, using almost identical phrases but putting them into other people's mouths. Don Jorge said that on the armada depended the fate of Christendom and of His Majesty's dominions; the king had embarked in it all his naval forces in those seas, and in any misfortune of battle or tempest, the whole might be lost. Don Francisco de Bovadillo, whose view was specially emphatic, said that any misfortune to the armada would cause the Indies to be lost, and Portugal and the Netherlands to be endangered too. This identity of argument suggests two possible reasons. Either the duke, or perhaps the secretary, was deliberately weighting the minutes, or – and this is much more likely – the idea of abandoning the whole project, and the reasons for it, had been more widely discussed than written records show.

The speech of Don Pedro de Valdes, the odd man out, was reported more fully than anyone else's: the Spaniards always made a record of minority opinions. But it seems typical of the sort of man who likes to be a minority of one in committee meetings. It was full of red herrings and non sequiturs, and arguments that cancelled each other out.

With his experience of English affairs, he said, it was perfectly obvious that the enemy's forces must be divided in two or three places. The missing ships would soon be heard of, or most of them, because the storm had not been so very severe, unless for reasons of their own any of them had wanted to make bad weather of it. The inspector had said the fleet had provisions for ninety days; if so, and if the sailing was not delayed beyond fifteen or twenty days, he thought they ought to go. But still he thought the provisions ought to be carefully examined again. He had gone round his own squadron and found they had enough biscuit for ninety days, but part of it was in bad condition. There was more than enough wine, but the salt pork, cheese, fish and vegetables were all rotten and very little use. The only usable victuals were the meat and fish received in Corunna, and he did not think there was enough of that for ninety days. While the fleet was in port, the men should be given fresh meat, so that the stores on board should be preserved. It would strengthen them and set them up.

It was not at all clear why all this had led him to think they should sail and enter battle with the forces they had. But at least the speech had the merit of bringing up the question of food, and it led the duke to ask another question: Would they estimate how long the provisions of their squadrons would last, and say what they thought should be done if there was not enough for ninety days? Nobody explained why they had hit on ninety days as the minimum period they would need. The armada had started by being stocked for six months, and all they had achieved so far was a voyage that was often done in a week. Perhaps they were thinking of the season. Ninety days would take them well into the equinoctial gales, and by then they would have to be home again, or in a safe winter harbour somewhere.

Anyhow, that was the time-span they were looking at. The duke's question seems to have raised a fresh outcry about the awfulness of the food. When it subsided, they all agreed they would like to hear the opinion of the Inspector General. He confirmed what they had been saying: everything except the biscuit, wine and vegetables was rotten because it had been on board so long. He had made an account of what remained, and estimated that at the very most there was not enough for more than eighty days, except in the squadron of Castile, which might last out for three months.

It was unanimously agreed that the stores were insufficient, and that a full report should be sent to His Majesty by a special messenger, so that he could adopt such measures as seemed best.

Everyone signed this resolution, including Pedro de Valdes. They had passed the buck back to the king, which indeed was all they could do. But their own joint opinion could not have been clearer: the armada had not enough food for its journey, and even if the food could be collected, it should not sail until it was as strong again as it had been in Lisbon. Everyone must have known that might mean never. Nobody mentioned miracles.

The duke had to wait ten days for the king's answer to his letter. He must have dreaded it. A commander-in-chief who advises his monarch to sue for peace cannot expect anything less than dismissal, with whatever degree of punishment and ignominy the monarch's whim decides. Perhaps the duke would have welcomed dismissal, and willingly paid the price of ignominy, or even faced a charge of treason.

While he waited, with his nerves on edge, he had some kind of argument with Pedro de Valdes. De Valdes complained to the king that as his opinion at the council meeting had differed from everyone else's, the duke had been looking on him with an unfriendly eye, and had used expressions which greatly grieved him. This is the only sign of discord in the records.

When at last the king's letter arrived, the duke undoubtedly took it to his cabin with a sinking heart to open it alone. It was very long and surprisingly mild. Less surprisingly, it took no notice at all of the argument the duke had presented with such anguish. The king had no intention of giving up the enterprise. On the contrary, he intended to carry it forward, overcoming whatever troubles might arise. Provided the missing ships came in, the armada was to sail again by 10th July (that was five days after the letter was written, and probably the very day when the duke received it), 'For I hope,' the king wrote, 'that our Lord will change these difficulties at the start to the triumph of His cause in the end.' If ships had been damaged by the storms, the duke had permission to leave behind twelve or fifteen of them, those that would need prolonged repairs. Only their hulls should be left: their crews and contents should be transferred to other ships.

There was a gentle rebuke about the rotten stores. Fresh meat, fish and bread was to be served out while the fleet was in port. The duke could use cash to pay for it. So the remaining stores would be preserved for the voyage. The king made no comment on the council's unanimous report that the stores were not sufficient. But in this part of the letter he added, in his own handwriting, 'You must take great care that the stores are really preserved, and not let yourself be deceived, as you were before.' He pointed out that the reports given to the duke in Lisbon, which the duke had passed on to the king, had been quite misleading. The same applied to the water. 'You were informed you had enough water for two months; and I now find that on the very day you arrived in Corunna you discovered that some of the ships had no water left. All this makes it necessary that you should be very careful to keep the officers up to their duties.'

About the ships that were still missing, especially the urcas, the king surmised that some trick might have been played by the foreign sailors on board. He hoped the duke had been wise enough to put at least a couple of trustworthy Spanish sailors in each of them, who with the help of the soldiers could have forced the foreigners to resume their proper course.

The letter ended by repeating the royal orders: to keep the stores intact by using fresh food in harbour, to assemble the ships in Corunna, or at least so many that the missing ones would not be important, and to be ready to sail by 10th or 12th July. It was written with an air of conscious magnanimity; the duke was forgiven this time, but reminded that he could be blamed for anything that went wrong. It totally disregarded the duke's opinion, and the joint opinion of the Council, as if they were not even worthy of discussion. The king, as usual, had not budged an inch; and as usual, one cannot tell whether to call it brave determination or stubborn pig-headedness. But the letter is not unkind. For all his faults, the king was not vindictive to his servants.

The duke made no direct reply to this letter – or if he did, the reply has disappeared from the archives. But by the time he received it, things had changed for the better. He had resigned himself to the prospect of going on, and probably regretted he had tried to speak his mind. He ought to have known, after all, that the king would not listen. He had even regained his faith, by one of those tortuous arguments that were the refuge of people who

looked for an act of God in everything: 'I am consoled to think
that He who had this expedition in His hand has deigned to take
this course with it, to instil even more zeal in Your Majesty and
more care in your officers. I am convinced of this because He has
been pleased to send into port all the missing ships except two
Levanters and two urcas. The refitting of these ships shall have my
personal attention, for I am more anxious than anyone to hurry
things on and get away from here.'

The best of the good news was on 5th July, when one of the
pinnaces the duke had sent to the Scilly Islands came back, closely
followed by twelve ships she had rounded up in the mouth of the
Channel. Recalde said they came in 'smelling of England'; and
they had in fact been in sight of the coast of Cornwall, from the
Lizard to Lands End. There they had searched for the armada in
heavy weather, but found nothing except a couple of small barks,
rounding Lands End on their way from Dublin to Biscay with
cargoes of hides, wheat and coal or charcoal. They set upon these
little ships, sank one and took the other in tow; in the process, the
Spanish admiral boarded one of them, and broke two of his ribs
when he was scrambling back to his flagship. The sailors who were
captured, and two Irish priests, told them the rumours that were
going round Dublin: that ashore in England, great preparations
were being made for defence, and that Drake had a hundred and
eighty ships in three squadrons, one in Plymouth and two to the
east of Dover. During the night the ship in tow seemed to be
sinking and they cut it adrift. But it was not, and three men and a
boy were still hiding on board. After watching the Spaniards
standing away to the southward, they went on their voyage. A day
later, off the coast of Brittany, they met an English pinnace that
belonged to Drake, and told their story.

The ensign commanding the pinnace the duke had sent out,
whose name was Esquival, brought back a brief report of a classic
sea-adventure. 'At dawn on Friday, 1st July,' he wrote, 'we
sighted St Michael's Bay and Lands End, five or six leagues
distant. We took in all sail and rowed inshore about four leagues.
We then lay to for night to come, and a sail passed to leeward of us.
I wanted to chase, but the pilots opposed it because it was late and
we were not sure of catching her. The general opinion was that, so
close to the land, we would be sure to catch a fishing boat during

the night. But the wind rose in the south west, with heavy squalls of rain, and in the night we had violent gales from every quarter of the compass. We had a struggle, with constant changes of tack, to keep off the shore. At daybreak the wind settled in the north, and we tried to reach across towards Ireland to carry out our orders; but the wind was too strong, and the sea so high that the pinnace was shipping water at every wave. We then ran to the southward, with such a gale astern that we could only carry our foresail, set very low. At four p.m., after we had already received several heavy seas, a wave passed clean over us and nearly swamped the pinnace. Our gunwales were flush with the water and we were almost lost, but all hands turned to bailing, and we threw everything overboard. We had already jettisoned a pipe of wine and two barrels of water. We lowered the mainmast to the deck, and so lived through the night under a closely reefed foresail.

'On Sunday, we were running under the foresail only, and at nine a.m. we sighted six sail, three to the north and three to the south east, although they appeared to be all of one company. We ran between them, and two of those in the south east gave us chase. We hoisted our mainmast and clapped on sail, and after they had followed us until two o'clock they took in sail and resumed their course. At nine p.m. we sighted another ship lying to and repairing, with only her lower courses set. On Monday 4th July we made land off Rivadeo (sixty miles east of Corunna).'

In spite of their solemn letters and reports, they must sometimes have laughed at the moments of farce in their predicament. No large body of men can exist for weeks without finding something to laugh about. Looking back, it is tempting to see something funny in the prodigious number of priests – even more had joined up, and there were now a hundred and ninety-eight of them. It was agreed that every man should confess and seek absolution all over again. This could not be done on board the ships: there was simply not space enough. Nor could the men be allowed ashore, in case they compounded their sins by mass desertion. A compromise was found by ordering all the priests to land on an island in the bay. There, dozens of tents and altars were put up, to be manned by relays of priests, and the men were ferried to the islands in companies to take their turn, while a careful watch was kept to see that none escaped to the mainland. By 15th July eight thousand men had passed through this production line of penitents. But this was no laughing matter at the time; it was part of the earnest search for divine approval, and the duke wrote of it as an inestimable treasure, which he valued more highly than the most precious jewel he carried in the fleet.

However, there certainly was macabre comedy among the new recruits collected by the local nobility. These were meant to replace the men who had died or gone missing, and the five hundred who were then lying sick with fevers in a hospital of tents on shore. They turned out to be very old men, incapable and useless, even as labourers. 'They are nearly all married and have large families,' the duke wrote to the king, as if he expected this humourless man to see the funny side of it. 'Their wives have been coming in with their troubles and lamentations, to such an extent that it goes against my conscience to ship the men. The captains themselves have refused to have anything to do with them – it is obvious all the use they would be is to die on board the ships and take up space. Not a soul of them knows what an arquebus is, or any other weapon, and already they are more dead than alive. Some have not eaten anything for two days. So I have thought it best to send the whole lot away, and they have all gone home again.'

And he left the king, and posterity, to imagine the scene: the duke and his captains and grandees besieged and routed by regiments of elderly peasant women, and the old ladies in triumph taking their tottering husbands back where they belonged. He also, without apparent intention, left a glimpse of his own compassion and common sense.

By 10th July almost all the missing ships had been traced. Not all of them made Corunna: some came in to the harbours of Vivero and Gijon, farther along the coast, and the flagship of Recalde's squadron, the *Santa Ana*, turned up in Santander, over two hundred miles to the east. Most of them brought problems. The galleon *San Luis* crept into Vivero on 4th July 'much knocked about', with a split mast and not a drop of drinking water. Most of the urcas had damaged masts, sails and rigging. The Levantine ship *Trinidad de Scala* reached Gijon by what was judged an authentic miracle: in some places, her planks had gaped four inches apart. In Corunna, the *Santa Maria de la Rosa* had to be remasted: it took six hours to get the new mast upright. Twenty-six coopers were at work repairing water barrels which had been thrown about and damaged in the gale. All these ports, in the first two weeks of July, must have rung with the sound of carpenters', caulkers' and coopers' hammers as everyone laboured to meet the king's impossible deadline.

Meanwhile, news or rumours of the armada's disaster spread through Europe as fast as ships or horsemen could carry them, or as fast as people could invent them. On 6th July the Queen Mother of France announced at a supper party that the armada was not in Spain but had the plague on board and had landed troops in Scotland. The story of a Scottish landing was also told in Le Havre by the crew of a small ship laden with oranges. The Duke of Parma, who needed more than anyone else to learn what was happening, heard nothing but vague rumours until 20th July, when Queen Elizabeth's emissary at the peace talks, of all people, told him the armada was in Corunna. When the King of France was told, at another party, that an outbreak of plague had forced the armada back to Corunna, he replied very loudly, 'That's a fine story! It was only because they had seen the English fleet and were frightened!' Mendoza, credulous as ever, reported from Paris that Lord Howard and Drake had told Queen Elizabeth the armada was so strong that they could not hope to fight it. In Rome, on 8th July, Count de Olivares was very anxious because he had heard no news since the armada left Lisbon. The pope, he said, was terribly put out because he had not been told it had sailed. De Olivares, who was a champion liar, told him the letter had been lost in the post; but the pope remained furious, refused to listen to reason and would not speak of the million ducats until he heard the Spaniards were in England. He was always like that, de Olivares said, as the bitter hour approached when he would have to part with some money.

Yet no news, no rumours, seem to have reached Corunna from the outside world. There was a great sense of urgency there, because the summer was passing, the king was impatient and the

Duke of Parma's army, they believed, was waiting for them. The armada was helpless, lying in that open bay with its ships impossibly disorganized. But there is no evidence of a sense of danger; no letters mention its vulnerability. Even the king, who liked to attend to the smallest details, sent no orders that it should prepare to defend itself where it was. Esquival's encounter with hostile ships, only a day's run from the Spanish coast, caused nobody to express alarm. The duke had vaguely supposed that the English would hear what had happened. But he did not suspect the truth: that their pinnaces had searched the coasts of Biscay and questioned every northbound merchantman they met, and that Drake knew exactly where the armada was.

On 20th July, after a month in Corunna, everything was ready again, or as ready as it would ever be. The duke called another council, to decide whether they should sail. All the high commanders were there, thirteen of them, and most of them were still hesitant. The duke asked if they judged the weather was settled enough to get the fleet out of the bay and safely clear of Cape Priorio, at its northern corner. There was much learned talk of the change of wind that might be expected with the new moon in two days' time. Recalde produced an old adage: Never look for bad signs in summer or good signs in winter, but make the best of a chance when it comes. The general opinion seemed to be that if they were going at all, they had better get on with it; but there was so much uncertainty that the duke called in all the principal pilots too.

Yet they must all have known it was much more than a question of local pilotage, however the duke might phrase it. The problem of food had not been solved or even answered by the king, and they had no more than when they had told him it was not enough – less, indeed, because they had not been able to get fresh bread in Corunna and had had to eat the biscuit from the stores. If anyone at that meeting had dared to re-open the question of food, the armada might have been abandoned. But Spanish councils were disciplined affairs, and nobody did. When everyone had spoken, the duke decided, unless the weather looked more threatening, to sail at dawn the next day. A signal gun was fired to make preparations. Another was ordered for midnight, when anchors would be raised and the leading ships would get out and leave the way clear. At daybreak, all ships would make sail and proceed on their voyage with God's blessing.

At that very moment, while they were solemnly weighing pros and cons, Lord Howard, Drake, Frobisher, Fenner and the finest of the English fleet were within a day's sailing of Corunna and bearing down on them, intent on catching them in harbour.

7

The English Fleet

t is time to turn to the English side of the story, and to begin by mentioning the calendar.

Six years before the armada Pope Gregory XIII was told that the ancient Julian calendar, in the course of centuries, had lagged ten days behind the seasons, because it reckoned a year as just over eleven minutes shorter than it really was. He decreed that ten days should be omitted from the year 1582, and founded the new Gregorian calendar which has been used ever since. By 1588, the whole of Catholic Europe, including Spain, was using this new calendar. But England and Protestant Germany, rejecting anything of papal origin, stuck to the Julian calendar long afterwards, and remained ten days behind. So Spanish reports put the duke's council meeting on 20th July, and English reports of the voyage to Spanish waters say they were approaching Corunna on 10th July. This was the same day. Likewise, English history says the fleets finally met, off Plymouth, on 21st July, and Spanish history makes it 31st July. To use both calendars is confusing, and I have decided to use the Spanish dates throughout, because they correspond to present-day experience of the seasons. As autumn approaches, ten days make quite a lot of difference. It is worth remembering that when the armada fought its way up-Channel it was already August, the days were drawing in, and very few weeks were left to clear the seas, to get in touch with Parma, bring his boats across and find a safe harbour before the equinox, 23rd September, when winter weather was expected to begin. Through all the delays, the voyage had become a race against the seasons, more so than the dates in English history suggest.

Ashore in 1588, the English waited for the armada, not in panic, but certainly with healthy apprehension. They had heard the kind of rumours one might expect, half bred by fear and half by propaganda: that the armada had orders to kill all Englishmen except boys under seven, that it was led by Inquistadores and laden with instruments of torture; that it carried nooses to hang the men and scourges for the women; and, most ingenious of all, in a report from one of Mendoza's men in England, that it was bringing two or three thousand wet nurses to suckle the infants orphaned by the massacre.

At sea, on the other hand, they waited with cheerful confidence. 'My good Lord, there is here the gallantest company of captains, soldiers and mariners that I think ever was seen in England.' So Lord Howard, the Lord High Admiral, wrote to Lord Burghley from Plymouth on 7th June. 'And God send us the happiness,' he added, with a sailor's air of superiority, 'to meet with them [the Spaniards] before our men on land discover them, for I fear me a little sight of the enemy will fear the land men much.'

The self-esteem of English sailors had been growing for twenty years. By a paradox, history finds its beginning in the fight at San Juan de Ulua in 1568, which the Spaniards won. A few English ships had put in for repairs to that Spanish harbour on the coast of Honduras, after being caught out in a hurricane on a slave-trading voyage. A large Spanish fleet approached the harbour too, and agreed on a truce, although the English, strictly speaking, had no business to be there. For some days, the two fleets lay side by side in peace, and then the Spaniards attacked without warning. By that treachery the Spaniards started a generation of trouble for themselves; for the English commander was John Hawkyns, and the captain of his smallest ship was Francis Drake, who was twenty-two years old. They both escaped and reached England separately after awful privations. When they got home, they were not on the best of terms – Hawkyns accused Drake of deserting him – but the episode left both of them, each in his own way, burning to take revenge on Spain. Drake did it in the series of voyages that made the Spaniards dread his name; and Hawkyns did it less directly: he worked his way up ashore until he was treasurer of the Queen's Ships, and in that position he controlled the design of a new kind of fighting ship to overthrow the Spaniards.

Of course neither of them acted alone. Many other sea-captains made half-piratical voyages like Drake's, some with success and some without; and Hawkyns was helped by other practical seamen, and by a generation of shipwrights who were willing to make experiments. But Hawkyns and Drake were leaders of nautical opinion, and probably deserve most credit for the sailors' confidence. Hawkyns created the new kind of ship, and Drake created the way of commanding it.

In all Drake's youthful expeditions to rob the Spaniards in the Indies he was in sole command. That was something of an innovation, even in England. In earlier Tudor times, in ships on official or warlike missions, sailors and sea-captains had been subservient to soldiers, as they still were in Spain. The first purely English voyage of exploration, for example, to the North East Passage in 1553, was led by Sir Hugh Willoughby, who was a knight, a gentleman and a soldier but not a sailor, and the ships' masters took their orders from him. So it had always been since medieval times.

Only one attempt had been made to impose a landsman's authority on Drake. That was in the voyage round the world, when Thomas Doughty, who was a gentleman and not a sailor, claimed a right to share the plans and decisions at sea, and in Drake's opinion stirred up trouble against him. In the harbour of San Julian near Cape Horn, farther from home than any English ship had ever been, Drake put Doughty on trial for mutiny and treason and had him executed. Drake's furious unstudied eloquence in that trial changed, once and for all, the status of English captains: 'My masters, I am a very bad orator, for my bringing up hath not been in learning . . . Here is such controversy between the sailors and the gentlemen and such stomaching between the gentlemen and the sailors, that it doth even make me mad to hear it. But, my masters, I must have it left. For I must have the gentleman to haul and draw with the mariner, and the mariner with the gentleman . . . To say you come to serve me I will not give you thanks, for it is only Her Majesty that you serve.'

He was insisting that under God and the queen, a sea-captain at sea had sole authority, not to be overridden by soldiers or by social rank. After his triumphant return from that voyage, the English had only tried once more to send out a sea expedition under a soldier. That was Edward Fenton's voyage in 1582, and it was a total failure because the sailors – many had sailed with Drake – disobeyed, misled and mocked the commander. By 1588 Drake's principle was fully accepted in English ships. It was true that rich or influential men could still become sea-captains without much knowledge of the sea. It was true that a great national fleet in any crisis needed a nobleman to represent the queen in its command: captains would not take orders from anyone less. And it was true that in the crews of the queen's ships some men were listed as sailors and some as soldiers. But when the ship was at sea, the captain was in sole command of it and everybody in it; and most captains, like Drake himself, were men of long experience but humble origin.

With this new-won prestige, English captains began to express their own opinions about the queen's ships of war. They did not like them. What they wanted was a kind of ship that would be a sailor's weapon, not merely a floating fort for soldiers. They evolved a concept of fighting at sea which was revolutionary: to give up the age-old idea of grappling and boarding, and instead to fight at a distance and rely entirely on their guns. So they would get rid of two encumbrances, the soldiery and its castles. The ships could be built with only a single aim: to sail as well as knowledge of the art permitted. It was the most daring innovation ever made in navies.

The result, under Hawkyns' guidance, was the race-built ship. Its name did not mean it was fast, though it was; the phrase came from the same root as the verb to raze, and it meant the castles were razed, as one might say a castle on land had been razed to the ground. Its opposite, the older kind of ship with castles, was called high-charged. Discarding the idea of boarding gave a free hand to the shipwrights. The forecastles of these ships were only a single deck in height, and the aftercastle was reduced to a poop to shelter the helmsmen and accommodate the officers. Amidships, they did not need a high freeboard. So they were lower throughout – they 'lay snug to the water'. The windage of the hulls was less, and therefore they sailed better to windward. To improve them still further, they were built with a much higher ratio of length to beam; and their sails were cut flatter than sails had ever been before, so that they could be set more closely to the wind. A race-built ship could probably make good a course two points to windward; at least a point better than a Spanish galleon, and four points better than the armada as a whole.

Of course if they had ever been boarded by a galleon they would have been at a disadvantage; but the English intended to avoid that situation, never to close to the distance they called 'at push of pike'. They intended to use their speed, their weatherliness and their quickness on the helm – and their own skill in seamanship – to choose their range and always to keep upwind of enemies. After the galleons, the race-built ships must have been a delight to handle, and no doubt this was one cause of the sailors' confidence. They knew they could sail rings round a high-charged ship, and thought they would have it at their mercy.

In the English legend that grew up in later years around the armada battle, it was said the English ships were smaller than the Spanish, which gave a David-and-Goliath air to the story. Perhaps they looked smaller to landsmen who watched the fleets from the cliffs of southern England, because they lay lower in the water. But it is very doubtful whether they really were.

Ships are difficult to compare in size, and the ways of measuring them are arbitrary. Tonnage is the accepted measure, and the tonnage of sixteenth-century ships is given in many lists. But it has always been a confusing measurement, even for sailors. In medieval times it was simply the number of tuns or barrels of oil or Bordeaux wine that a ship could carry. Today there are several ways of working it out, and only one of them, displacement tonnage, has anything to do with a ton in weight. In the sixteenth century, tonnage had been reduced to formulae, but there were several in use which all gave different answers. A document of 1582, which has annotations that look like Hawkyns' hand-writing, instructs one to multiply together the length of the keel in feet, the beam, and the depth from the point of greatest beam to the top of the keel. The product was then multiplied by 160 and divided by 15,552, a strange and useless exercise. Having done all that, you ended up with a tonnage figure which was much too small, so you increased it by one third. Another simpler formula was to divide the product by 100 without adding the final third. Of course this gave a lower figure.

Obviously these formulae gave no idea of the visible size of a ship, in which the most important element is the length overall.

For one thing, they did not count the overhangs at stem and stern, which might add anything up to fifty per cent to the length of the keel. For another, a small difference in beam or depth, invisible to the eye, would make a disproportionate difference to the tonnage. The queen's ship *Elizabeth Jonas* was 100 feet in length of keel, 40 feet in beam and 18 in depth, and her tonnage was recorded as 986. Another, the *Golden Lion*, was 102 feet in keel, but only 32 in beam and 14 in depth, and her tonnage was 614. So the *Golden Lion* was longer than the *Elizabeth Jonas*, but her tonnage was only two thirds. (Although these figures are in the same document as the formula, neither of the sums comes out exactly right. Elizabethans were not very good at arithmetic.) In those days a ship could easily be recorded in one official list as 200 tons more or less than she was in another.

However, the dimensions of the *Jonas* and the *Lion* do reveal something: the *Lion* was a race-built ship and the *Jonas* was not. In fact they were both old ships, the *Lion* was built in 1557 and the *Jonas* in 1559; but when these figures were issued the *Lion* had just been rebuilt, and evidently given the slenderer lines of a race-built ship. Probably she was sawn in half and lengthened, by pulling the two halves apart and building a new bit in the middle. The *Jonas* was also rebuilt but not until 1592. Any race-built ship, being less in beam and depth, would be longer than an old-fashioned galleon of the same tonnage. Howard's *Ark*, the flagship of the English fleet in 1588, and Drake's *Revenge*, were race-built. Using the simpler formula and the proportions of the *Lion*, the *Ark* would have been 120 feet in length of keel, and the *Revenge* just under 100. One report says she was 92 feet.

It is even more difficult to compare the sizes of English and Spanish ships, because the Spanish system of measurement was quite different. It was reckoned from the half-beam instead of the full beam, and the length overall instead of the length of keel. There is some evidence that the Spanish system gave higher tonnage figures than any of the English systems: occasionally, the English captured a Spanish ship, and the tonnage they gave it was always smaller than the Spaniards had given it. The *San Salvador*, which was captured from the armada, was listed by the Spaniards as 958 tons, but estimated by the English as 600. Most authorities agree the difference was from twenty-five per cent to forty per cent. So, though the figures in Spanish lists of the armada are higher than those in lists of the English fleet, this does not prove the Spanish ships were bigger. Spanish ships were listed up to 1200 Spanish tons, but the English *Triumph* of 1000 English tons may have been the biggest by tonnage in either fleet; and Howard's race-built *Ark* of 800 tons may well have been the longest.

In any case, sheer size was no advantage, except in boarding. A fighting ship, as the English saw it, had to be big enough to carry a respectable outfit of guns, and enough men to fire the guns and work the ship; but within that limit, the smaller she was the better. A small ship was handier and – to use an Elizabethan word – more nimble. Drake fought in a ship of only 500 tons, but it was his own deliberate choice. He must have thought this was the ideal size – and nobody knew more about fighting. The David-and-Goliath idea was a later heroic addition to the story, and quite untrue.

Not all the ships that fought the armada were race-built – far from it. Altogether, about a hundred and forty ships, great and small, assembled in the Channel. But the queen only owned about twenty-five ships and ten pinnaces. A few more were warships that were privately owned. The rest were armed merchantmen. And of the queen's ships, some were too small to be reckoned first-liners, and some were old-fashioned high-charged galleons like the *Triumph*. Perhaps a dozen could be reckoned as first-class race-built ships. But it was these that led the fleet and, except on the last day, did most of the fighting, while the rest sallied forth with boundless confidence astern of them.

Guns are even harder to compare than ships. Everything in sixteenth-century gunnery was inexact: the names of the guns, their calibres, their range, the quality of their powder, and above all their aim. But roughly speaking there were seven kinds of guns that could have done some damage to a ship (*see opposite*).

There were several other smaller guns, down to the muskets and arquebuses the Spanish soldiers carried; but all those were designed to injure men, not ships. All the big guns fired a round iron ball except the cannon perier, which fired a ball of stone. It is doubtful whether this stone shot could have done much damage to a ship, except the rigging, because it broke up on impact, or sometimes even in flight, and formed a kind of shrapnel.

	Calibre (inches)	Weight of shot (pounds)	Point-blank range (paces)	Range at random (paces)
Cannon	$7\frac{1}{4}$	50	340	2000
Demi-cannon	$6\frac{1}{4}$	32	340	1700
Cannon perier	8	24	320	1600
Culverin	$5\frac{1}{4}$	17	400	2500
Demi-culverin	$4\frac{1}{4}$	9	400	2500
Saker	$3\frac{1}{2}$	5	340	1700
Minion	$3\frac{1}{4}$	4	320	1600

Buying and selling guns was an international trade, although it was sometimes contraband, and the medieval names of guns were more or less the same in every European language – some even in Arabic too. One can at least be sure that what the English called a culverin, the French a coulevrine and the Spaniards a culebrina, was substantially the same thing. Indeed, they all came from the same foundries, mainly in England, the Netherlands and Italy. The best of them were cast in bronze, a technique which had long been in use for church bells, and were elegantly decorated with coats of arms and dolphins; but most, by the latter half of the sixteenth century, were cast in iron, which was not so strong or accurate but was cheaper. The Spaniards still had a few guns of wrought iron, made by welding bars together to form a tube and strengthening it with hoops shrunk on the outside; but that sort of gun had long been obsolete in England.

The three sorts of cannon were short guns in proportion to their calibre: a 'whole' cannon, with its $7\frac{1}{4}$-inch calibre and 50-pound shot, was usually about 11 feet long. A 'whole' culverin, on the other hand, with a calibre of $5\frac{1}{4}$ inches and a shot of 17 pounds, was sometimes 15 feet long. For this reason, the culverin family had generally a longer range than the cannon family, although their shot was smaller.

King Philip put things back to front when he said the English would choose to fight at a distance because they were superior in artillery. In fact, they had made their choice of tactics and then provided themselves with guns to suit it. They concentrated on the long-range guns, from culverins downwards in size, and neglected the heavier guns of shorter range. Two estimates have been made of the numbers of guns in the rival fleets, one for the whole fleets and the other for the warships – the queen's ships on one side and the galleons and galleasses on the other:

	Whole Spanish fleet	Whole English fleet	Galleons and galleasses	Queen's ships
Cannon and Demi-cannon	163	55	163	55
Cannon perier	326	43	196	38
Culverin	165	153	165	130
Demi-culverin	137	344	47	200
Saker	144	662	27	220
Minion	189	715	132	40

So the Spaniards had the best of it in the heavy short-range guns, and the English in the long-range demi-culverins. The two sides were almost equal in culverins, and the English were greatly superior in the smaller sakers and minions – most of which, in both fleets, were carried by the merchant ships.

One speaks of short-range and long-range guns, but the figures for range are extremely vague. For one thing, the range of a gun depended on the quality of the powder, and also on the 'windage' – the gap between the outside of the ball and the inside of the barrel, which might be as much as half an inch. So every gun, and almost every shot, was different. For another thing, the range was measured in paces, and nobody really knows what Elizabethan gunners meant by a pace – perhaps even then there was no exact definition of it. One authority says it was 5 feet, which would give a culverin an extreme range of nearly $2\frac{1}{2}$ miles; but another, which seems more likely, says it was $2\frac{1}{2}$ feet, and the range therefore $1\frac{1}{4}$ miles.

Point-blank range, of course, was the distance at which a gunner could point his gun at the enemy and fire without much regard for elevation. The random range was the greatest distance the gun could carry when it was elevated, and 'at random' was a vivid expression for long-range gunnery; for this depended on guessing the distance, guessing the elevation and choosing the moment to fire as the ship rolled. It meant firing as many shots as possible, literally at random, in the general direction of the enemy, and hoping for an occasional hit.

What matters in comparing the fleets is not the real range but the relative range. The English expected to use their more nimble ships to choose their range, to keep out of the way of the Spanish cannons, and yet to be able to hit with their culverins. But it was a narrow margin, a delicate theory for the defence of a kingdom. Beyond 2000 paces, they were safe from cannon shots: beyond 2500, they could not use their own.

Most of the famous English captains of the age were met in Plymouth that summer, and ships with names that have come down through generations of warships ever since: Lord Howard, as Lord High Admiral, flying his flag in the *Ark* or *Ark Royal*, which the queen had bought from Sir Walter Raleigh; Drake as Vice-Admiral in the *Revenge*; John Hawkyns, Rear Admiral in the *Victory* at sea again after twenty years ashore; Frobisher in the *Triumph*; George Beeston in the *Dreadnought*; Drake's captains Thomas Fenner and Robert Crosse in the *Nonpareil* and the *Hope* – ten thousand men and nearly a hundred sail. They had been there since May; and at the other end of the Channel in the Thames and the Straits of Dover, another forty sail, commanded by Lord Henry Seymour, were watching the narrows in case the Duke of Parma made a foray.

Lord Howard and Drake had endless troubles, but not quite the same troubles the Spanish fleet was having. One was a chronic shortage of food and ammunition; the other the vacillating orders of the queen. The shortages were really nobody's fault; it was simply that the English had no experience of keeping such a fleet in being for so long, and the shore organization was not up to the job. Nor perhaps can the changes of mind of the queen be called a fault; she had often found strength in being unpredictable. She dreaded the unforeseeable hazards of war, and until the last moment she clung to the hope that negotiations with Parma would find a peaceful solution. But it was a fault that neither she nor her council understood the tactics of naval war, much less its strategy.

Naval strategy, in fact, had scarcely existed before; to exist, it needed a certain mastery of the sea itself. Drake was its founder. He had come into the queen's ships with a wider experience of the sea than any Englishman had had before, and with an unrivalled confidence that he could keep the sea whatever weather came. So his strategic ideas had a freedom nobody had dared to express before. He passionately argued, all that summer, that the proper place to fight an enemy in defence of England was not off the English coast but off the enemy ports – the same strategy, based on the same confidence, that guided the navy of Nelson's time in the great blockade before Trafalgar.

As early as March, before the armada left Lisbon, he had written a long despatch from Plymouth to the queen. He never learned to express himself clearly on paper, and the thoughts he wrote down are tangled. But phrases stand out among them: 'To seek God's enemies and Her Majesty's where they may be found . . . With fifty sail of shipping we shall do more good upon their own coast than a great many more will do here at home . . . If there may be such a stay or stop made by any means of this fleet in Spain, so that they may not come through the seas as conquerors, which I assure myself they think to do, then shall the Prince of Parma have such a check thereby as were meet.'

Perhaps the despatch was even less clear to the queen and her council than it is to the modern reader. It made them think he proposed to attack the armada in Lisbon itself, which was impossible. He was summoned to court to explain, and found Lord Howard himself opposing the idea. But he was far more convincing as a talker than a writer. He persuaded the queen, and Howard came round to the idea when he understood it: not to attack Lisbon, but to lie off the port and challenge the armada to come out. It was after the meeting, in May, that Howard was sent down Channel from the Thames, where he had been lying, to join his own forces with Drake's and take the whole lot under his command.

Like the duke in the armada, Howard formed a council of war, but it was smaller: it had only four members – Drake, Hawkyns,

Frobisher and Thomas Fenner. At its first meeting the question of sailing to Spain was opened again, and one of the members opposed Drake's strategy. It could not have been Fenner, who came from a famous seafaring family of Chichester (three Fenners were captains against the armada) and was one of Drake's most trusted followers. Nor could it have been Hawkyns, who was certainly of the same mind as Drake. So it must have been Frobisher, a brave but illiterate and obstinate Yorkshireman best known for his explorations of the North West Passage. There was a long discussion, but in the end they all left the council convinced.

Yet they had to wait. The wind was a strong south westerly, Howard's ships had only three weeks' food and his supply ships were stuck up the Channel. 'God send us a wind to put us out,' he wrote, 'for go we will, though we starve.' At the end of May, the wind showed signs of changing and the whole of the fleet put to sea, to find the armada and fight it where it lay. Before they reached Ushant they met with a southerly gale. They fought it for seven days; then it veered to the west. While it was blowing they spoke with a merchant ship northbound which had sighted the armada standing out from Lisbon. The same weather that held the English might bring the Spanish into the Channel at any moment. Howard saw a danger of being driven to leeward of Plymouth and leaving it unprotected, so they put back to the Sound.

There in Plymouth were new despatches from London: the queen had changed her mind. They were not to go to Spain, but to 'ply up and down in some indifferent place between the coast of Spain and this realm'. Drake's reasoning was still not understood at court. Howard replied with an angry sarcastic letter that no lesser man would have dared to write, explaining it all again in simpler terms. He waited for an answer, and for a shift of wind. Every day the armada was expected. In the wind that was blowing it would certainly have arrived – unless it had been scattered and driven in disorder to Spanish or Biscay ports. Now was the moment to strike: so Drake insisted, and there was nobody in the fleet who disagreed. Another attempt was made; but in the face of another gale, and perhaps in deference to the queen's decision, it was carried no farther than the coast of Brittany.

Back in Plymouth again, new orders were received: the queen had relented and confirmed that Howard should use his own judgement, subject only to the advice of his council of war. Pinnaces and horsemen were constantly coming in to report they had seen Spanish ships, but nobody claimed to have seen the whole armada. What they had seen, in fact, were the ships that had pressed on to the Scilly Islands when the armada was scattered off Corunna. Among the pinnaces was the one that had spoken south of Ushant with the Irish bark that had been captured and towed by the Spaniards and then cut adrift when they thought it was sinking. The four survivors said the Spanish ships had clearly been sailing to the southward, back to Spain. Merchant ships coming up from the Biscay ports of France reported nothing there. Drake was convinced the armada was lying badly damaged in Corunna or possibly Vigo.

At the end of June, when the armada in fact was helpless in Corunna, the weather in Plymouth began to lift. Howard's supply ships came in, and men worked without sleep or rest to get the stores on board. On 4th July the wind came fair from the north east. They did not wait to finish the victualling, but gave orders for the store ships to follow, and stood away for Spain.

Off Ushant, the wind headed them again – a fair wind for the Spaniards, foul for them. They beat against it for ten days, between Ushant and the Scillies, with pinnaces out to port and starboard to watch the widest front, and provisions running shorter all the time. Then again it changed, and stood fair for Spain. But Howard hesitated: those ten days could have brought the Spaniards out. Evidently Drake was desperate: aboard the *Revenge*, he wrote a protest – an act he would have condemned in anyone else – and sent it across to Howard in the *Ark*. The message itself is lost, but it must have been emphatic. Howard called a council of war at sea, and on 17th July there was a long discussion. The question they had to answer was clear, but the answer needed a kind of inspired conviction. Was the armada still in port, or had it been fit to use those ten days of wind to put to sea again?

If it had, and the English fleet stood south, there was every chance of missing it on the way – and England, behind them, was unprotected except by Lord Henry Seymour in the Thames. Moreover, most of the English ships had barely enough provisions to reach the coast of Spain, and certainly not enough to lie there. Drake insisted: from his own intuition, from all the meagre intelligence they had gleaned, from his own knowledge of the sea and of the Spaniards, he had convinced himself the armada was still in harbour recovering from the gale, and open to an attack that would cripple it for ever. As for provisions, he had always fed his crews by plundering prizes. He won the argument: that evening, Howard signalled the fleet to make sail, and the whole of it set course down wind across the Bay of Biscay.

It was perhaps the greatest gamble ever taken with the fate of England at stake, and it failed. Some sixty miles off the coast of Spain the wind fell away and left the fleet becalmed; and then it got up again from the south. Without food, there was no chance of hanging on the the teeth of the weather and waiting for it to change. And sixty miles off was just too far to be sure of intercepting the armada if the new shift of wind had brought it out. There was nothing to do but put about and run for the coast of England.

This was on 20th July, the day the duke called his council and asked them whether the armada should sail.

8

The Hostile Shore

The duke had to cancel his sailing orders after the council meeting in Corunna: the weather again was too bad. But on the morning of 22nd July the armada got out of harbour with a very light south westerly wind. That afternoon, before the fleet was clear of the bay, the wind fell away to a dead calm, and there were some anxious hours when the mass of ships seemed likely to drift ashore. They were saved by a land breeze at three o'clock in the morning of the 23rd, which grew to a brisk south easterly wind as the day advanced. The galleass *Zuniga* broke her rudder pintles while she was making sail (the galleasses were always in trouble with their rudders). But when that was repaired, the fleet stood out at last for England; and for three days it basked in summery weather and a perfect following breeze.

On board, most people seem to have thought of this final departure from Spain as the real beginning of the voyage, as if they preferred to forget the frustrations of the past two months. At any rate, it was only after leaving Corunna that the duke began to keep a diary, and most of the other private accounts of the adventure also begin on that day. All of them mention the beautiful weather; but it only added to the duke's impatience. In the *San Martin*, he reckoned, he could have been in the mouth of the Channel by the 25th, but he had to wait for the slowest tubs in the fleet – 'and some of them are really dreadfully slow'. Yet even he must have had some feeling of pride when he stood on his poop in the sunshine and looked at the forest of sail astern of him – the fleet with its troubles, to all appearances, left behind and every ship on its station. One can even imagine a holiday air, among the more privileged people, on that crossing of the Bay of Biscay.

The fleet was reorganized now in eleven squadrons. About sixty-five ships, roughly half the total, were warships, or merchantmen more or less converted as warships, and their squadrons were geographical: Portugal, Castile, Andalusia, Biscay, Guipuzcoa (the north east corner of Spain) and Levant (Italy and the Adriatic). In separate tactical units were the four galleasses and the four galleys. Each fighting squadron had a few small pinnaces attached to it for communications; and the fighting ships were escorting a squadron of twenty-three urcas, another of twenty-six pinnaces, and a third of nine small ships now listed as water caravels. Essentially, therefore, the armada was not a fighting fleet. It was a convoy.

The duke had gathered a team of friends and advisers round him in the flagship *San Martin*. Recalde, the admiral, left the flagship of his own squadron, the *Santa Ana*, and joined the vice-flagship of the duke's squadron, the *San Juan*, where the duke might expect to have him close at hand in battle. In Corunna, Don Diego Flores de Valdes, as one of the oldest and most experienced seamen, did the same, and joined the duke in the *San Martin* herself; so did the senior general, Don Francesco de Bovadillo. Diego Flores was therefore always on hand with advice about the management of the fleet, and Don Francesco about its battle tactics. In addition, the duke had the captain of the *San Martin* and four pilots, one of whom was said to be English – not to mention the gentlemen of his own entourage, and the most senior among the priests. In practice, therefore, the armada was commanded by a permanent council, to which the duke (much younger than most of them) brought nothing but his own common sense and the authority the king had given him – and, one must add, a very positive degree of personal courage.

For the moment, as they set the long course out of sight of land across the Bay towards the coast of Cornwall, decisions lay with the pilots; and throughout the voyage it is an advantage to understand the knowledge and equipment the pilots had.

In the sixteenth century the art of finding one's way at sea was already divided in two parts: in the open ocean it was navigation, by compass and observation of latitude, and inshore it was pilotage, which was mainly a matter of 'caping', or following the coast from cape to cape. The voyage the armada foresaw called for almost nothing but pilotage. It was only in crossing the Bay of Biscay that they expected to be out of sight of land.

Their compasses were very much like a modern compass, except that they were not filled with liquid and were more roughly made. The cards were already divided into thirty-two points, and the north was marked by a fleur-de-lys, as it still is; but the east was marked by a cross, which had something to do with the Star of Bethlehem. They were mounted in a round wooden box inside a binnacle, or bittacle, in front of the helmsman, and were lit at night by a candle or oil lantern. The needle, stuck on the underneath of the card, was not a permanent magnet, and ships carried a lump of magnetic iron ore, a lodestone, which was used to 'feed' the compass from time to time by rubbing it on the needle. Rough though the compass was, it probably showed the course as accurately as a sailing ship could be steered.

Ocean navigators used the cross-staff or the astrolabe for observing the elevation of the sun at noon, or the pole star at dusk or dawn or on moonlit nights when the horizon was visible. They had almanacs, from which they could convert their observations into estimates of latitude. In good weather, with luck and care, they could find their latitude to within about half a degree, or thirty nautical miles. But there was no way of finding their longitude; that did not come until the eighteenth century.

When an ocean navigator was approaching land, the most important and most ancient instrument was the lead. On long voyages, ships carried two different leads and lines. The dipsie (or deep-sea) lead weighed 14 lbs, and it had a line with the astonishing length of 150 or even 200 fathoms – 1200 feet. But to use it one had to stop the ship or put off in a boat. For lesser depths, there was a lighter and handier lead of 7 lbs with a shorter line, which a leadsman could use while the ship was under way. With a dipsie lead a navigator could tell when he had crossed the continental shelf and was entering pilotage waters. Both leads were 'armed' with a lump of tallow stuck in a hollow at the lower end, which picked up a sample of the sea bottom; and this, from previous experience, could tell the pilot roughly where he was.

This kind of experience was recorded in books of sailing directions which the English called rutters, from the French *routiers*. Rutters had existed for centuries in the Mediterranean, where they were known as *peripli*. In northern waters, through the middle ages, each captain had made his own rutter in a private notebook, if he could read and write, and probably bequeathed it to his son. But in 1528 the first printed rutter in English was published, and a new extended edition appeared in 1541. It was still in print and in use in the 1580s, and by then another, with woodcuts of the shape of the land as it was seen from seaward, had been translated from Dutch into English, and undoubtedly into Spanish too.

These rutters were meant for coastal pilots 'caping' round the shores. But they included instructions for the voyage the armada was making from Finisterre to the Lizard in Cornwall, because this was one leg of the regular trade route round Europe – the longest cape-to-cape passage a coastal pilot ever had to make, and the only one that took him out of soundings. The rutters told the armada pilots what course to set when they were clear of Corunna, and in the fine weather of the first few days that was about all they had to do. There was no need to observe their latitude. They estimated their speed simply by looking over the side and watching the bubbles go past; and a dead reckoning of the distance they had covered would have been more exact than a celestial observation. Three days out, on 26th July, they told the duke they were in 48°N, which is almost the latitude of Ushant. Even with that favourable wind they were making only two knots. The king had told the duke, and he had told the pilots, to be sure to take soundings when they were nearing the end of their crossing; and the rutter told them what to look for: 'When ye be at LXXX fadome ye shall finde small black sande and yee shalbe at the thwart of Lezarde [i.e. in the longitude of the Lizard]. When ye be at LX or LXV ye shall fined white sande, and white soft woormes, and ye shall be very nigh to Lezard.'

Hitherto, coastal pilots in northern waters had not used charts. The rutters gave them all they needed: the compass courses from cape to cape, the worst of the hidden dangers, the landmarks for entering harbours, the state of the tides in each port at full and new moon, and the navigational beacons and buoys, of which there were few. None of the information was exact – for example, the only distances given in rutters were not in nautical miles or leagues but in kennings, and a kenning was the range at which a seaman might expect to ken or recognize the coast. Thus the width of the straits of Dover was one kenning, and the width of the mouth of the Channel was five. Some coastal skippers affected to despise the rutters, perhaps to disguise the fact that they could not read. They liked to rely on their own local knowledge and use their own landmarks – church spires, woods, hilltops, headlands and houses – to see them safely into port. It was this attitude of mind that made the duke take the trouble to find an English pilot.

Just before the armada sailed, however, there was a great innovation in northern pilotage. This was the first atlas of sea-charts of western and northern Europe. It was published in Holland by Lucas Janszoon Wagenhaer of Enchuysen – for the Dutch at that time were leaders in cartography. The first volume, from Cadiz to the Zuider Zee, appeared in 1584, and the second, of the North Sea and the Baltic, in 1585. A Latin edition of both parts was published in 1586. An English edition, entitled *The Mariners Mirrour*, was commissioned by Lord Howard in 1586 but was not published until the armada had come and gone, in October 1588. Wagenhaer's work was an immense success – so much so that all sea charts were called Waggoners by English seamen for at least a century afterwards. In 1588 it was much the best thing of its kind in existence, and there is no doubt the armada pilots had it, either in Dutch or Latin, or perhaps with the relevant parts put into Spanish. The English, on the other hand, did not. But of course they hardly needed it. Most of the time, they were in their own home waters, and they knew the Channel coast by heart.

Wagenhaer's volume was not only an atlas, it was also an almanac and a manual of navigation. It summed up very clearly all the techniques of ocean navigation that were known. In addition, each chart had a rutter, which gave courses and distances from cape to cape and from one port to another; the means of telling the time from bearings of the sun or moon, and of working out the state of the tides and tidal streams at any hour; and meticulous instructions for entering every major harbour.*

*But his instructions would have been very difficult for a stranger to follow. For example, those for entering Spithead on the way to Portsmouth were enough to scare any pilot:

'If you will enter at the east end of Wight, keep the Castle right against the Lime-kill that lies above Portsmouth until that Culver Cliff come within the point of the Ile, for

The charts themselves, which were engraved on copper, look unfamiliar to anyone who knows the coasts today, because they show all the harbours and inlets as bigger than they really are. But this was deliberate. These were the parts that mattered most, the parts where most detail was needed; and they were drawn bigger in an attempt to combine the different uses of a general chart and a set of harbour plans. The charts were elegantly decorated with the coats of arms and scrolls, sea monsters and ships that custom demanded. They had views of the coast from seaward, much better than the older woodcuts, and they were the first to use standard symbols for sunken rocks, anchorages, buoys and beacons. They were also the first to have scales, not now in kennings, but in Spanish, Dutch and English leagues.* Of course they were not strictly accurate, because they were based on the observations of hundreds of seamen; but even now, a small-boat sailor could make the armada's projected voyage and safely find his way with nothing but a compass, a lead and a copy of the sixteenth-century Waggoner.

There is one thing, however, that he would have to remember: the compass variation in English waters in the 1580s, as one can see from the compass roses on Wagenhaer's charts, was about a point and a half, or $17°$ more easterly than it is now. Throughout the armada story, one has to allow for this difference. All the courses and wind directions recorded by either fleet were a point and a half away from what would be shown by a modern chart or compass.

The only exception in Wagenhaer's instructions – as things turned out, a crucially important one – was the coast of the Netherlands. There, the atlas reported, the sandbanks shifted so

then you shall have brought the Lyme-kill to the east end of Portsmouth: which you must hold until the Castle which standeth to the westward of Portsmouth do appear on the east side of the wood: and then ply sometimes towards St Helens Abbey, keeping your marks in this sort, you shall then take no hurt on the Shoaldes or Sands. But if you cannot see the Lime-kill, then shall you keep the Castle on the west side of Culver Cliff, until you have brought St Helens church with out the point of the Island a ship's length. Then you freely sail North west, without danger of the Riffe or tail-sand that lieth out. Then keep the square tower between the east end of Portsmouth and the Castle: until you may see the Castle which standeth in the west side of Portsmouth, eastward of the wood: and so you go inwards.'

*A Spanish league was $3\frac{1}{2}$ nautical miles, a Dutch league 4 and an English league 3.

often that it was forbidden to approach the coast without using the lead.

Thinking of pilotage raises the question why the armada's leaders, crossing the Bay so cheerfully in the summer sun, had already decided to make landfall in Cornwall and sail up-Channel in sight of the coast of England. The pilots would certainly have wanted to be in sight of one Channel coast or the other. By their methods of ocean navigation they could only know their north-and-south position within about thirty miles, and their east-and-west position not at all; so they could hardly have sailed up the middle, out of sight of land. But why choose the English side? It seems obvious that if they had made the opposite choice and followed the coast of France, they might have reached the Straits of Dover before the English knew they were there, or at least before the greater part of the English fleet, which they knew was in Plymouth, had time to catch up with them. But to sail along the English coast as they did, past each of its harbours, gave the English every possible advantage.

The answer to this question, as to so much else, is that the king had given the order. 'You must keep away from the French and Flemish coasts,' he had written in his orders of 1st April, 'because of the shoals and banks.' He was quite wrong, of course; there are no shoals or banks off the French coast, and never were, except in the Bay of Boulogne which the armada would not have entered in any case. Perhaps he had misunderstood what he had been told or read. Perhaps he expressed himself badly, and was thinking vaguely of the shoals beyond Calais, beyond the border of France. Possibly, in his belief that the English would welcome the armada, he wanted them to see it coming. But there it was, a categorical order; and as usual, the duke did not query it – he had no opportunity. He obeyed it; and by this single sentence the armada was doomed to fight a running battle half the way up the Channel and make its rendezvous with Parma when almost all its ammunition was already spent. All that way, moreover, the armada would be at hazard. Its merchantmen were unable to sail even at right angles to the wind, and so if the wind came southerly they would be driven ashore.

*

On the third of those sunny days, the duke sent off a second pinnace to run the gauntlet of the Channel and take a report to the Duke of Parma, telling him of the delay in Corunna and the successful voyage since. The pinnace, much faster than the bulk of the armada, vanished into the summer haze ahead.

But the good weather did not last. At dawn on 26th July the wind fell calm, and all that morning the fleet lay wallowing motionless in a fog. After noon a northerly wind sprang up and forced the fleet off course. At first, the ships fell off to the eastward. But somewhere down that way were the rocks of Ushant, and nobody could tell how far away they were; so the duke fired a gun to turn to the other tack. The fleet made its clumsy and time-consuming manoeuvre and set a course of west, away from its objective, beset by heavy squalls of wind and rain. That day, someone noticed that one of the galleys was missing. The duke sent a pinnace to ask the other galleys what had happened to her, and was told she had been making so much water she had had to turn back for Spain.

The wind rose in the night, and the next day it blew a gale. 'The sea was so heavy,' the duke wrote to the king, 'that all the sailors agreed they had never seen its equal in July. The waves mounted to the skies, some seas broke clean over the ships, and the whole of the stern gallery of Diego Flores' flagship was carried away. We were on watch all night, full of anxiety lest the armada should suffer great damage, but we could do nothing more. It was the most cruel night ever seen.'

That was frankly a landsman's description in writing to another landsman. In his diary the duke was more reticent, only mentioning a 'very heavy sea'; and the chief purser Pedro Coco Calderon, who was also keeping a diary, wrote: 'A strong wind, and the armada kept its course.' But still, it had certainly been a dirty night; and anxiously counting the ships in the light of a clear morning the duke was aghast to find forty missing. It looked like Corunna all over again.

In fact, it did not turn out so badly. The storm, after all, had been short, and the missing ships could not have gone very far. Pinnaces were sent out to hunt for them, some ahead and some astern, and the fleet shortened sail and waited. The squadron of Pedro de Valdes was already close to the English coast, and it waited there for the rest to catch up. Two days later, all the other ships had been found except four: one galleon, and the three remaining galleys.

The galleon was the flagship of Recalde's squadron, the *Santa Ana*. There must have been something wrong with this ship. Either her crew was mutinous, or her captain half-hearted, or her pilots less than competent — or perhaps there was merely some ironwork close to her compass. It was she who, after the storm at Corunna, had finished up farther away than anyone else, in the harbour of Santander. Now she had lost the squadron she was supposed to be leading; and she was next heard of, after the battles were over, in the French harbour of Le Havre. How and why she got there was never explained; but she must have started 90° off course, and sailed half-way up the Channel, but on the wrong side and all alone. Nobody ever offered an explanation of this mystery. She was said to be carrying fifty thousand ducats belonging to the king.

The galleys were more comprehensible. The sea was too much for these light craft, with their low freeboard and their banks of oars, and all of them turned before the wind and made for the coast of France. But their disappearance provided one of the strangest stories of the armada, which found its way into Dutch history and thence to an English history book of 1860. The strange thing about it is that it was a pack of lies.

It was told by a Welshman called David Gwynne, who was an oarsman in one of the galleys. These oarsmen are usually known as galley slaves, but in Spain they were not really slaves, they were convicts. Gwynne did not say what he had been sentenced for; but he was a seaman, so he had probably been captured in some enterprise the Spaniards judged was piratical. He claimed to have been at the oars for eleven years.

In the storm, he said, one of the galleys, named *Diana*, went down with all hands at sea. He was in the *Bezana*, and her captain lost his head and begged Gwynne, as a seaman, to tell him what to do. Gwynne said the only hope was to take in sail, send the soldiers below decks out of the oarsmen's way, and row for the coast of France. All the slaves, according to him, had been in the habit of making toothpicks, which they sold, out of bits of broken swords, and all of them had secretly made themselves stilettos. When he had got the galley shipshape, he threw down his cap as a signal and stabbed the captain to the heart, and the slaves rose up and killed every Spaniard on board.

Then they were attacked by the flagship of the galleys, but Gwynne laid his ship alongside her, leaped aboard, liberated her slaves and finished off all her Spaniards too. Thereupon everyone acclaimed him as captain, and he took both ships to Bayonne in France, marched to La Rochelle at the head of four hundred and sixty-six men, French, English, Turks and Moors, and was rewarded by King Henry of Navarre. He went home to England, and was commended by the queen.

All this was a glorious invention. In fact, when the galleys could not weather the storm they all ran before it in good order and made the coast of France. Gwynne was in the *Diana*, not the *Bezana*. She was not lost at sea, but entering the harbour of Bayonne she ran aground and was wrecked. Most if not all of the men in her were saved. There was no mutiny and no fight at sea or anywhere else, and the other three galleys safely returned to Spain. Ashore in France, the convicts of the *Diana* were set free, or ran away.

The only important thing about Gwynne's mendacious tale is that when he reached England people at first believed it and made him a hero. He turns up again in this story. When scattered armada ships began to reach Ireland he was sent there, because he spoke Spanish, to extract confessions from prisoners. Those unfortunate shipwrecked men were interrogated by an ex-convict with a powerful personal grudge against Spain – until at last the English discovered he was a rogue, a thief and a liar, and sent him back to England in disgrace.

The storm had made havoc of the pilots' dead reckoning. As it subsided they did not know where they were. A pinnace was sent to take soundings, and if possible to find the land; and at noon on Friday the 20th the duke told the pilots to take a sun sight. They did, and reported the depth as fifty-six fathoms and the latitude as '50° bare'. 50°N is the latitude of the Lizard itself. They had not sighted the Scilly Isles. Now they were somewhere very close to the hostile shore, but they could not see it.

The storm had also put an end to the holiday air. That gave way, among the host of men, to suppressed excitement. They were acutely aware they were now in enemy waters, and committed to the voyage up the Channel, from which there was no turning back. It was not an unpleasant feeling; the men, the duke said, were so cheerful it was a joy to see them. They crept on under shortened sail, the look-outs alert, with a gentle westerly wind and a hazy horizon, feeling their way the last few miles to England in the silence of sailing ships when the breeze is fair, at a speed that a man on shore could achieve in a leisurely stroll. At one time the whole fleet had to heave to because another of the galleasses had broken her rudder – this time the flagship or *capitana* of the squadron, the *San Lorenzo*. 'These craft are really very fragile for heavy seas,' the duke noted. No strange ships were sighted, not even a fishing boat: the emptiness of the seas seemed ominous. 'In the whole voyage so far, we have not fallen in with a single vessel from whom we could get information, so we are groping in the dark. As we pass Plymouth, I shall try to pick up some intelligence with our pinnaces.'

At four o'clock in the afternoon of 29th July, the look-outs sighted land on the port bow, and said it was the Lizard. The duke hoisted to the maintop an ensign with a crucifix and the Virgin and Magdalen on either side of it, presumably the one that was blessed in Lisbon, and he fired three guns and called all hands to offer a prayer of thanks for God's mercy in bringing them so far. The first part of the undertaking was over. They had arrived – and they knew they were observed. That night on every hill-top of the shore they saw the beacon fires.

During the night the duke completed a long letter to the king describing the voyage, and despatched it by a pinnace back to Spain. With it he sent a second letter, in code. He said he was astonished to have had no news from Parma. He had sent two pinnaces to Dunkirk, and there was plenty of time for the first at least to have come back.

'Without information from him,' he now wrote, 'I can only proceed slowly to the Isle of Wight, and go no further until he informs me of the state of his forces. All along the coast of Flanders there is no harbour to shelter our ships, and if I took the armada there from the Isle of Wight it might be driven on the shoals, where it would certainly be lost. To avoid such an obvious danger, I have decided to stay off the Isle of Wight until I know what the duke is doing, as the plan is that the moment I arrive he should come out with his fleet, without making me wait a minute. The whole success of the enterprise depends on this, and to make sure the duke understands it I will send him another pinnace as soon as I am in the Channel, and yet another when I arrive off the Wight.'

It was not one of his most coherent letters, but it shows he was already worried at hearing nothing from Parma – a worry that was to grow in the next few days to something bordering on panic. The cheerful men knew nothing about it; but for him it was certainly a daunting prospect, even as early as this, to enter the English Channel with no idea of what he might find at the other end. The last word he had had from Parma was dated 22nd March, four months before, in the letter Captain Moresin had brought to Lisbon. Almost anything might have happened since then. The king had told him nothing. Parma could have been fighting battles somewhere else. He could have come up against untold problems and abandoned the enterprise altogether. If he was not ready when the duke arrived, what was to happen to the armada? It could not stop in the Straits of Dover, or fight its way into the Thames without Parma's aid. And beyond that was the enigmatic coast of Flanders, mainly held by the English or the Netherlands rebels. It was not quite true that there were no harbours there that could have sheltered the armada, but there was none that anyone in the armada knew. This was the blank in Wagenhaer's instructions; and nobody had thought of providing the Spanish fleet with Flemish pilots, because nobody had intended it should go so far.

The king had always insisted on hurry, and had specifically told the duke not to stop at the Isle of Wight. But he had to know. Rather than go on in ignorance, he had made up his mind to disobey this order.

Of course the duke could not have made a decision like that single-handed. He must have discussed it with his experts, and it was probably the decision of a council of war which he called that night or early in the morning of Saturday 30th July.

*

The minutes of that council have never been found, and there are conflicting reports of it. Apparently the duke called it to make final decisions on the order of battle, not on strategy, which had already been decided long before. But after the voyage ended in disaster, Spanish public opinion had to find a scapegoat, and its most obvious target was the duke. One critic in particular was a priest called Juan de Victoria, who sailed on the voyage and wrote a very badly-informed account of it, in which he called the duke a fool and a coward and blamed him for everything that went wrong. This man was not present at the council, nor was his informant; but his third-hand story was that every expert wanted to make an attack on Plymouth and that the duke refused – and so through his cowardice deprived the armada of victory.

But the duke was not a fool, nor were the dozen members of his council. It underrates those men to think that they could have argued hotly for such a drastic plan at the very last moment, when Plymouth was almost in sight. There are only two firm bits of evidence that Plymouth was mentioned at all. The first comes from Captain Alonso Vanegas of the *San Martin*. In his account he said that de Leyva suggested they should attack the place and that some of the others agreed. But the duke pointed out that this was against the king's orders, and that the channel was narrow and well defended; and the decision not to try was unanimous.

The second report was from Don Pedro de Valdes. By the time he made it he had been captured and was raging with animosity against the duke. So he might have been expected to disagree with anything the duke had said or done. But he did not; he said he had agreed the entrance was too narrow and the attempt should not be made.

History has usually assumed that a naval attack was what they mainly discussed, and that the English fleet, caught in harbour, was vulnerable to the kind of headlong attack that Drake had made on Cadiz and proposed to make on Corunna. But that is impossible to believe. To begin with, the armada was not a highly mobile fighting fleet, like Drake's at Cadiz, and its commanders knew very well that it was not. Nor is Plymouth harbour anything like Cadiz or Corunna. There are miles of inland water beyond the town where the English fleet could have retreated, and the narrows to east and west of the town were commanded by the strongest shore batteries anyone could devise. Moreover, the tidal stream in the Sound runs up to a knot and a half, and in the narrows two and a half. If the armada had ventured in, it could only have done it on a rising tide, and would have had to wait for a change of wind and an ebbing tide to get out again.

Finally, the armada was encumbered by its convoy of merchantmen. It certainly could not take them all in; nor could it abandon them outside, in case a part of the English fleet, under Lord Howard perhaps, was patrolling the Channel or lurking in Dartmouth or Torbay. Plymouth, in fact, was impregnable by sea, and no seaman would have wasted time, so late in the day, in arguing about it.

But de Leyva was not a seaman; he was a cavalry soldier with a gallant reputation. It may be he was tempted for a moment by the emptiness of the sea and the apparent emptiness of the shore. In that company, the only thing he could have suggested was a land attack: not to take the fleet into the Sound, but to put him and his troops ashore outside it, perhaps in Whitesand Bay to the west or Wembury Bay to the east, or both. It was not impossible that Spanish troops could have fought their way inland and enveloped the town and the anchorage while the armada lay offshore and blockaded it.

It seems much more likely that this was the project they discussed, after quickly discarding any idea of sailing in. It would certainly have re-aroused the belief Recalde had expressed in his letter to the king – that the armada ought to capture a west-country port for its own safety after the invasion, and to protect the reinforcements that would have to come from Spain. The king had not answered that letter, unless the copy has disappeared from the archives of Simancas.

But the duke knew perfectly well what he would have said: that the armada's first duty was to proceed as fast as it could to the junction with Parma. He was bound to oppose the plan, because it would take time and also – perhaps an even more cogent reason – because it would use the troops he was ordered to give to Parma. It was no use capturing Plymouth unless he left a large part of his army to hold it.

With such meagre reports, one cannot do much more than guess the trend of the argument; but this at least is a logical trend, which does not assume – as the English liked to believe – that the Spanish commanders were stupid. And one may take the guesswork a little further. There was now a new element to be argued. What was the use of hurrying on, somebody may well have asked, while they did not even know if Parma was ready? The duke could have had no ready answer. But duty and common sense would have made him insist that they ought to give Parma as long as they could to send them a pinnace, and not pause in executing the orders of the king until the last possible stopping-place: the Isle of Wight. It is likely that this was what satisfied them all, and this was the reason why the duke wrote his coded letter to the king.

Anyhow, the decision had only just been made when the choice was taken away from them. The duke had sent off a pinnace, as he had proposed, to try to pick up some information. It was commanded by a young man called Juan Gil, an ensign who spoke English. He came back during the night with four Falmouth fishermen he had captured. These bewildered anonymous men, prodded or hoisted up the towering side of the *San Martin* and confronted by Spanish grandees, said Drake and the English fleet were already out of the harbour and waiting in the lee of its western point, Rame Head.

The castle of Simancas, where King Philip established his archives and where most of the documents quoted in this book were found.

Overleaf: The last page of a letter of instructions sent by the king to the duke on 20th February. The postscript in the king's hand reads: 'I can only think this letter will find you nearer Lisbon than San Lucar, since the trust I place in you obliges you to do no less. I trust in God that with His aid, through you, the task which we desire and propose to do will be accomplished. I the King.'

Overleaf: The river at Lisbon in the sixteenth century, where the armada assembled.

lleua enla Empressa y como se ha de guiar y el
modo dela correspondencia conel Duque de Parma mi
Sobrino, os esperara los alcancara en lisboa Instrucion y
aduertimientos muy particulares despachados por esta via,
y por la del cons de guerra delo que en lisboa se ha de haser.
yo os teneys muy probada la Intencion enla dilig.a y cuydado
y pues nunca tanto fue menester lo uno y lo otro como agora
disponeos y afinaos como espero para haser me este serui
cio y ayudar me a haser a Dios el que principal mente pre
tendo enlo que se trae entre manos y auisad me luego de
quanto sucedes haziendo. de Madrid a 20 de hebrero
1588

el que sabe que la esta carta no
os aya de tomar mas cerca de lis
boa que sant lucar pues no os o
bliga a menos mi confiança y
espero en dios el con su ayudo se lo
he de haser por vra mano lo que se de
sea y pretendo

yo el Rey

LISBONA.

Sir Francis Drake, who created the concept that warships were
commanded by sea-captains, not by soldiers.

Lord Howard of Effingham, Lord High Admiral of England.

Sir John Hawkyns, who pioneered the creation of a new kind of warship, the race-built ship.

9

The Encounter

The best-known of all the armada legends has the marks of truth: the game of bowls on Plymouth Hoe. It was on Friday 29th July (new calendar) that the frigate *Golden Hinde*, captain Thomas Flemyng, came sailing up the Sound with the news that they had sighted the armada off the Lizard. No contemporary report says what time of day it was, or how long it had taken Flemyng to come from the Lizard, fifty miles away. Nor can one deduce this from the Spanish story, because what he had seen was not the whole armada but Pedro de Valdes' squadron, which had run ahead of the rest in the storm and had been waiting somewhere near the Lizard for several days. But it is a fair enough guess that the sighting had been at dawn (most sightings are) and that he reached port the same afternoon. Afternoon is also perhaps the most likely time to play a game of bowls.

The story of the game has been traced right back to a pamphlet of 1624, well within living memory of the event; but Drake's alleged remark is a later addition: 'Plenty of time to finish the game and beat the Spaniards after.' This does not appear in a written history until 1736. One can only say it was just the sort of thing he would have said, if other people were getting over-excited. After all, he was expecting the armada. He knew it had had a fair wind since the moment nine days before when he had turned back from Corunna. If it was coming at all, it was sure to come soon. Whatever anyone else might do, he was not the man to let them imagine he was surprised. It is much easier to believe he said it than that somebody years afterward made it up.

Besides, it was not just a gesture of gallant nonchalance. There really was plenty of time. If it was mid-afternoon, it was dead low water. Some of the ships were probably aground alongside the quays, and the fleet could not possibly get out against the flood that was just beginning. There was nothing much to do until the tide began to slacken in the evening. It is doubtful if it occurred to

Drake or his companions, knowing Plymouth as they did, that the armada would try to enter the harbour. But if they did intend to try, they could not conceivably do it until the flood tide the following afternoon, and by then the English had every intention of being outside to stop them.

Late that evening, therefore, at high water, they warped the ships out of the inner harbours and towed them through the narrows with rowing boats. The wind was very light, but some ships may have begun to beat down the Sound in the dark. Most came to anchor south of the town and waited for daylight and the morning ebb, which began about eleven o'clock. With the day, the wind came up from the south west.

It has often been acclaimed as a great feat of seamanship that they succeeded in gaining the open sea. The only descriptions they left were laconic. 'Upon Saturday,' Howard wrote the next day, 'we turned out very hardly, the wind being at south west.' A semi-official account said, 'The greater number of ships . . . with that wind were very hard to be gotten out of harbour, yet the same was done with such diligence and good will, that many of them got abroad as though it had been with a fair wind' – a strangely contradictory statement. Drake wrote a letter next day, but said nothing about it at all.

The fact is that nobody now can judge how difficult it was, or whether the feat was outstanding. This is one of the moments in the story when the compass variation makes a difference. What they reported as a south west wind would be nearer west south west on a modern compass. It was therefore not quite such a contrary wind as it looks on a chart today. In still water and a west south west wind, a ship which could make two points to windward would need four or five tacks to clear the Sound, and would need to be pretty smart in going about. Only the best of them, the queen's race-built ships and the pinnaces, could have done as well as that. But the tide was helping them all. One would suppose they used easy sail, just enough to give steerage way, and let the tide take them out – which it would have done unaided in about three hours. That would have minimized the need to tack. Hard work it may have been, and tedious, but it does not really sound exceptional. Perhaps the most worth-while comment is that phrase 'with diligence and good will'. It is worth remarking that nobody made excuses and that every ship put out enthusiastically.

By three o'clock that afternoon, still beating against the wind, Howard and Drake with fifty-four sail were near the Eddystone Rock. Thirteen miles, four or five of them due to the tide, in four hours: like the armada's first few days out of Lisbon, it gives a measure of the fleet's ability to windward.

There off the Eddystone, through a break in the squalls of rain, they had their first glimpse of the armada, upwind of them, 'to the westwards as far as Fowey'. At about the same moment, the Spaniards sighted them: 'A number of ships,' the duke wrote in his diary, 'but as the weather was thick and rainy they could not be counted.'

The first principle of naval tactics – in so far as any tactics existed – had always been to get to windward of the enemy, because in that position a captain could choose his moment to bear down and attack. In the new English scheme of fighting by gunnery, that remained as important as ever, and this first evening and night both fleets manoeuvred to 'win the weather gauge', to be upwind of the enemy in the morning. The duke sent a pinnace round his fleet to order everyone to close up in the battle order he had decreed, and then he came to anchor. As the armada could not sail to windward, this was the best he could do. Howard also took in all sail for a while, hoping no doubt that the armada would pass him in the night. But during the night he made sail again and stood farther out to sea, close-hauled on the starboard tack; then when he judged the moment had come, he changed tack to a course somewhere near north west.

Frobisher in the *Triumph* had come out of the Sound astern of the rest, with ten other ships. The *Triumph* was a high-charged galleon, and he probably had more of a struggle against the wind. Nevertheless, he also was working up to windward in the night by making short tacks inshore of the Spanish fleet. By dawn, both parts of the fleet had succeeded in their maneuver. Howard and Drake were to windward of the armada, five miles to the west of the Eddystone, and Frobisher only needed one more tack to join them.

*

In the revelation of that dawn, both sides had an unwelcome surprise. The Spaniards were astonished by the way the English beat to windward. The English were astonished by the massive compact formation of the armada.

The original accounts of the fights which started that morning off Plymouth and lasted half-way up the Channel are brief and vague and sometimes plainly wrong. It is not surprising. Before the end, two hundred and fifty ships were involved, all moving, though very slowly, and scattered over many miles of sea, and nobody on board any one of them could possibly watch them all and comprehend what all of them were doing. So everyone who wrote about it at all wrote only what he had done himself, and what he thought he had seen. Moreover, men who survived this battle had a good story to tell for the rest of their lives, so of course their imaginations flourished and rumours grew. The Spaniards made no attempt to correlate eye-witness stories, and the English made very little. The only thing approaching an official report was called the *Relation of Proceedings*. It had two versions, the first apparently based on talks with Howard, and the second with divergent views from Drake; but it was written by an Italian, Petruccio Ubaldino, who was not a seaman and had not been there, and it has utterly confusing mistakes in it, like writing east for west or leeward for windward.

In the last hundred years naval tacticians have analysed the contradictory stories with the greatest care, and tried to deduce in modern terms what really happened, what movements were made and why by squadrons or single ships. But however cleverly that is done there has to be guesswork in it, there is so little firm evidence to go on.

The object of this account is not to offer a novel study of tactics (except on a single occasion) or to repeat the old ones, nor to try to work out exactly what happened. It is rather to try to discover what people thought was happening and what they felt about it; and especially to follow the dilemma of the armada's leaders, which grew day by day until at last they were forced to recognize the shattering truth.

Accounts of the fight that morning are typical of the rest. 'At nine of the clock,' Howard wrote, 'we gave them fight. In this fight we made some of them bear room to stop their leaks.' That was all he wrote at the time, and even that was a hopeful guess: he could not know his shots had made them leak, and in fact it was very unlikely. On the same day Drake wrote, in a letter he sent up-Channel, marking it 'Haste, post haste', to Lord Henry Seymour, who commanded the fleet that was waiting in the Straits: 'We had them in chase, and so coming up to them, there hath passed some cannon shot between some of our fleet and some of them, and as far as we perceive they are determined to sell their lives with blows.' The *Relation of Proceedings*, written later, added some meagre details. Lord Howard, it said, began the fight by sending his pinnace *Disdain* 'to give the Duke of Medina defiance' – a picturesque act like a knight throwing down the gauntlet. Thereafter he fought with the Spanish flagship, while Drake, Hawkyns and Frobisher took on the vice-flagship, which they supposed was commanded by Recalde. The fight is given the air of a formal challenge.

The Spanish accounts are more detailed and quite different. Purser Calderon wrote one, the duke wrote two and other men wrote their own, and none of them fits together. Calderon named seven Spanish ships engaged in the fight. He also said that 'during this morning certain ships basely took to flight, until they were peremptorily ordered by the flagship to luff and face the enemy'. The duke in his diary said Recalde luffed up to repel the attack, supported by some ships of the rearguard. 'The enemy attacked him so fiercely with gunfire (but without coming to close quarters) that they crippled his rigging and hit his foremast twice.' Then he himself lay to and waited until Recalde rejoined the fleet. But in a letter he wrote that day to Parma he said 'My flagship became so closely engaged that we had to attack the enemy in force; whereupon they retired, although they still continue within sight of the armada, with the object, apparently, of delaying our voyage. If their object had been to fight, they had a good opportunity today.'

They might all be accounts of different battles. All one can say for certain is that they shot at each other without doing any damage except to Recalde's rigging, and a few Spaniards who were wounded (one officer had his leg shot off). The significant thing is that both sides had caught a glimpse of the other's strength. The duke had not yet grasped that the English meant to fight only with gunfire: he did not count that as fighting. But he had observed that he could not attack them, 'the English ships being very fast and well handled, so that they could do as they like with them'. As for Howard, he was baffled by the armada's close formation. 'We durst not adventure to put in among them, their fleet being so strong.' So he wrote that day to Walsingham; and he added in a postscript, 'Sir, for the love of God and our country, let us have with some speed some great shot sent us of all bigness, for this service will continue long; and some powder with it.'

Nothing like the armada's battle formation had ever been seen before, or indeed has ever been seen again. At the time, it was described by the English as a half-moon. This idea seems to have started with the contemporary historian William Camden, who, like Ubaldino, was no seaman; and it was repeated in the famous set of charts drawn in 1590 and made into tapestries for the House of Lords. These show the armada always in the form of a tidy crescent moon. But naval historians are sceptical, for two good reasons: it would be extremely difficult, if not impossible, for any fleet to keep formation in a curve; and even if they could do it, there would be no point in it. The leaders of the armada did not say specifically what their formation was, but a much more likely version of what they intended was published in Rome while they were at sea. It was more like a bird than a moon. The main body of the urcas and other transports was in the middle, with the duke's squadron of Portuguese galleons and the four galleasses ahead, and Don Pedro de Valdes' squadron astern; and on either side a mixed 'wing' of galleons and other ships in echelon formation – slanting, but in straight lines. The whole fleet was about four miles wide. To a landsman on a cliff-top, or indeed to an English seaman following behind, this might have looked like a moon.

One surprising thing about the armada's formation is that its lines were certainly abreast. Ships' guns were already on the broadside, but it had not yet occurred to the Spaniards, and scarcely to the English, that a line ahead, not abreast, was better to give a clear field of fire for their guns. For the Spaniards, the explanation perhaps is that they were not thinking of guns as a primary weapon, they were thinking of boarding. Besides, their formation was not meant to be offensive, it was defensive; their job was to get up the Channel intact. For defence, the formation was very strong, in fact impregnable. The ships were so close together – in theory fifty paces apart – that no enemy could penetrate the ranks without immediately being boarded on both sides.

That very morning, it seems, the high commanders of both fleets had begun to understand the unique situation they were in, a situation that never occurred again in the history of naval war. Here were the two most powerful fleets in the world, intent on fighting each other, and there was no possible way they could do it. They had chosen and armed themselves for different ways of fighting, and neither of them could be made to work. The Spaniards wanted to board, but the nimbler English could always slip away to windward. The English wanted to cannonade, but their longest shots could only reach the nearest edges of the Spanish fleet, leaving the mass of it unscathed. The kind of battle each had imagined was simply not going to happen. There was no way they could come to grips, and neither side could hope to beat the other – unless one side ran out of ammunition or the Spaniards, somehow, somewhere, abandoned their close formation.

In the afternoon when the fight had ended, Howard called a council of war. The English did not take minutes of their meetings, as the Spaniards did, and the only report of it is in the *Relation of Proceedings*, which says that 'His Lordship's considerate advice was much liked of, and order delivered unto each captain how to pursue the fleet of Spain'. To pursue it, not to fight it: his advice can only have been to follow so closely that the armada would not have a chance to land, and to attack any ship that fell out of formation. Anyhow, that was what they did, or attempted to do.

At the same moment, a mile or two away, the duke was writing to Parma, the letter in which he described the morning's fight. 'I intend with God's help to continue my voyage without letting anything divert me, until I receive instructions from Your Excellency of what I am to do and where I am to wait for you to join me. I implore Your Excellency to send someone with the utmost speed, bringing replies to the points on which I have written to you; also to send me pilots for the coast of Flanders, for without them I am ignorant of the places where I can find shelter for ships as large as these, in case I should be overtaken by the slightest storm.'

He did not mention his plan to wait at the Isle of Wight, only that he would carry on until he heard from Parma. Perhaps he already suspected that with the English on his heels, to stop at the island or anywhere else would be easier said than done.

This letter, dated 'Two leagues off Plymouth, 31st July, 1588', was to be carried by Juan Gil, the ensign who had captured the fishermen. He must have been a highly trusted young man. But next day the duke wrote briefly again: 'I could not send Gil yesterday, but he leaves today. I have nothing to add, except that the enemy continues to harrass our rear, and that their ships now seem to have increased to over a hundred sail. Some are excellent vessels, and all of them very fast sailers.'

Gil's voyage, from Plymouth to Dunkirk with the English thoroughly alerted, must have been a very perilous adventure. There is one clue to how he did it, in a report written by two English couriers who sailed from Rye on 4th August. After they had left port, they said, they fell in with some fishermen, who told them that shortly before a large Spanish ship, with many oars, and full of Englishmen, had passed. 'They said she bore a banner of Santiago, and another flag of the Queen of England over all. The people on board had spoken with them and told them the English fleet had met the Spanish fleet on Sunday and fought it, and they were going to warn Lord Harry Seymour to take care that the Duke of Parma did not come.'

At that time and place this could only have been Gil, pretending to be an English ship as he entered the Straits of Dover. Of course his pinnace was not full of Englishmen, but if he spoke to the fishermen in English and told his crew to keep quiet, they would have assumed the crew was English too. He had not discarded the sacred banner of Santiago, which no Spanish sailor would like to do, but was flying an English flag. It was a bluff that deserved to succeed, and it did. He delivered the letters to Parma in Bruges. But Parma did not reply.

The armada's precise formation must have been very hard to

maintain, with ships of such diverse ability, and only possible with a light wind astern and a reasonably calm sea. To keep station so closely would need unremitting attention to helms and sails. It is surprising, after their ragged performance so far, that they were able to do it, and it speaks very well for their sailors.

But the duke and his advisers decided a drastic threat was needed to keep the captains alert and up to the job. On the second day, 1st August, all sergeant majors (*sargentos mayores*, who acted as officials of discipline) were summoned to the flagship and then sent out in boats with written orders to each ship which specified its station. They were also ordered to hang any captain whose ship left its proper position, and Provost Marshals and hangmen went with them ready to carry out instant executions.

This gruesome order must have had a reason, right or wrong. Admirals seldom threaten to hang their captains, and it does not seem to fit the duke's pacific nature. One has to remember two things: first that a Spanish sea-captain was the servant of the army he carried, and second that the armada was not entirely Spanish, as the English fleet was entirely English. Many of its ships and their captains and crews were German, Italian and Portuguese, and many had been dragged into service against their will. Technically, most were subjects of King Philip, but the allegiance of some was pretty thin; they were not all equally eager to give their lives for him or the cause he thought was God's. When the fleet was scattered off Corunna, everyone, even the king, had suspected some might have deserted; and the disappearance of the *Santa Ana* was suspicious too. Perhaps the ships that 'basely took to flight' the day before had been a more serious threat of mass desertion than Calderon made it seem. Anyhow, the duke appeared to think some of his ships would desert if they had half a chance – another nagging fear to weigh on his mind. But a fleet that had to be kept together by a threat like this could not have been a happy one; unlike the English, skirmishing behind it, puzzled but cheerful, with hardly any orders at all.

Desertions apart, there had been two serious accidents the evening before which imperilled the all-important formation. First, the flagship of Don Pedro de Valdes, *Nuestra Senora del Rosario*, 1150 Spanish tons, fell foul of two other ships, one after the other, and they carried away her bowsprit and forestay. Of course Don Pedro blamed the others, but it looks as if he or his captain were not being careful enough. Soon after that, a great explosion shook the fleet. The *San Salvador*, vice-flagship of the Guipuzcoan squadron, had blown up and was seen to be on fire. The duke's other ships put about to help her, and in the confusion Don Pedro's foremast went by the board and fell against his main yard-arm. Suddenly the duke had three lame ducks on his hands: Don Pedro dismasted, Recalde with his damaged rigging, and worst of all, the *San Salvador* with her stern blown out, the two upper decks of her poop in ruins, and a great many dead and wounded. Recalde managed to get himself into the centre of the fleet, where he was safe to make his own repairs. The *San Salvador* was taken in tow, and men from frigates helped to put out the fire (no small achievement in a wooden ship) and tried all night to take off wounded men. But Don Pedro had taken in all his sail and drifted astern of the fleet, firing guns to draw the duke's attention. The wind and sea were rising.

What happened that night is full of mysteries: everyone told different stories. The duke said he put about to try to get a hawser across to Don Pedro to tow him, but weather made it impossible. Don Pedro's cousin, Don Diego Flores de Valdes, whom he hated, was in the flagship as nautical adviser to the duke, and he told the duke he should not wait and stand by Don Pedro: if he did, in the falling dusk, some of the ships would see what he was doing and some would not, and by daybreak the fleet would be fatally scattered. On that advice, the duke told off two galleons, four pinnaces and a galleass to stand by and get a hawser on board, and if that failed to take off the crew; and then he made sail and took his position again in the vanguard of the fleet. But in that windy night, neither operation succeeded.

The next witnesses were John Fisher, John Nash and Richard Tomson, captain, master and lieutenant of one of the merchant-men in the English fleet, the *Margaret and John*, of 200 tons and a crew of ninety, who came up with Don Pedro's ship just after dark. Afterwards, these men made a highly literate deposition to the queen's council. They said they saw a galleon, a galleass and a pinnace standing by Don Pedro, but when they approached all three sheered off and left him. There was no light and no sign of life in the ship. They tried to board her, but she was too big and the sea was too rough. To find out if anyone was aboard they fired a volley of muskets. 'Presently they gave us two great shot, whereupon we let fly our broadside through her, doing them some hurt, as themselves have and can testify. After this we cast about our ship, and kept ourselves close by the Spaniard until midnight, sometimes hearing a voice in Spanish calling us; but the wind being very great, and we in the weather [i.e. to windward] the voice was carried away, that we could not well understand it, but were persuaded by our mariners, to be the voice of one swimming in the sea; whereupon we put off our ship boat with eight oars, to seek, call, and take them up; but found nobody.'

At midnight they saw the *Ark*, a couple of miles away in the moonlight, making sail to follow the main fleet of the enemy; and 'fearing his Lordship's displeasure if we should stay behind the fleet, we made all the sail we could, and followed my Lord to overtake him'.

It was an eerie scene, the great dark galleon seeming to be deserted, the small determined ship that tried to board, the foreign voice in the wind, the not ungallant venture in the boat. It was made the more eerie by the discovery at dawn that the whole of the crew of four hundred and twenty men had been lurking on board all the time without making any attempt to save themselves – neither to fight off their small assailant, nor to repair their damage, nor even to make sail on their three remaining masts.

This discovery was made by Drake in the *Revenge*, who had no business whatever to be there, astern by then of most of the English fleet. The evening before Howard had appointed him to lead the fleet through the night, and at dusk he began to do so, the rest of them following his stern lantern. But during the night he put out his light and sheered off to starboard, leaving the fleet to grope in the dark without a leader. His story was that he sighted suspicious ships to seaward and thought they might be Spaniards doubling back to gain the wind. When he came up with them, he found they were German merchantmen, and at dawn, by the purest chance, he happened to find himself close to Don Pedro. Nobody else had seen the suspicious ships, and probably nobody fully believed the story: they believed he had left his station simply to be the first to claim the prize. The duke was prepared to hang a captain for less, but Howard let him get away with it – though it is noticeable that his *Relation of Proceedings* never mentions Drake as taking any further part in the fighting in the Channel. Most English sailors probably wished they had done it themselves. One such was Martin Frobisher. Ten days afterwards, in a towering rage, he called Drake a cozening cheat: 'Like a coward he kept by her all night, because he would have the spoil. He thinketh to cozen us of our shares of fifteen thousand ducats; but we will have our shares, or I will make him spend the best blood in his belly.'

At dawn, anyhow, Drake was on the spot and called Don Pedro to fight or surrender. He surrendered, with flowery speeches. Drake took him on board the *Revenge* with forty of his officers and gentlemen, and lodged him in his own cabin. Don Pedro witnessed the whole of the subsequent battles from either the *Revenge* or the *Ark*. The captured ship was taken into Torbay and then to Dartmouth where legend says her timbers were used to build the present gallery in the church.

The helpless behaviour of Don Pedro and his crew remains a mystery: one cannot believe they could not have followed the fleet down wind if they had tried. And they certainly did not try: they took in all sail to make repairs, but they made no repairs and never set sail again. A partial explanation may be that Don Pedro was furious with the duke – so furious that he may have felt like washing his hands of the whole enterprise and ordering his crew to have no more to do with it. A month later, he had not calmed down. He wrote to the king from his comfortable confinement in England, where he was waiting to be ransomed. The duke, he said, had basely refused to help him. 'Although he was near enough to me, and saw in what case I was, and might easily have relieved me, yet would he not do it; but even as if we had not been Your Majesty's subjects nor employed in your service, discharged a piece to call the fleet together, and followed his course, leaving me comfortless in the sight of the whole fleet, the enemy being but a quarter of a league from me; who arrived upon the closing up of the day; and although some ships set upon me, I resisted them, and defended myself all night, hoping still that the duke would send me some relief, and not use so great inhumanity and unthankfulness towards me; for greater I think was never heard of among men.'

This was a contemporary translation from the Spanish. It was certainly far from the truth. For one thing he had not defended himself all night, he only fired two shots. It has been suggested that he made this verbal attack on the duke in the hope it would rebound on Don Diego Flores, his old enemy. If he was really being so deviously cunning, he succeeded; for the king never censured the duke for this or anything else, but when Diego Flores came home he was put in prison.

Because of Drake's escapade, there was no fight on the next day, Monday, 1st August. The armada was left to make its stately progress across Lyme Bay. Howard in the *Ark* was close astern of it, with only two other ships. All the rest had been confused by the disappearance of Drake's light and had not known whom to follow. From the *Ark*, as dawn broke, only the masts of the nearest could be seen on the western horizon, and most were out of sight. It took them all day to catch up.

Not a soul in the armada recorded what he thought of the heretic land of England when he saw it. Yet very few had ever seen it before, and one would imagine they stared inquisitively as they passed so slowly along it (on average, two miles an hour) through those summer days. Even when there was fighting the vast majority of them took no part in it; except the sailors on watch, they had very little to do and plenty of time to stare. They did not know what was happening or what was expected to happen, and had no idea of the devastating worry that was starting to oppress their leaders. Sometimes they were only two or three miles offshore. They could easily see the gentle hills, the rocky heathery headlands, the unmistakably cosy villages of whitewashed cottages, the spires that marked the scenes, so they had been told, of such devilish rites. Perhaps most of them thought of it only as a source of plunder, but surely some saw the beauty of it and the aspect of homely peace, and wondered what there could be behind it that made it a mortal enemy.

The only disturbing event that day was at eleven o'clock in the morning, when a message came from the *San Salvador* that she was sinking. The duke gave the order to take off her crew and scuttle her.

Sixty-four seamen and 319 soldiers had been aboard the ship and over 200, Calderon said, were killed or jumped overboard and drowned. Among those rescued was the chief paymaster of the armada, with his papers and a large sum of money.

The duke's order to empty and sink her could not be done. The captain was badly wounded, the remainder of the crew was in a hurry to abandon ship, and she still had burnt and wounded men on board who could not be moved. So they let her drift. Towards evening, Howard and some of his ships came up with her. He sent his kinsman Lord Thomas Howard and John Hawkyns, two of the senior officers in the fleet, in a small skiff together to board her; 'where they found a very pitiful sight,' the *Relation* said, 'the deck of the ship fallen down, the steerage broken, the stern blown out, and about fifty poor creatures burnt with powder in most miserable sort. The stink in the ship was so unsavoury, and the sight within board so ugly, that the Lord Thomas Howard and Sir John Hawkyns shortly departed.' It is interesting that pity is what they felt. Howard sent Thomas Flemyng in the *Golden Hinde* to tow the tragic remnant to whatever port he could, and next day he brought her in to Weymouth.

There were stories afterwards that the ship had been blown up on purpose. Only one of them has Spanish authority: it was told by Calderon, who ought to have known because he took the vice admiral and about thirty men into his ship, all badly burnt. He said one of the army captains had beaten a German gunner, who then went below saying that one of the guns had got wet and would have to be fired. He fired it, and then threw the slow match into a barrel of powder. Other versions made the gunner a Dutchman or an Englishman, and one, which Ubaldino repeated, said the captain had made advances to the gunner's wife, who happened to be on board.

Later historians were inclined to deride the stories of the vindictive foreign gunner, especially Ubaldino's version of the gunner's wife: it seemed incredible that after the rigorous searches for women the duke had ordered in Lisbon, and after all those weeks at sea, a gunner should still have his wife concealed on board. But the end of the story had a very curious twist in it, which neither Ubaldino nor the sceptical historians had noticed. When the Mayor of Weymouth came to make an inventory of the ship, he reported fifty-three barrels of wine but no food except three casks of beef, bad, and one of beans. He also asked what he should do with the survivors. Twelve had died since the ship came into port, leaving only ten Spaniards, four Germans, two Frenchmen – and a German woman. So perhaps it was all true; and perhaps she had preferred the romantic captain, and driven her gunner husband to a classic and spectacular action of despair.

All the following night the fleets lay becalmed in sight of each other, drifting back and forth with the tide in Lyme Bay. A calm, when nobody else could move, was weather for the galleasses, and the English apprehensively saw the four of them emerge together from the fleet. But they did nothing and soon went back again. One explanation afterwards was that their commander, Don Hugo de Moncada, was in a huff with the duke. That morning, it was said, he had seen the *Ark* almost alone astern and had offered to go and attack her; but the duke had said no, because attacking the rival admiral was his own prerogative. Don Hugo, who was a very proud knight of Catalonia, was said to have felt so insulted by this rebuff that he refused to fight that night, although Recalde, de Leyva and Oquendo all joined in begging him to go. In all the welter of rumour, one cannot tell whether to believe this sort of thing or not. But evidently it was not incredible at the time. Silly conventions have often influenced battles, and so has excessive pride; and in fact, the galleasses played a disappointing part in all the fighting.

Next morning, Tuesday, 2nd August, the wind came out of the north east and suddenly gave the Spaniards the weather gauge. Off Portland Bill the biggest battle so far began – and in the telling the most utterly confused: 'A wonderful sharp conflict,' the *Relation* said. 'There was never seen a more terrible value of great shot, nor more hot fight than this was; for although the musketeers and harquebusiers of crock were then infinite, yet they could not be discerned nor heard for that the great ordnance came so thick that a man would have judged it to have been a hot skirmish of small shot, being all the fight long within half musket shot of the enemy.'

And Sir George Carey, governor of the Isle of Wight, listening from far away in Carisbrooke Castle to the battle the following day, wrote the same thing more compactly: 'The shot continued so thick together that it might rather have been judged a skirmish with small shot on land than a fight with great shot at sea. In which conflict, thanks be to God, there hath not been two of our men hurt.'

About the hurts, he was merely being hopeful; perhaps that rumour was going round ashore. And the *Relation* was exaggerating when it mentioned half musket shot: most of the shooting was still at long range. However, it was true that an immense amount of powder and shot was blazed away that day and very little hurt was done to anyone.

It was the noise that impressed those two witnesses, and probably most of the rest; apart from that, nobody wrote much about their own experience. But perhaps imagination can be allowed to fill the gap; perhaps one can say it was much more exciting than dangerous.

Down in the gundecks the noise was certainly hellish: in naval gunnery battles it always was. In the major English ships, gun drill was fairly well organized, and men could load their guns and fire them quickly – the Spaniards said three times as fast as they could do it themselves: sponge out the gun to stop it getting too hot, load with powder and ball and ram it down, lay the trail of powder to the touchhole, run the gun forward to its firing position, sometimes turn it with crowbars to aim at a visible enemy and drive the wedges in or out to change the elevation, and then stand clear of the recoil. When it was done, the gunner was itching to put his slow match to it, and often did not wait for an order but let fly as soon as he saw a target, although it was sometimes hopelessly out of range.

It was the upper decks which had most of the excitement, where men could see the flashes from the enemy gunports and then the splashes far and wide of his random shots. Once in a while there might be a thud when a ball hit the hull, or the twang of a cut stay, or a crash when a halyard was cut and a yard fell down – or worse when a shot came through the upper works and sent splinters of wood humming across the decks, splinters that wounded more men than the shots themselves; and sometimes, but rarely enough, a cry of agony.

The greatest excitement, especially for the English, was not when the shot was falling; it was in the exercise of seamanship. It was just the same sort of excitement modern yachtsmen get in maneuvering for position at the start of a race. Success and safety depended on the captain's eye for the situation and the skill of the crew. The captain would pick out an enemy who looked as if he might be isolated, and set a course if he could to cut him off. As he came into range there were quick decisions: could he luff up a little more without losing too much speed, and cross the enemy's bows where his own broadside could be brought to bear and the enemy's could not? Or should he pay off, tempt the enemy to fire his broadside at long range, then close and cross his stern before he had time to reload? And what was the enemy going to do, and what were all the rest of them doing? The English had wanted a sailor's weapon and that is what they had. To use it tested a sailor's judgement harder than ever before.

When the fight began off Portland, there was no sort of organization in the English fleet, nothing to resemble the Spaniards' fleet formation. Most junior captains attached themselves to one of the leaders they knew, Howard, Hawkyns, Drake, Frobisher, Fenner, and more or less followed him; but that was their personal choice and no orders were given. However, through the fog of confusion of the conflicting accounts, there are signs that day that they were learning. The first thing they had to learn was to take the risk of closing the enemy. Things were not going to work the way they seem to have hoped. It was no good using demi-culverins at random range, still less the smaller sakers and minions. They still did it, especially perhaps the merchant ships, but a minute proportion of the shots were hits, and they began to see that a ball at long range did not have the momentum to make a hole in the solid Spanish hulls. It could cut the rigging, or penetrate the castles, which were lightly built; but if it hit the hull it only went part way through and stuck there. Later experience showed it was very difficult to sink a wooden ship with solid shot; a well-built hull could be battered all day and still be afloat at the end of it. To sink or disable a solid phalanx of a hundred and thirty ships would take months, and need more powder and shot than had ever existed in England.

But that day it does seem they started to venture farther in and found they could do it in safety – partly because the Spaniards' aim was even worse than their own, and partly because they were learning to choose positions where the Spaniards' guns could not be brought to bear. There also is a glimpse of tactical organization: they seem to have started to use the line ahead. 'His Lordship,' the *Relation* says, 'called unto certain of Her Majesty's ships then near at hand and charged them straitly to follow him, and to set freshly upon the Spaniards, and to go within musket-shot of the enemy before they should discharge any one piece of ordnance . . . ; which was very well performed by the *Ark*, the *Elizabeth Jonas*, the *Galleon of Leicester*, the *Golden Lion*, the *Victory*, the *Mary Rose*, the *Dreadnought* and the *Swallow* – for so they went in order into the fight.'

It is slender evidence, but for once the duke's diary told a story which could be recognized as the same: 'When our flagship saw the enemy's flagship leading towards her, she lowered her topsails; and the enemy's flagship passed, followed by the whole of his fleet, each ship firing at our flagship as it passed.' It does look as if Howard had invented the line of battle which became the whole basis of naval tactics and remained so until the Battle of Jutland.

But on that first attempt it was not as successful as it deserved to be. Calderon also described what seems to be the same engagement. The duke's flagship, he said, engaged the enemy's fleet for an hour and a half alone. She 'fired over eighty shots from one side only, and did great damage to the enemy. The latter shot at the duke at least five hundred balls, some of which struck his hull and others his rigging, carrying away his flagstaff and one of the stays of his mainmast.' It is illogical but human to think one's shots are hitting and hurting, while the enemy's are wasted. But the English admitted no damage at all; and a flagstaff and stay were not much reward for five hundred shots. Certainly, for all the 'terrible value of shot', neither side in the whole of the day had any damage the crews could not quickly repair.

All round, it was disappointing and frustrating. The fighting died away in the afternoon, when the wind went back to south west and the Spaniards lost the weather gauge. The armada re-formed and went on its way, to all appearances as strong and compact as ever. There seemed to be no way the English could hinder it, they could only hang on until they found where it was going and what it intended to do.

But for the Spaniards the disappointment had been worse,

because they knew what they were meant to do, and knew now, the more percipient of them, that they were going to fail to do it. The day had proved they could not catch and board a single English ship even with the wind behind them. How then could they ever clear the seas for Parma's crossing? The vast number of soldiers they carried, the core of their strength, were never going to have a chance to do their job. All that day the soldiers had stood to their arms, their muskets, pikes and swords, waiting for the moment they had been told to expect when their ship would crash alongside an enemy and they would swarm across and slaughter its crew hand to hand. But every time it looked like happening, the enemy put about and was off with a speed and dexterity their sailors could not match. The soldiers were left with nothing to do except stand there and be shot at, and once in a while let off a volley of musketry they knew was a waste of powder. They were beginning to grumble.

The next day, Wednesday, 3rd August, was another without any fighting, except a skirmish at dawn. But the reason was different. All the English fleet was there, hovering on the edge of gunshot in the lightest of breezes; but most of the ships were short of ammunition. Howard sent barks and pinnaces urgently in to the ports to ask for more.

During that night, the armada crept very slowly past St Alban's Head. At dawn on the 4th, the duke saw the chalk cliffs of the Isle of Wight ahead of him, and knew the time of decision had come. There had not been a word from Parma.

10

The Isle of Wight

It is said the duke had scarcely slept at all since England was sighted, and had eaten nothing but hard tack and cheese that were brought to him on the poop. No doubt a good many other people had gone without a good night's sleep or a square meal. But certainly nobody else had such insoluble problems on his mind.

Looking at the past three days, he could have told himself he had done his best and had nothing to be ashamed of. There are some hints in his diary that he felt remorse at leaving Don Pedro behind, and guessed he had made an implacable enemy of him; but he had done it on the advice of Don Diego Flores, which he was bound to treat with respect. And perhaps he had missed a good chance, and made another enemy, when he told Don Hugo not to attack the enemy flagship with his galleasses; history has said he did, but whatever the reason had been there is no evidence he had regretted it. Without any question, he had set a good example. All accounts, both Spanish and English, agree his ship was in the thick of every fight, and was always among the first to put about and give support to anyone who had lagged behind and got into trouble.

He could tell himself too that, so far, things had not gone badly at all. He had carried out to the letter the orders the king had given him. Counting the four galleys, he had lost seven ships, but none to enemy action. He had also expended half a dozen pinnaces in sending letters to Parma and the king; but that was what they were for. As for men, a few had lost their lives to gunshot, but only a tiny proportion of the thousands he commanded. The armada was in good order, and half-way up the Channel.

Yet looking ahead, the future was utterly black. Perhaps in the calm of Wednesday night, when every ship was still and every sail was hanging idle, he gave orders he should be called if any breeze came up, and lay down in his cabin and hoped to sleep – and instead of sleeping lay awake in a nightmarish premonition of disaster. The facts that he knew that night could only have banished sleep.

First, the design of the armada had proved to be fundamentally wrong: it could not damage the English because, as he wrote in his diary, 'our ships are too heavy, compared with the lightness of the enemy's'. On the contrary, the enemy fleet was growing all the time as ships came out from every port to join it – and the intelligence reports had told him there was another fleet down wind, estimated at eighty sail, so far untouched, awaiting him in the Straits of Dover. It was already certain his central mission was going to fail. Whatever he did, however hard he tried, he could not clear the seas for Parma's crossing. He had not been given the weapon to do it with.

Second, from Parma, who should have provided a gleam of friendship in that hostile world, nothing had come but a bewildering silence. The duke did not know if Parma was ready, or where he was. He had begun to suspect he was not at Dunkirk where he ought to have been, because none of the messages he had sent there had come back. Had all of them been captured? Were the English patrolling the Straits so strongly that no pinnace could get through? Did Parma even know he was coming?

Third, there was no harbour ahead beyond the Isle of Wight, so far as he knew, except the Thames, and he could not hope to fight his way into the Thames unless Parma were there with his army. Nor could his clumsy fleet even enter the river mouth, changing course from east to west, unless God sent a miraculous change of wind at the crucial moment.

Yet fourth, he had to fight and win, if only to capture stores to replenish the miserable eighty days' supply he had brought from Corunna. And the longer the fighting went on, the less his hope of winning. The English could be stocked with powder and shot from the shore, but already the armada's enormous supply of shot was running low. Ships were beginning to ask him for more, and he had nowhere he could look for more – unless possibly Parma could give him some. The only resolve he made in that restless night was to write yet again to Parma in the morning and ask for shiploads of shot.

The final weight on his mind was the decision he had to make in the coming dawn: whether or not to attack the Isle of Wight and seek a defensible anchorage in the Solent, where he could wait until he knew what Parma was doing.

Of course Lord Howard and Drake had worries too, in that day and night of calm, but nothing like the duke's despairing premonition. They were disappointed that the English policy of gunnery had done so little damage; but they still had their confidence, they were still thinking positively and hatching hopeful plans. At least, the armada so far had done no harm to England. If they could keep it moving, it could never do any harm, and if it stopped and came to anchor they had other ideas to attack it.

During the day when the fleets were lying becalmed, Howard called a council in the *Ark*. As usual, they made no minutes of it, so there is no way of knowing who made which proposals; but after all, they knew each other well and the problems were obvious to them all. There was probably not much need for discussion.

The principal long-term worry was ammunition. Howard had already done what he could to get more from the shore, and knew the shore people would do their best. But even in the coastal forts the stocks were small, and whatever was sent it would never be enough for the unprecedented battle he was fighting. They would have to economize, and there is some evidence they resolved that day to do it by coming to closer quarters.

But it was one thing to resolve, another to enforce it in the fleet. The fleet had grown too big to organize. It seems never to have occurred to the English before to subdivide a fleet; they had never before put to sea with anything like that number of ships. Perhaps they observed that the Spaniards were in divisions. They needed to do the same, if only to stop the minor ships wasting powder and shot at impossible ranges. 'This day,' the *Relation* said, 'the Lord Admiral divided his fleet into four squadrons, whereof he appointed the first to attend himself, the second his Lordship committed to the charge of Sir Francis Drake; the third to Sir John Hawkyns, and the fourth to Sir Martin Frobisher.' It was the second new naval concept, born in those days of battle, that was to last for centuries: first the formation in line ahead, and now the division into squadrons.

The more immediate worry was the Isle of Wight. When Lord

Henry Seymour, waiting off Dover, received Drake's letter from Plymouth, he wrote, '[As] to our opinions here, we conjecture still their purpose may be to land in the Isle of Wight, to recover [i.e. capture] the same, which God forbid.' Probably this was a general opinion, and Seymour happened to be the only one who wrote it in a letter at that moment which has survived (he was always expressing ideas about Spanish strategy). At all events, it was an obvious risk, and the moment had come. The armada was lying close to the south west of the entrance to the Solent. If the south westerly wind got up again and coincided with the flood tide, the armada could be in through the Needles channel in an hour or two, and nobody could stop it.

So the council thought up a novel plan to disrupt the armada that very night. 'This afternoon his Lordship gave order that, in the night, six merchant ships out of every squadron should set upon the Spanish fleet in sundry places, at one instant, in the night time, to keep the enemy waking.' It was a brilliant idea, and proved the English still had initiative. Only a few of the merchant ships had done any good so far, except to 'make a brag', to give a show of strength. Nobody before had thought of provoking a sea battle in the dark, and nobody thought of it again for generations afterwards. It might have worked and caused chaos in the armada's ranks, leaving them disorganized for the warships at dawn. But they had no chance to try: 'All that night fell out to be so calm that nothing could be done.' By morning, the armada had drifted to the east, and the risk of the Needles channel had passed. The risk remained that they would try the eastern entrance by Spithead.

All the way from the Lizard, the armada had been creeping along so slowly that news of what was happening had plenty of time to spread all over the south of England. A horseman on land, or even a man on foot, could travel much faster, and so could a pinnace at sea. The pinnace Drake sent from the Eddystone Rock 'late in the evening' of 31st July reached Seymour, lying at anchor off Dover, on 2nd August – an average speed of at least five knots and probably more. Yet the armada, in the same wind, hampered by its slowest merchantmen, took twice as long to cover half the distance.

Ashore, Howard's urgent calls for ammunition were answered with surprising speed. Everybody's first idea was the windfalls in the captured Spanish ships. The first of Howard's barks or pinnaces came into Weymouth on 3rd August. The Mayor of Weymouth wrote to the Mayor of Lyme Regis, who received the letter the same day. Don Pedro's ship was then in sight of the town and moving westward, so the Mayor sent on the letter to the Deputy Lieutenants of Devon, who were in Torbay. It reached them, after something like seventy-five miles, still on the same day, and at nine o'clock in the evening they despatched a man to intercept the ship at Dartmouth. Two days later they reported they had taken out of her 1600 shot and 88 barrels of powder and sent them by sea to Lord Howard. They had also helped themselves to two barrels of wine, but that was only reported later by somebody else.

The *San Salvador*, which had exploded, was brought into Weymouth Bay on the same day, the 3rd. Four days later, the queen's council, meeting at Richmond, west of London, had heard of it, discussed it, and written to the mayor an order to take her powder out and send it in some suitable bark to Dover. But Captain Flemyng of the *Golden Hinde*, who had towed the Spaniard in, had already used his common sense, off-loaded 140 barrels of powder, 2000 cannon, demi-cannon and culverin shot and a ton of match, and sailed again to catch up with the fleet.

The Earl of Sussex, who was Warden and Captain of Portsmouth, sent out all the powder and shot in the town as soon as the armada had safely disappeared beyond it, and wrote post haste to London for more to be sent to him or to other ports in Sussex to the eastward; and one may imagine all these horsemen, changing their sweating horses in post houses west and east, telling the eager crowds what was happening at sea, and making perhaps a good story even better. Both powder and shot were sent to the coast from the Tower of London, and the queen ordered the best musketeers in Kent to be sent to the seaside in case Lord Howard needed them. But men were not what he needed, nor were ships. Early in the proceedings, he had written to the Earl of Sussex to send out all the ships that were ready for sea in Portsmouth, and 'as many tall men as you can get in so short a time'. Since then, volunteers who came out to see the fun had become an embarrassment, and so had the small ships that brought them, armed only with the half-dozen little guns they carried in case of pirates. When Sir George Carey, Governor of the Isle of Wight, sent out a pinnace with a hundred men, Lord Howard sent them back with hearty thanks and a message that he had as many men as he wanted or could use.

All this ready help for their enemy was the price the Spaniards paid for their decision to sail along the English side of the Channel.

There is nothing in the duke's diary or anywhere else to tell whether he would have entered the Needles channel if the wind had come fair that day. No doubt he re-read the king's orders, even if he knew them already by heart. The island, the king had said, was apparently not so strong as to be able to resist, but could be defended if he won it. It would provide a safe harbour, and if he took it he should fortify it strongly. The order was strict that he was not to attack it on the way up-Channel. 'If you resort to this plan, it will in consequence of some doubt, or the failure of the main design which may lead you to return from Margate. On no account will you enter the Wight on your way up, nor before you have made every possible effort to carry out the main idea.'

The duke had already made up his mind to disobey that part of the order. Perhaps he relied on the words 'some doubt'. There was certainly some doubt when he had heard nothing from Parma. But the king had added, with his usual excessive attention to detail, 'If you should have to adopt this course, you will take notice that you should enter by the east side, which is wider than the west.' Quite possibly the duke, disobeying one part of the order, would have taken extra care to obey the rest and neglected the western channel.

But in writing this, with his air of omniscience, the king was childishly wrong. He had sailed into the Solent thirty-four years before on his way to marry Mary Tudor, and he always liked to show off his knowledge of England. Perhaps he remembered seeing the entrances, or perhaps he had looked at a map. From shore to shore, the eastern entrance is indeed much wider, but its navigable channel, between the hidden sandbanks, is not; and in those days, without the buoys and beacons that mark it now, it was far more difficult to find. Moreover, the king in his orders never took any account of the wind, but assumed his armada could move in any direction it pleased – or relied on his prayers that God would send whatever wind it needed. In fact, with the south westerly wind which is much the commonest in a normal August in the English Channel, the westerly entrance, past the Needles, would have been the obvious one to choose. But the choice did not arise, because that Wednesday there was no wind at all. The armada could not have approached the entrance against the ebb, and if it had entered on the flood it would have lost its steerage way and gone out of control.

Instead, it drifted back and forth offshore with the tides. After the frequent westerly gales, the Channel current which flows to the eastward would have been stronger than usual, and at each high tide the fleet would have been a little farther east. In fact, with the aid perhaps of a catspaw now and then, it moved about sixteen miles in twenty-four hours. When dawn broke on 4th August, the duke found himself off the southern tip of the Isle of Wight, still without a breath of wind on a glassy sea, and the English on three sides of him.

The accounts of what happened that day are just as confused as usual, but they have an air of special drama and suspense. It was a day of crisis, the only day when the armada with a little luck, for all its faults, might have won a partial victory.

At dawn, it was not a dozen miles from the entrance to Spithead, and thence to Portsmouth, Southampton and the ample harbour of the Solent. Whether it could enter hung on the wind and tide. The wind was unpredictable, it might come up with the day from any quarter. The tide was not. The west-going tide which could have helped the armada in was due to begin that morning soon after seven o'clock and last until half past twelve. After that, it would be running out against it till almost dusk. The Spanish pilots would have known the time of the tides, roughly at least, from Wagenhaer, and everybody except the soldiers would have known it from observation: nobody can sail up the Channel without noticing when the tides change. They would not have known the speed of the tidal stream in the entrance, but any seaman's common sense would have told him it was strong, and they certainly knew there were only three days to go before spring tides.* In fact, the stream at springs is well over two knots. Nobody would have dreamt of trying to take a sailing fleet into Spithead against that, except perhaps with an easterly gale behind him. In other words, if the armada was going to enter the Solent, it had to be in and at anchor soon after midday. If the wind came southerly, there was a chance.

For both sides, nothing that early morning could have been more awkward than a calm. The armada was getting nowhere, and the English were deprived of their only advantage, their speed of manoeuvre. Lord Howard saw drastic action was needed and he took it. He called up rowing boats to tow the principal ships into battle. Again, two Spanish ships had lagged astern in the night, this time the *San Luis*, one of the galleons of the Portuguese squadron, and one of the urcas called (like several other ships) the *Santa Ana*. Hawkyns was closest to him, and the first in the fray. The boats towed him in until the oarsmen were harassed by musket shot. Thereupon, three of the Spanish galleasses emerged from the fleet, one of them towing a galleon for extra fire-power. Howard in the *Ark* and Lord Thomas Howard in the *Golden Lion* came up, both pulled by boats. 'There was many good shots,' the *Relation* says, 'made by the *Ark* and *Lion* at the galleasses in the sight of both armies, which looked on and could not approach, it being calm, for the *Ark* and the *Lion* did tow to the galleasses with their long boats.' The galleasses were 'much damaged, that one of them was fain to be carried away upon the careen; and another, by a shot from the *Ark*, lost her lantern, which came swimming by, and the third his nose'. Once more, it is astonishing how little damage was done, though the ships this time were certainly within musket range – Howard, in his first brief report, puts it at 'two or three score' paces. One stern lantern and one nose, a figurehead or beakhead, were really nothing to crow about; and as for the one that was 'upon the careen', which meant listing, she showed no later sign of serious hurt. Perhaps she had had to move some of her oarsmen across so that she could fire her broadside.

Meanwhile Frobisher was lying north of the armada, between

*Spring tides, as opposed to neaps, are the specially strong tides which occur twice in each lunar month, when the pull of the sun and moon are in conjunction.

it and the shore: he had got himself into a similar awkward position at Portland. He also called for boats to get himself clear, and at one time he was being towed by eleven of them.

At length, a breeze began. The *Relation* calls it a 'little gale', but gale did not have the same connotation then that it does now, and it was certainly not very strong. Nobody says what time it started. The only clue is in the *Relation*, which says the *Ark*, the *Lion* and the galleasses fought a long time. Since they started at dawn, it can scarcely have been much after seven – when the tide turned. Nor does anyone specify its direction; but it quite clearly left Frobisher in the lee of the armada, so it must have been somewhere very close to south. Anywhere else on the voyage along the coast, an on-shore wind might have been fatal. But at that very moment it was just what the armada needed to carry it round the east of the island and into Spithead.

With the wind, the accounts of the fight dissolve into typical mystery. For a time, the Spaniards' hopes were high, and they thought they were going to grapple and board an enemy flagship, which seems to have been Frobisher's. 'We were sure,' the duke's diary said, 'that at last we would be able to close with them, which was our only way of gaining the victory.' But he added, 'At this moment the wind freshened, and we saw she was getting away from us and had no further need of the boats that were towing her.' Calderon wrote of the same gloomy disappointment: 'Our flagship and other ships sailed towards her; but she got out so quickly that the galleon *San Juan* and another fast-sailing ship – the two fastest in the armada – although they gave chase, seemed in comparison with her to be standing still.'

The duke also wrote, 'While the skirmish was going on in the rear, the enemy's flagship, with other large vessels, fell upon our royal flagship which was leading the vanguard.' This was another English flagship, not Frobisher: the Spaniards were inclined to call any conspicuous ship a flagship. Perhaps it was the *Ark*, but it is far from clear how she managed to attack the Spanish vanguard. At any rate, the duke added a very significant sentence: 'They came closer than they had on previous days, firing their heaviest guns from the lowest deck, cut the trice of our mainmast and killed some of our soldiers.' The inference is that the English, up till then, had not fired their lowest tiers of guns, which were the biggest; or at least, the duke had not seen them do it. It seems extraordinary, but it is not impossible. Early warships had often been built with their lowest gunports so close to the waterline that when they were heavily laden they could only open them in the calmest seas and the lightest winds. Ten miles from where they lay that day was the wreck of the *Mary Rose*, which had sailed from Portsmouth in 1545 with her lower gunports open and had flooded and sunk and drowned most of her crew as soon as the wind filled her sails. There was a second *Mary Rose* in the present fleet, and nobody had forgotten the first. But if this was the first day calm enough to open the lowest ports, it follows that all the English long-range bombardment so far had used only the smaller guns, nothing bigger than a demi-culverin with a nine-pound shot; which goes a long way to explaining why it was so ineffective.

This fight, while the wind and tide were fair for the Solent, called for the greatest effort the English could make, but no English account of it mentions what Drake was doing. Probably he and his squadron were out on the southern wing, and possibly Howard could not see them: in the still air and the 'little gale' that followed it, the powder smoke may have hidden them. Only one Spanish account mentions fighting on the seaward edges of the fleets. It was written by an anonymous captain of a galleon of Seville, and tells of an attack which made the outermost galleon give way and retreat to the body of the fleet. 'Seeing that, the enemy took heart and turned with his whole fleet or the greater part of it, and charged upon our wing, so that we who were there were driven into a corner.'

The greatest of the nineteenth-century tactical analysts, Sir Julian Corbett, built on this a theory that Drake, who was his hero, was trying to force the armada on to the rocks called the Owers, which are on the north side of the approaches to Spithead. This is a far-fetched hypothesis. First, there is no evidence that any attack could divert the bulk of the armada from its chosen course. Secondly, it meant driving them right across the entrance to Spithead on the ingoing tide, while everyone else was trying to drive them out. And thirdly, the armada pilots knew the Owers were there: they are marked on Wagenhaer's chart – nearer the

middle of the channel than they really are, but a hazard clearly to
be avoided.

It is much more likely that Drake attacked the southern wing
merely because that was where he happened to be. If he was really
trying to drive the armada north instead of east, it invites a more
interesting speculation: that he was not averse to seeing them go
into harbour in the Solent. Drake was well-known for heretical
but far-sighted naval opinions, and it is possible that he saw the
Solent as a trap for the armada, not a refuge. This is equally far-
fetched; but looking back with the knowledge of later history, one
may wonder what would have happened if the armada had gone
in, as the duke had proposed and the king had suggested, and
anchored somewhere perhaps in Cowes Roads. No doubt they
could have landed their army, advanced on Carisbrooke Castle in
the middle of the island, which was the headquarters of its defence,
and captured it all. But the armada itself would never have
escaped. It would have been harassed day and night by the English
fleet, based securely in Southampton, Portsmouth and the creeks
and rivers of the mainland; the exits would have been blocked and
commanded by cannon from the shore; and lying at anchor, the
armada would have been open to attack by fireships floated down
on it with every tide, which were the surest way to destroy a
wooden fleet. Bit by bit it would have been burned or sunk or cut
adrift and wrecked, until the army was stranded and starving on
the island. It is hardly likely that anyone, even Drake, saw things
in this light then; but now, it seems the duke was lucky that he
failed to enter there.

Fail he did: not because the English stopped him, but because
the southerly wind shifted to south west. That made a fatal
difference. One cannot tell exactly when he gave up the idea, but
some time that morning he must have had an earnest discussion
with the pilots. They would certainly have told him it could not be
done in a south west wind. The course as far as the mouth of
Portsmouth harbour is north west. They might possibly have
managed that with the wind abeam on the last of the ingoing tide,
but only with the risk that the urcas would be driven on to the
northern sands and stranded far from shore, where they would
have been sitting ducks. Further in, the course is almost west, and
not even the galleons could have made it.

Before midday, the duke had abandoned that tenuous ray of hope. He 'fired a signal gun and proceeded on the voyage, followed by the rest of the armada in good order'. His diary does not say with what foreboding he committed himself to the unknown hazards of the Straits of Dover.

The English followed him, quite a long way astern. Once past the island, they were not in a hurry. There was nowhere on the Sussex coast where the armada might make a landing. Howard decided to save his ammunition until he was joined by Lord Henry Seymour and saw what the armada meant to do when it came to the Narrows. He expected to pick up powder and shot from the Sussex ports as he went along.

The duke wrote to Parma before the Isle of Wight was far astern, and sent the letter on ahead in the hands of a captain named Pedro de Leon. It was a perfectly calm and sober letter, explaining he had made slow progress because of the calms and because of the enemy's bombardments. The enemy had resolutely refused to come to close quarters, although the duke had tried his best to make him. 'Sometimes some of our ships have been in the very midst of the enemy's fleet, to induce one of his ships to grapple and begin the fight; but all to no purpose, because his ships are very light and mine are very heavy.' It is odd that he could write of beginning the fight, as though everything that had happened so far had not been fighting, but only some kind of preliminary sparring: he, and perhaps the Spaniards in general, had not yet grasped that they were up against a new kind of warfare, and that the English were never going to grapple and fight in the old-fashioned way. 'The enemy,' he went on, 'has plenty of men and stores. My stores are beginning to run short with these constant skirmishes; and if the weather does not improve and the enemy continues his tactics, as he certainly will, it will be advisable for Your Excellency to load a couple of ships with powder and ball of the sizes noted in the enclosed memorandum, and to despatch them to me without the least delay. It will also be advisable for Your Excellency to make ready at once to put out to meet us, because by God's grace, if the wind serves, I expect to be on the Flemish coast very soon.'

The sizes of shot he asked for were small, 4, 6 and 10 pounds.

Thereafter he wrote to Parma every day, letters which first became impatient, then desperate and frantic, but always remained polite. No answer came; no pinnace was sighted approaching from the east.

Friday, 5th August was another day of calm, and out there in the sunshine off the Sussex coast, Lord Howard seems to have been in a festive mood. The armada was visible ahead. It was edging away from the coastline, and seemed to be heading for the French side of the Straits; it looked as if it was aiming to join with Parma before it tried an attack on England. He summoned a lot of his senior captains on board the *Ark*, and used his prerogative to confer knighthoods on half a dozen of them, as though a victory had already been won. Lord Thomas Howard, Lord Sheffield, Roger Townsend, Martin Frobisher, John Hawkyns and George Beeston all became knights that day, 'as well in reward of their good services in these former fights, as also for the encouragement of the rest'. If Howard was angry with Drake for deserting his post to take Don Pedro as prize, perhaps it was just as well that Drake was already knighted.

During that day, somebody in the armada had a new idea: Parma must surely have plenty of the fast light ships that the armada lacked. Why should he not send them out, full of soldiers, to grapple with the English ships and bring them to real battle? Accordingly the duke sent off another pinnace, carrying this time a pilot called Domingo Ochoa. Ochoa was told to repeat the request for shot, and to press on Parma the need to be ready to come out and join the armada the very day it was sighted off Dunkirk. He also carried a request to Parma to send out forty fly-boats immediately to join the armada. Fly-boats were Dutch coasters, built with light draught and flat bottoms so that they could cross the shallow banks off the Flemish shores; armed, they were said to make effective and handy warships. This was the first outward sign of the total misunderstanding between the two dukes, Medina Sidonia and Parma. Medina Sidonia had been led to believe that Parma had a sea-going fleet, but he had not. Forty fly-boats! The request was pathetic. Parma did not have one that was ready for sea. There were indeed many at sea at that moment, but they belonged to the rebel Dutch and were patrolling offshore, intent on catching Parma if he tried to come out.

At sunset that Friday, a westerly breeze came up and the armada began to make good progress. By the morning of Saturday the 6th the English had caught up and were close astern. Howard's hope had been justified: barks had come out from the little Sussex harbours bringing new stocks of powder and shot. But he did not attack; he merely followed, with insulting confidence, as if he knew the armada was running into danger. At ten o'clock the coast of France was sighted, and at four o'clock that afternoon both fleets were approaching Calais. And here a new, unexpected and devastating problem was brought to the duke.

All through the voyage everyone had assumed that their destination, whether or not they waited at the Isle of Wight, was Dunkirk, the port that Parma held. That idea went right back to the council meeting off Lisbon, when Recalde had pointed out the defects in the king's proposal that they should meet with Parma off the Cape of Margate; they decided then to go to Dunkirk, fetch Parma and his army and escort them across. Only the day before, the message the duke had sent by Ochoa had spoken of the armada arriving 'in sight of Dunkirk'. Now, at the very last minute, the pilots told the duke they could not take him there.

They were certainly right. There was nowhere the armada could shelter on the Flemish coast. The row of harbours – Calais, Gravelines, Dunkirk, Nieuport and Ostend – have artificial breakwaters now; but then they were shallow creeks. Moreover, only two of them, Dunkirk and Nieuport, were held by Parma: Calais and Gravelines at the western end were French, and Ostend at the other end was an enclave held by the English. As Wagenhaer said, the sandbanks off that shore are liable to shift, but the general formation of them is the same as it was when he charted it. Beginning east of Calais there is a series of narrow banks parallel to the coast which are three fathoms deep at low water, or less – too shallow for any of the armada's major ships. Off Dunkirk they extend twelve miles to seaward.

There is only one navigable channel, very close inshore, which leads to Dunkirk; but it is very narrow, not more than a third of a mile across, with invisible banks on each side of it. Wagenhaer mentions it, but does not recommend it: 'You may safely sail along the coast of Flanders, between the shore and the shoals at five or six fathom, but it is dangerous for great vessels because the waves in the ebbing and flowing do for the most part set thwart over the shoals.' That channel, of course, is buoyed now, but it was not then, and nobody could have found it without very expert local knowledge – not even in a single ship, let alone a fleet of a hundred and twenty. Not one of the armada's pilots had that local knowledge. The duke had asked Parma for Flemish pilots but received no answer. If by a miracle they had succeeded in getting in, they would have been embayed by the outer banks and stuck there, unsheltered and unprotected, until they got an easterly wind, which might not have happened before the winter.

Nobody had thought of this, neither the king, nor the duke, nor Diego Flores, nor even Recalde. If the pilots had known they had not told the duke until this last moment, and if Parma had known he had not told anyone at all. But it was a fact: the armada, after coming all that way, could not approach within a dozen miles of Dunkirk. Its draught was too deep.

The immediate result was an argument, probably a very angry one, as the fleet sailed up towards Calais. Even the duke in his diary says the majority was in favour of pressing on. It is not surprising if they refused to believe such extraordinary lack of foresight; not surprising either if they were furious and looked for somebody to blame. But the duke believed the pilots, overrode the objectors and gave the order to anchor off the French coast about four miles short of Calais and twenty-four short of Dunkirk. The English came to anchor a culverin shot astern of him, still to windward.

Parma

The Duke of Parma's behaviour is the central riddle of the armada story: one can read or deduce what he did, but only guess why he did it.

To try to see the thing through Parma's eyes one has to pause and go back to February. That was the month when Queen Elizabeth's commissioners came to Flanders to negotiate peace with him, and the negotiations had been going on ever since. All that time, on the king's express instructions, Parma had been living in a world of deliberate deceit. It has sometimes been said the king, like the queen, wanted peace, but his letters to Parma disprove it. He wrote to him many times to say the negotiations must not on any account succeed: they must only be a means of wasting time and keeping the English guessing until the armada was ready. It is enough to quote from one of those letters, in which he told Parma to insist on an apology for Drake's attack on Cadiz: 'When you have got this, you are to act as if you were completely deceived by it, and pretend to believe anything they tell you: you will then renew the negotiations, name commissioners, and propose a meeting on neutral territory. As for powers . . . say that you have had full powers for many months, but cannot exhibit them until conditions worthy of my acceptance have been offered. Say this only for the sake of appearance. It is the best way to take them in, so that the peace commissioners may meet. But to you only, I declare that my intention is that these negotiations shall never lead to any result, whatever conditions the English may offer. On the contrary, the only object is to deceive them, and to cool them in their preparations for defence, by making them believe such preparations will not be necessary. You are well aware that the reverse of this is the truth, and that on our part there is to be no slackness but the greatest diligence in our efforts for the invasion of England, for which we have already made abundant provision in men, ships and money.

'Although we enter thus into negotiations, without any intention of concluding them, you can always get out of them with great honour by taking umbrage about some point of religion, or the other outrageous proposals they are likely to make . . . Thus you will proceed, now yielding on one point, and now insisting on another, but directing all to the same object – to gain time while preparations for the invasion are completed.'

It would be hard to find a more cynical royal command in any century. One cannot tell whether Parma disliked being told to lie and deceive, but one would imagine he did. After all, he was a very distinguished soldier, and soldiers even then had their code of honour. However, he did it very successfully for six months. It was pathetically easy, because the queen firmly believed he was honest and sincere and because the commissioners she had chosen were not remarkable for astuteness, and incapable of subtlety or cunning. They were two aristocrats, the Earl of Derby and Lord Cobham; and three aged and supposedly learned men, Sir James Croft, Dr Dale and Dr Rogers. Sir James, one early historian wrote, 'exhibited himself with very anile characteristics' – in other words, he was in his dotage; and the two doctors were adept at wasting time with speeches in Latin, full of ancient sophistries and classical allusions, that nobody else understood, which were unbelievably long and boring and had nothing to do with any practical question.

Parma also appointed commissioners, and between them they contrived to spend three months in exchanging compliments and presents and debating where to meet. The English wanted to meet in Ostend, which was held by an English garrison. Parma refused, on the ground that the town by right was Spain's. In May, the first meeting was held in some discomfort on the sandy shore, just out of range of the guns of Ostend, which satisfied everybody. Parma himself took no part in it, but he was there; he had gone disguised as a servant, in order to enter the town and inspect its defences from inside. Nothing was decided or even discussed, because the English insisted on seeing Parma's commission, his written authority from the king.

He had been telling them for months that he had a commission, but in fact he had not. He had written to ask the king to send him one; otherwise, he said, the English might break off the

talks. Indeed, the queen was impatient. 'Be plain with the duke,'
she wrote to her commissioners in the middle of May, 'that we
have tolerated so many weeks in tarrying a commission, that I will
never endure more delays. Let him know he deals with a prince
who prizes her honour more than her life. Make yourselves such as
stand of your reputation.' The commission arrived just in time. It
was written in French, which made it more confusing (the
argument had been in Latin, Italian, Spanish and English) and was
accompanied by a letter from the king reminding Parma that it was
'on no account to be used for anything but show'. Parma's
commissioners showed it to Dr Dale but would not give him a
copy. After all that Parma had said, it was embarrassing that it was
dated 17th April, less than a month before.

So the negotiations went on, a kind of black comedy, with one
side naïve and the other intent on time-wasting and deception.
Often Parma was driven to the most scandalous lies: for example,
when he assured Dr Rogers, who had noticed the warlike
preparations, 'On the honour of a gentleman, I declare really and
truly [he spoke in Italian but said these words in Spanish] that I
know of no plans of the King of Spain against Her Majesty or her
realm.'

True to his king's orders, they agreed on absolutely nothing.
They were still talking when the armada anchored off Calais and
Parma wrote with an air of innocent surprise, 'The peace
negotiations with the English have ended in the recall of the
commissioners by the queen. My efforts to persuade them to
continue the negotiations, notwithstanding the presence of the
armada, were unavailing.'

He had done what he was told, but the experience had changed
him. At the end of those six months his opinion of the armada plan
was different; even perhaps his opinion of the king.

He had received all the letters the duke had sent him during the
voyage, but had not tried to send any answers. Of course, the
letters had arrived telescoped together in time, because the earlier
ones had farther to go than the later. The first had been sent from
the Bay of Biscay on 25th July, and the last on 5th August, and
they all arrived between 2nd and 7th August. The only one he
answered was the first, and he did not send that answer until he

heard the armada had arrived at Calais. On the 7th, he had them all copied and sent to the king. With them he sent a long letter of his own.

'There is no need for me to dwell on these communications,' he began, 'except to say that I have acceded with all speed and energy to the request for pilots and ammunition. I have done this to the full extent that our poverty here permits.' He was always having to beg the king for money, and – with good reason, perhaps – he never missed a chance to rub it in. But the speed and energy did not amount to much. Three days later he had to confess that the ships with the pilots and ammunition had not left port, with the excuse that the sea was too rough. Yet the sea was not really rough. The boats of both fleets were plying from ship to ship without any trouble, and the duke's boats were constantly going ashore.

When Ensign Gil arrived on the 5th, Parma continued, he had ordered the boats that comprised his fleet to be brought alongside and the embarkation begun. By now, he expected it was finished. Meanwhile, he had remained at Bruges (which is forty miles from Dunkirk) to wind up affairs and write despatches, and he hoped to leave for the coast on the following day, the 8th. He promised the king he would help the duke in any way he could. But the core of the letter was this: 'To judge from what the duke says, it would appear that he still expects me to come out and join him with our boats, but it must be perfectly clear that this is not feasible. Most of our boats were built only for rivers, and they cannot weather the least sea. It is quite as much as they can do to carry the men across in perfectly fair weather, but as for fighting as well, it is obvious they cannot do it, however good the troops in them may be. This was the principal reason why Your Majesty decided to risk sending the armada, as in your great prudence you saw the enterprise could not be carried out in any other way.'

The next day, after he had heard the armada was at Calais, he repeated this all over again in different words, and added: 'If the duke were fully informed on the matter, he would be of the same opinion, and would busy himself in carrying out Your Majesty's orders at once, without letting himself be diverted into a different course.'

It was a theme he kept returning to: that his boats were only fit to cross in perfect weather, and only after the duke had done his job and cleared the enemy off the seas. That was the plan the king had made, and if anyone wanted to change it, he washed his hands of any responsibility. It seems he had never been told of the change Recalde had proposed before the armada sailed – that the armada should go to Dunkirk first and pick up Parma's fleet and escort it across. Unluckily, one can never be sure that a letter is not missing from the archives, but among the many letters the king had sent to Parma, none has come to light which gave him this vital information.

Nor had Parma understood, from all the letters the duke had sent him, that the armada was simply unable to clear the seas. This looks like a wilful misunderstanding. Nobody could have mistaken what the duke had said so many times. He had never suggested Parma's transports should join in battle, only the fighting fly-boats he supposed he had. The duke had escorted the helpless urcas all the way up the Channel. If Parma had tolerably seaworthy boats, there was every chance (given a fair wind) that he could escort them too, in spite of the active opposition, for the forty-odd miles from Calais to the entrance of the Thames. And if he had not, no doubt the army could have been packed into the armada ships for that short voyage. All the duke was asking was that they should come out quickly and join him off Calais. It was not unreasonable. Indeed, it was the only hope there was.

But Parma refused to see any reason for hurry. The duke should go and do his duty and defeat the enemy at sea. If he succeeded, Parma would wait for perfect weather and cross unopposed at leisure. Until then, he would not try. His letters all suggest he had believed for some time that the enterprise was doomed.

If the two dukes had met for ten minutes, they could surely have sorted it out and agreed how to make an attempt, if it was to be made at all. Given the pilots, the armada could have gone another dozen miles along the coast. Parma's boats, however bad they were, could have come out of the harbours at high water and drifted down on the ebb. But twenty miles of sea still separated them, and an even wider gulf of misunderstanding. The misunderstanding was mutual, and the fault for it lay far away in the secret rooms of the Escorial; for the king had given each of them false information, or no information at all, about the other. He had led Medina Sidonia to think Parma had a reasonable fleet, good enough to meet him off Margate, and led Parma to think the way would be cleared for him so thoroughly that he could cross without firing a shot.

The very minute the duke had come to anchor he sent his secretary, Jeronimo de Arceo, ashore with yet another letter to Parma, which Arceo had written in his name. It was much more acid than anything the duke ever wrote himself: 'I have constantly written to Your Excellency, and not only have I received no reply, but no acknowledgement of their receipt has reached me. I am extremely anxious at this, as Your Excellency may imagine; and to free myself of the doubt of whether any of my messengers have reached you safely, I am now sending this boat with the information that I am at anchor here off Calais with all the armada, the enemy's fleet being on my flank and able to bombard me, while I am not in a position to do him much harm. I feel obliged to inform Your Excellency of this, and to beg you, if you cannot at once bring out all your fleet, to send me the forty or fifty fly-boats I asked for yesterday. With this help, I shall be able to resist the enemy's fleet until Your Excellency can come out with the rest, and we can go together and take some port where this armada may enter in safety.'

That same evening the duke sent a captain ashore to call on the Governor of Calais to explain why he had anchored there; for the governor of course was French, and there was always doubt which side a Frenchman would favour, if he favoured either. The captain found the governor in a carriage on the seafront with his wife, expecting to see a battle. But he was friendly, so friendly that in the morning the duke sent his steward and paymaster ashore with six thousand ducats in gold to try to buy food, and the governor sent out his nephew with a present of fresh provisions. This nephew told the duke, as local busybodies will, that he had chosen a dangerous place to anchor because of the tides and currents and the lack of shelter. This was true – in fact, the place they had chosen to stop has stronger tides than anywhere else in the eastern half of the Channel. But the duke already knew. When the fleet anchored it had been slack water, but during the night the spring tide had been racing past at three knots, and every ship had had to drop a second anchor.

The next day, Sunday 7th August, the duke wrote two more letters to Parma; and in them one can plainly see the death of all hope in his mind. In the first, he said he would have to leave the anchorage at the least sign of bad weather. He begged Parma to help him find a port: 'As the season is so advanced, and my ships so large, I am obliged to be very careful, so that I may be able to give a good account of myself in the fulfilment of the task entrusted to me . . . I therefore beg you to hasten your coming out before the spring tides end, as it will be impossible for you to get out of Dunkirk and the neighbouring ports during the neap tides.'

On this letter Parma wrote a somewhat sour note, presumably to some underling: 'With regard to the Duke of Medina's remarks about getting out of Dunkirk during the spring tides, he may be informed that there will be no difficulty in Nieuport, or in Dunkirk either. It is true that in certain states of the wind the water goes down, and the spring tide is necessary, but there are only a very few boats that run this risk. Even if we should not be able to use them, there has never been the slightest question or idea of waiting for the spring tides, or deferring the enterprise on this account.'

This was the last time the duke asked Parma to hurry, and the last time he mentioned fulfilment of his task. The snippet of information about the tides in Dunkirk must have been brought to him by Don Rodrigo Tello, the man he had sent with the first of his letters from the Bay of Biscay. Don Rodrigo had turned up from Dunkirk at dawn that Sunday, having been at Bruges with Parma the day before when the news came in that the armada was at Calais. Parma had expressed great joy, but had not come down to Dunkirk, and when Tello left there on Saturday night the embarkation of men and stores had not begun.

Later that day, Secretary Arceo sent a message: Parma had still not arrived, no stores or guns or ammunition had been shipped, and carpenters were still at work on the boats. In Arceo's opinion they could not be ready to sail within a fortnight.

It is not recorded how much more of the appalling story Don Rodrigo told the duke: of the river barges Parma had provided, totally unsuitable for a sea crossing, some new and badly built, some ancient and rotting, some uncaulked so that they sank in harbour as soon as they were loaded; of the very few fly-boats, unarmed, some without masts, some without rigging, one at least lying on her beam ends in the mud. This came out later, and it is doubtful if the duke ever knew it all. But a fortnight to be ready! That was enough to know. He could not possibly wait where he was for a fortnight. Nor could he put to sea and continue to fight the English without more ammunition. He had to find a harbour, even if that meant abandoning the enterprise until the spring. Only Parma's pilots could help him to find it, and the pilots had not come.

To carry his final letter, he sent the Inspector General Don Jorge Manrique, who had spoken with such authority in the council meetings in Corunna. He did not ask for fly-boats, or suggest that Parma should hurry out. He was sending Don Jorge, he wrote, 'to give you an account of the state of the armada and to represent to you the urgent need to find a harbour for it, without which it will doubtless be lost as the ships are so large. In every way, I believe this course should be adopted as quickly as possible. The season is so far advanced that we must be very careful. Besides, it is impossible to continue cruising with this armada, as its great weight causes it always to be to leeward of the enemy, and we cannot do any damage to him however hard we try. Don Jorge will give you as full an account as I could do in person.'

In fact, there was a harbour in Parma's control not far away, which could have sheltered the armada, even for the winter: the river Schelde, leading up to Antwerp. The southern side of it and the city of Antwerp were in Parma's hands. The northern side, and the port of Flushing near the mouth, were held by the Dutch. The armada was strong enough to fight its way in past Flushing, and to have a good chance of defending itself off Antwerp; but without the pilots it had not a hope of finding the entrance channel, which is called the Wielingen and extends between immense sandbanks, shallow but invisible, almost twenty miles out to sea.

There was one good reason why Parma could not come out, apart from the preposterous quality of his boats. This was the Dutch fleet, which had its nearest base in Flushing. The Dutch had a few big ships, and a great many fly-boats. Neither the English nor the Spanish really understood how strong they were. The English seldom saw them and never saw them all, because they were ships of shallow draught which sailed among the sandbanks where galleons could not go. So the English from time to time expressed resentment that the Dutch were not doing enough. The Dutch were equally resentful, for an opposite reason: that the English fleet under Seymour kept appearing off the coast in ample strength to stop Parma coming out. The Dutch were longing for him to come out. They had been patrolling all summer in the shallows off Dunkirk and Nieuport, but far enough out to tempt him to put to sea. (They only did it at spring tides because they knew what Parma apparently did not – that his boats could not get out of the harbours on the neaps.) They wanted him to come because they knew the kind of boats he had, and were perfectly certain they could demolish them once and for all, and his army with them; and the farther offshore they met them, the farther the soldiers would have to swim.

The Dutch have seldom been given the credit they deserve for the defeat of Spain at sea. But in fact they posed a quite insoluble problem. Even if the armada had beaten the English fleet, it could never have beaten a fleet of fly-boats, which could retreat in perfect safety among the sandbanks where it could never follow. There was a good chance Parma's boats could have safely made their way to Calais close inshore: the duke's boats did it with impunity. He had only to come out of harbour at high water and drop down the coast on the ebb. But if he had waited for the armada to sweep the English off the seas, and if he had then set course to make the shortest crossing, he would have been slaughtered before he reached deep water where the armada could protect him. Indeed, if the English fleet had been beaten England could still have been defended by the Dutch. Parma knew the Dutch ships were there, but he saw it as part of the duke's job to get rid of them. No doubt they would disappear, he wrote, as soon as the armada arrived. Neither he nor any other senior Spaniard seems to have grasped the difference between ships of deep and shallow draught, or between the deep and shallow seas.

'The men who have recently come here from the duke,' Parma wrote in his letter of 8th August, 'seeing the boats unarmed and with no artillery on board, and the men not shipped, have been trying to make out we are not ready. They are mistaken. The boats are, and have been for months, in proper order for the work they have to do, namely to take the men across. We have not as many seamen as we ought to have; but enough for the job. The boats are so small that the troops cannot be kept on board for long. There is no room to turn around, and they would certainly fall ill, rot and die. Putting the men on board these low, small boats can be done in a very short time, and I am confident that in this respect there will be no shortcoming in Your Majesty's service.'

Yet the day before, he had written that he had ordered the embarkation to begin on 5th August, and expected it was completed. Both these letters were sent before he left Bruges, and that may be the clue to his complacency. So far as one can discover he had not been down to the coast since May, and then not to Nieuport or Dunkirk. He had left the building of the fleet to his underlings, and several people suggested afterwards that they deliberately let him down. Boatbuilders had been imported from Italy and the Baltic, but the manual work was done by Dutchmen who had the bad luck to live in the part of the country he had captured. Their hearts would certainly not have been in the job, and there was even talk of sabotage. Another Manrique, not Don Jorge but Don Juan, who was with Parma's army, wrote to the king's secretary: 'You may think it bold on my part, but I cannot refrain from saying how the most blessed expedition in the world has been defeated. The day we came to embark, we found the vessels still unfinished, not a pound of cannon on board, and nothing to eat. This was not because the Duke of Parma did not do all he could (it would be difficult to find another man in the world who works half as hard) but because the seamen, and all those who had to do the detailed work, openly and undisguisedly directed their energies not to serve His Majesty, for that is not their aim, but to waste his substance and prolong the war; besides which the common people put every obstacle in the way.'

Another letter which reached the king, this one anonymous, said much the same: 'There has been very bad management with the Flemish ships. They cannot be ready for another fortnight because of the neglect of the commissaries, whose only care has been to steal everything they could. The ships are short of sailors, because the sailors have been neglected and dreadfully ill-treated.

If the ships had joined the armada, no doubt they could have carried out the design.'

It seems clear that Parma had not taken the trouble to supervise the building of the fleet, and thought it was ready when it was not. But that does not explain everything. He was a man of enormous energy, and did stupendous deeds with armies; he had even built canals to take his barges from the Schelde to Dunkirk without the need to go to sea. Why then had he been so futile in this one respect? Why build river barges instead of sailing boats? Why hazard everything on the unlikely event of days of perfect weather? And how on earth did he hope to propel the barges? By oars perhaps; but had he provided oars and rowlocks, and taught enough soldiers to use them, or found out if anyone could really row a river barge, designed to be towed by a horse? Nobody answered these questions, least of all himself; and the only guess one can make is that he had lost interest in the enterprise, and after so many months of waiting had given up expecting it to happen. The barge-building seems a pretence, a make-believe to cloak some other intention, just as the negotiations with England were meant to cloak the king's intention to invade.

This is not impossible. Parma had conducted the negotiations under the strictest orders from the king that they must not succeed. Yet in those months of discussion he had certainly come to believe that without his deliberate frustration they could succeed. At the same time, he had lost faith in the invasion because the delays had given the English plenty of time to prepare for it. As early as March he had put both these thoughts in a letter to the king: 'The conquest of England would have been difficult if the country had been taken by surprise. Now they are strong and armed; we are comparatively weak. The danger and the doubt are great; and the English deputies, I think, are really desirous of peace. Nevertheless, I am at Your Majesty's disposition, life and all.'

Nobody ever dared to *tell* the king what he should do, but no hint could have been much clearer. It was precisely the same advice the other duke had given from Corunna. Seen in this light, the collection of barges makes some sense. They were merely a threat, a bargaining point in the negotiations, and it was a long time since Parma had really expected to have to put to sea in them.

Parma had two advantages over the king. First, he was a more intelligent man, and his intelligence was not clouded by webs of intrigue and dogma. Also, unlike the king, he had met and had long discussions with Englishmen who, inept though they may have been, were Protestants and loyal to the queen. With his intelligence, and that experience, he may have seen what the king had failed to see: the futility of invading England – that even if he risked his life and countless others, and crossed the sea and won his battles, entered London, sacked it and deposed or killed the queen, the king at the end of it all would never be able to govern the country because the English, like the Dutch, would never submit. He was certainly sick of waging one endless repressive war on behalf of the king. He can hardly have wanted another.

Moreover, Parma seems to have been disenchanted with the king's authority because of his own royal lineage, or more especially his children's. Their claim to the throne of Portugal was as good as the king's, but the king had seized it. He felt he deserved a kingdom for his line, and had earned it. But the king never offered it; neither in Italy, where Parma's estates were, nor in Portugal, nor the Netherlands, where he had fought so skilfully and so long; and now the bloodier battle with England was solely to give the king another throne, with no suggestion of any reward for himself. Even in the armada, people had argued whether Philip or Parma would be King of England, and had said half-humorously that there would have to be another war to decide it.

Of course Parma had not seen the king's secret letter with its minimal demands – freedom of worship in England and withdrawal from the Netherlands – because he had not met the duke, who brought it; and he never saw it. If he had, it would finally have convinced him the invasion was a useless waste of effort, not to mention lives. He could have won the king's demands, except the forgiveness of the exiles, at any time in his months of negotiations; and the queen could have rewarded him more generously than Philip.

This then is one guess at the reason why he behaved as he did, and no better one has been made. The king had stretched him too far. He had had enough; his loyalty was near breaking point. A year before he had been persuaded, like everyone else, that invasion was the cause of God, and had willingly ordered the building of a fleet. Then he had slowly ceased to believe in it. The boat-builders went on building unsuitable boats, and he had not bothered to keep an eye on what was happening in the ports, because he thought and hoped the boats would never be needed. Peace by negotiation, he believed, was sure; invasion was dangerous and could not succeed. If only the invasion could be abandoned before it had gone too far, the king would have to let him negotiate sincerely, and that is what he wanted. Not that he was a pacifist in character, far from it; he was a fighter by trade and inclination. But great generals never fight battles if they can win their ends by talking.

But now the armada had come, far too late in the season to leave any reasonable hope of perfect weather for the kind of boats he had built. It was far too late also to tell the king what he had done, or failed to do. He could only tell him, over and over again, that he was ready, though all the observable facts proclaimed that he was not.

Perhaps one ought to sympathize with him. If he believed the negotiations could have succeeded, and that England could not be conquered by force of arms, then he was right and the king was wrong. The only unattractive thing about him is that he did his best, in every letter he wrote, to make sure the blame for the failure would fall on the duke – while the duke never blamed anyone but himself.

In the evening of Monday 8th, Parma mounted at last and rode for the coast, going first to Nieuport and then to Dunkirk. In Nieuport, he claimed, sixteen thousand troops had been embarked that day, and everything was practically ready – except, of course, that it was not the perfect weather he demanded, and the boats could not leave port. Nieuport was the minor harbour, and he had told the king before the armada sailed that he had only seventeen thousand men altogether, which was the reason why he needed six thousand from the armada; so it is difficult not to suspect his figures were elastic. In Dunkirk the following morning he found the men assembled on the quay and expected they would be shipped by the evening.

In Dunkirk also he met Don Jorge Manrique, who had been searching for him all the previous day and had seen for himself what was happening in the ports. Don Jorge was a more outspoken man than the others the duke had sent ashore, and he was so incensed by what he had seen that he was quite prepared to stand up to the Duke of Parma or anyone else.

It was a remarkable scene, a back-to-front kind of argument; for Parma had to try to convince Don Jorge that his own boats were unseaworthy. He did not explain, then or ever, why he had built unseaworthy boats. There are two versions of the meeting, neither by Don Jorge; a few days later, he wrote a report of the voyage, probably the first that reached the king; but it describes the adventures of the armada after he left it, which he heard from somebody else, and does not say what happened ashore.

The more dignified of the versions is Parma's. He told the king Don Jorge requested him to help the duke to capture a port, specifically the Isle of Wight, or else join him to engage the enemy. It is very difficult to believe that this is what Don Jorge said, and it was certainly not what the duke said in the letter Don Jorge brought; for the letter only begged his help in finding a harbour – any harbour. Nor had the duke proposed in any letters to go back to the Isle of Wight. One can only think Parma deliberately misrepresented Don Jorge, or did not listen. He had always supposed, he said, that the duke would have managed to find a harbour on the way up-Channel. The request only showed 'how badly informed the duke must be about the character of our small, weak boats, entirely unfit for fighting, or even to live in any heavy sea or high wind'. 'Nevertheless,' he continued to the king, 'my desire to serve Your Majesty is so great that I decided to discuss the possibility with the Marquis de Renti and practical sailors here, in the presence of Don Jorge Manrique, so that if it turned out to be impracticable he might be convinced that it really was so, and that the most we could hope for from these boats would be in fine settled weather, and with the Channel clear of enemies, to take our men across, as had been arranged. The general verdict was that it would be out of the question for them to undertake a voyage of seven or eight days as proposed by the duke.'

Seven or eight days? The duke had never proposed anything of the sort.

The other version was written by the priest Juan de Victoria. He is not a reliable witness and he was probably only repeating hearsay – nobody suggested he was there in person. But his story has a human air, and it is somewhat confirmed by the other Manrique, Don Juan, who simply wrote: 'Don Jorge Manrique is here, it is quite pitiable to see how he carries on.'

As Inspector General of the Fleet, Don Jorge (according to the priest) thought his authority included Parma's fleet, and he had a furious row with Parma's supply officer, who had not prepared any supplies or ammunition, or indeed anything else. The supply officer said they took their orders direct from the king, not from the armada. Don Jorge said he would go out to the fleet and get his authority confirmed, but before he could do so the supply officer went to Parma to complain. Then Parma himself arrived, and Don Jorge tackled him in person, which was brave or even rash. 'He was ill received by the duke,' the priest wrote, 'who was accompanied by other dukes and Spanish gentlemen. Don Jorge told him he ought to embark at once, but the duke said that was none of his business. The duke tried to hit him, but he was prevented by the other gentlemen and the presence of the Spanish troops. Instead, he ordered Don Jorge to go back to the fleet. Don Jorge replied that he would not go back until he had reported to his Majesty what was happening.'

While the ferocious argument was still going on, and men were still being herded aboard, a small boat came sailing in to the harbour and a young man scrambled ashore from it. It was none other than the Prince of Ascoli, King Philip's illegitimate son, shivering with cold, distraught and wet to the skin. He stammered out a story of disaster. A great and terrible battle had been fought the day before, and the armada had disappeared to the north.

It is extraordinary that nobody in Dunkirk had heard the gunfire of the Battle of Gravelines, which happened barely a dozen miles away, or seen the scattered ships of the armada. But it was so. Parma's charade of loading the men in the boats was on the day after the armada had been irrevocably beaten.

The Fireships

he English had approached Calais in a mood of contrition. They had not failed, but certainly they had not had much success. The gunnery they had relied on had done no mortal damage to any ship. Some weeks later, a master gunner named William Thomas proposed the founding of a corporation of gunners to improve the art. 'If it had pleased God that Her Majesty's ships had been manned with a full supply of good gunners . . . it would have been the woefullest time or enterprise that ever the Spaniard took in hand . . . What can be said but our sins was the cause that so much powder and shot spent, and so long time in fight, and, in comparison thereof, so little harm?' Skilful gunner though he may have been, Thomas's spelling was eccentric even for that era. His letter goes on: 'Yt were grettly to bey wesshed that yowr onors were more truly sartyfyed of that blynde exsarsyes and own skelfell techen by the name of skolors. In the artelayry.' Translated, 'it were greatly to be wished that Your Honours were more truly certified of that blind exercise and unskilful teaching by the name of scholars in the artillery.' The council Howard called when the fleet came to anchor would have agreed with that. The only comfort was that Spanish gunnery was worse.

But the moment when the armada anchored, everything was changed. Three hours later Lord Henry Seymour joined the fleet, bringing twenty-five fresh ships from the Thames, including the queen's newest race-built ships the *Rainbow* and the *Vanguard*, all fully stocked with ammunition. That brought the English fleet up to somewhere about a hundred and forty sail. The armada was outnumbered.

Howard sent a boat to the *Vanguard* to fetch Sir William Wynter, a sailor of life-long service and Rear Admiral of Seymour's fleet. (Wynter had the same relationship to Seymour as

Drake had to Howard, seaman to aristocrat.) He came with what he thought was a new idea: 'Having viewed myself the great and hugeness of the Spanish army, and did consider that it was not possible to remove them but by a device of firing of ships, which would . . . put many of them in danger of firing, and at least to make them to loose their cables and anchors, which could not be less than two for every ship, I thought it meet to acquaint my Lord withal at my coming to him at that time, which was about nine of the clock at night; and his Lordship did like very well of it.' Fireships: point was added to the plan while they were discussing it, for three other ships dragged their anchors in the tide and wind and drifted down, 'all tangled together', on the *Ark*. Both tide and wind were setting directly down towards the Spanish fleet.

Wynter was certainly not the only man to have seen the armada was in a classic position for a fire attack, anchored close together in a strong tidal stream; but Howard let him think he was. Fireships were a well-known weapon; the Spaniards had used them against Hawkyns and Drake at San Juan de Ulua, and against Drake at Cadiz, and the Dutch had used them against the Spaniards at Antwerp. They were no good against ships under way, because ships under way could always dodge them; but floated on wind and tide against a fleet at anchor, especially in the dark, they were the most destructive weapon there was, and the most alarming. Fire was the worst of all hazards for wooden warships. The whole of them, timber, tar and pitch, cordage and canvas, was highly inflammable, and if a fire got hold they were absolutely certain to blow up when their magazines were hot enough. Every sailor knew he lived on top of a bomb, and every sailor in the English fleet must have thought of using fireships when the armada stopped.

In later years, designing fireships was a science and they accompanied every fighting fleet. But in 1588 they were a do-it-yourself weapon, created simply by loading a ship with anything that could burn: old timber, old rope, old canvas, brushwood from the galley fires, and barrels of pitch and tar and the oil used for lamps. The English fleet had no fireships ready-made, which might be thought short-sighted; but an order had been sent from London to Dover for suitable ships and combustibles to be collected there. Early on Sunday morning Howard in council

decided to make the attempt, and a pinnace was sent to Dover to
bring the ships across.

After it had gone the council began to have a sense of urgency.
The Dover ships or boats could not arrive that day. If they waited
longer, the wind might change, the armada might get under way
again, or Parma might emerge from his harbours, and the chance
would be lost. 'It was thought meet,' Wynter wrote, 'that we
should help ourselves with such shipping as we had there to serve
this turn.' Volunteers were asked to provide the ships to be
burned.

It was not such an unpopular job as one might think. An
owner-skipper of a tired old ship was glad to offer it, because it
gave him a chance to claim more compensation than its market
value, and also to claim for whatever stores it might have had,
whether it had them or not. Eight ships were chosen, five of them
from Drake's squadron, each at least 150 tons. They were
surreptitiously filled with inflammable stores, and their guns were
loaded; surreptitiously because the Spaniards might be watching.
At eleven o'clock that Sunday evening the tide turned in their
favour. By midnight they were ready, and waiting for the gun that
would give them the signal to start.

The Spaniards were indeed watching. One who was in the *San
Martin* wrote, 'We rode there at anchor all night' – referring of
course to Saturday night – 'with the enemy half a league from us
also anchored, and we waited because there was nothing else we
could do. We had a great presentiment of evil from those fiendish
people and their arts. So we continued anxiously on Sunday all day
long.' They had seen the new fleet arriving from the Downs, and
believed it was commanded by Hawkyns, whose name, after
Drake's, was most familiar to them; and they knew they were
outnumbered and outgunned. The Spaniards described an
incident the English did not mention. 'At four in the afternoon we
saw a pinnace coming across from the enemy fleet to ours. It came
as close as it could to our royal flagship, fired four shots and then
sailed back to its own fleet. The flagship of the galleasses, which
was close to the royal flagship, fired twice, but I do not know if it
did any damage except that it seemed to take a piece out of the
main topsail. We were very much impressed by this daring. We

marvelled again at their well designed light ships, which could come and go as they pleased, a thing that none of ours could do.'

The devastating news from Parma was not allowed to spread around the fleet, where morale was low enough already. Some officers who described events long afterwards had still not learned the truth when they wrote. 'In the evening,' one wrote, 'Don Rodrigo Tello arrived with a message from the Duke de Parma. All the men were pleased that a reply had come so quickly and that we had decided to wait there for it.' And another: 'This same day news came for the duke that the prince was embarking his men with all speed in a hundred and fifteen ships, albeit small ones.' So hope was kept alive, and possibly nobody outside the duke's immediate staff knew what the messages from Parma really said.

But they all knew the danger of fireships. Their vulnerable position was as obvious to them as it was to the English, and they saw movements in the English fleet that made them more suspicious. 'They could not make their preparations so secretly,' one of them wrote, 'that we could not see what they were up to.' But there was nothing much they could do about it, unless they raised anchor and moved farther along the coast towards the unknown sandbanks – and that would only have meant the English would do the same and follow them. Their fear of fireships was exaggerated because an Italian engineer named Giambelli had had the idea, not long before in Antwerp, of making a fireship with an enormous charge of gunpowder in it. When it blew up it had scattered flaming wreckage half a mile and killed something like a thousand men of Parma's army. Now Giambelli was said to be in England, employed by the queen; and indeed he was, but not to make fireships, only to build a bridge of boats across the Thames to stop the armada coming up river.

The duke took the only precautions he could. At nightfall he stationed pinnaces between the fleets with grapnels, and ordered them to grapple the fireships if they came and tow them clear. He also sent officers round the fleet in boats to make sure that everyone was alert to the danger. If fireships broke through the line of pinnaces, every ship was to buoy its anchor cables and cut them, get clear of the fireships' track and anchor again; and then return with the change of tide in the morning and pick up its buoys again.

Soon after midnight the signal gun was fired in the English fleet and the ships made sail. Boats went with them to take off the skeleton crews when the fires were lit. The Spaniards saw them coming, eight ships in line abreast with only their mainsails set. For some minutes, nothing happened. Then, half-way across, they burst into flames with awful suddenness: fire spouted from the gunports, ran up the rigging and engulfed the sails. They were much bigger ships than anyone had expected. The pinnaces the duke had sent tried to get their grapnels on board and one or two succeeded, but before they could turn the ships in their courses the ropes burned through, and as the gundecks rose to the heat of a furnace the guns began to fire, scattering their shot at random and sending up fountains of glowing embers. 'It was a terrifying spectacle in the night,' a Spaniard wrote.

In the accepted English story the fireships caused a ludicrous panic in the Spanish fleet. Nobody said so at the time. Sir William Wynter came nearest to it when he wrote, 'This matter did put such terror among the Spanish army that they were fain to let slip their cables and anchors; and did work, as it did appear, great mischief among them by reason of the suddenness of it.' But he believed at least two of the Spanish ships had been set on fire, and he wrote not so much in scorn as in self-congratulation for the success of the idea he thought was his own. By the Victorian age the legend had grown. 'In a moment, all was panic,' Sir Julian Corbett wrote in 1898. 'Sidonia gave the fatal order for cables to be cut. The result was an indescribable confusion. Ship fell upon ship, and cries of panic and the crash of spars were mingled with the sound of the fireships' exploding guns.'

There may indeed have been a lot of shouting in the Spanish manner, especially from the soldiers and gentlemen. Some went so far as to tell the duke he should leave his ship and escape. Of course he refused. But undeniably the sailors kept their heads and succeeded in a very difficult maneuver with extraordinary speed. It may have been fifteen minutes since the signal gun was sounded for the fireships to get under way; ten minutes since the fires were lit; five minutes since it was seen that the pinnaces could not stop them. In those five minutes, lying head to wind and tide, the sailors had to heave the anchor buoys overboard, take an axe to their straining cables, climb the rigging, make sail, set the sails to wear the ships' heads round, and then re-set them for a course to get clear of the fireships' tack – and do it all in the pitch dark. Yet by the time the fireships reached the anchorage it was empty. No sailor will believe that was achieved by panic.

Of course, there were collisions. At first, the *San Martin* could not go about because other ships were crowding her on both sides. But only one ship was badly damaged. That was the *San Lorenzo*, flagship of the galleasses, and she had less excuse than most. With oars, one might have expected she could stem the tide without any need to wear; but she entangled her rudder with somebody else's anchor cable and tore it off. No ship was burned, and the fireships did not explode: they were not Giambelli's infernal machines. They sailed or drifted harmlessly across the anchorage and burned themselves out. But they had done their job. 'The enemy were lucky,' a Spaniard wrote with truth, 'their trick turned out exactly as they had planned. With eight ships they put us to flight, a thing they had not dared to attempt with a hundred and thirty.'

The duke himself did what he meant the whole of the fleet to do. He stood out to sea across the wind for a mile or so and dropped another anchor. From there, he hoped when the tide had turned to be able to go back and pick up the anchors he had buoyed. But dawn showed only three or four ships anywhere near him: Recalde and de Leyva and one or two of the Portuguese galleons of his own squadron. The rest were scattered down wind and tide as far as Gravelines ten miles away. Possibly most of them, having lost two anchors, had nothing better than a kedge on deck which could not hold against the wind and tide, and were labouring to get up whatever spare anchors and cables they had stowed in the holds. Nearly three hundred anchors were lying on the sea-bed off Calais, and no doubt they are lying there still; and losing their anchors in the end caused more destruction among the armada ships than anything else.

There were many moments when the duke deserved more admiration than he was ever given, just as his sailors did; and that dawn was one of them. He could easily have panicked and fled, and let his armada follow, but he did not. He sent off pinnaces to order the fleet to round up and rejoin him; and there was some hope it could, because the tide turned about five o'clock in the morning. He then began by running down wind to join them, which was the logical thing to do. But the relevant passage in his diary refers to 'his Flemish pilots', and subsequently to his 'experienced pilots'. Some time the previous evening the pilots had made their way out from Dunkirk at last, though nobody mentions them coming. These experts told him the fleet was already dangerously near the shoals. It seemed to him there was only one way to protect it until it could extricate itself. He turned and prepared to delay the English fleet by fighting it alone.

The Duke of Parma, appointed to command the invasion of England.

The armada in the Channel: design for a tapestry, showing the crescent formation which was probably an English legend. Drake is conspicuously absent from the portraits in the borders.

The rival flagships, *Ark Royal* (*left*) and *San Martin*. These modern drawings by Ray Woodward, based on contemporary paintings, are as near as one can get to the slender lines of an English race-built ship and the ponderous bulk of a Portuguese or Spanish galleon.

The armada in battle. This imaginative painting, by an unknown contemporary artist, belongs to the Society of Apothecaries in London. Its style is Spanish but it depicts an English victory watched by the Queen.

The thousand-foot cliffs of Achill Head project a hundred miles west of any land shown on the armada's charts. Many ships failed to round them and were wrecked in this region.

The end: as a symbol of disaster, the wheel of a land-type gun carriage lies on the sea bed off Donegal among the débris of the *Trinidad Valencera*.

13

The Battle of Gravelines

nglish accounts of the battle that began that Monday morning were as sparse as ever. Spanish accounts were much more numerous and detailed, but it is just as hard to sort them all out and fit them together. It is not surprising, because the battle itself was fought in almost total confusion and shrouded by gunsmoke, a gigantic free-for-all in which each English captain and each Spanish army commander did whatever seemed best to him, and never received an order unless he happened to come within shouting distance of a senior officer. A few horrific stories stand out clearly, because there was somebody there who saw them, and survived, and wrote what he had seen, and a few generalities can be deduced from all the individual versions. One is that it started about seven o'clock in the morning, reached its peak about nine, and lasted till four in the afternoon. Another is that the Spaniards, in spite of everything, succeeded in building up again the nucleus of their old formation. A third is that although two hundred and sixty ships were present, a very much smaller number took an active part in the fight – at the most perhaps thirty Spaniards and forty English. Most of the Spanish ships remained to leeward, fully occupied in clawing off the sands. What the remaining hundred English ships were doing was never specified, but it was nothing very useful.

One cannot be sure exactly where it happened, or of the answer to the all-important question of which way the wind was blowing. Both sides agreed that when it began the bulk of the armada was off Gravelines about seven miles out to sea, which was why the battle was given the name of that village. But the fighting was farther to the westward. It began at half-ebb, and during the day the tide would have carried a mass of fighting ships five miles in each direction, towards Calais on the ebb and towards Dunkirk on the flood. As for the wind, Sir William Wynter, who ought to have known, put it at south south west. But Calderon says it was west north west, which fits in better with the known facts, and the duke's diary says it was north west. Wynter adds that the galleons, when they were not in fight, were standing away to the north north west, which is what one would expect in a west north west wind if they were sailing close-hauled, as they certainly were, to keep clear of the sandbanks. If the wind had been south south west, nobody would have had to worry about the sandbanks. Probably it was veering and increasing all the time – Wynter's south south west at the time of the fireships, Calderon's west north west in the early morning and the duke's north west by the afternoon. But these, of course, were directions by the compass of the 1580s. A compass in the 1980s would show the duke's direction as almost north; and that was dead onshore. The thing they must have dreaded all the way up the Channel had happened at last. They were caught on a lee shore.

The difference in the Spanish and English commands is most noticeable in the reports of this fight. In English reports, the names of the captains and their ships are almost synonymous: they speak sometimes of Drake, for example, and sometimes of the *Revenge*. But Spanish reports do not mention the sea-captains unless they did something wrong. They use the names of the ships or of the army commanders, or sometimes both. Clearly the battle was fought between English sailors and Spanish soldiers. But a final thing one cannot exactly explain is why the English won.

During the night the English had not been able to see what had happened. The fireships had not started the conflagration they had hoped for, and they must have feared the plan had failed entirely. Their jubilation was all the greater in the dawn, when they saw the anchorage empty and the armada scattered. Howard at once gave the signal for a charge: that was the word they used, like cavalry. At utmost speed, anchors were weighed and sails were shaken out, and the whole of the maritime might of England was launched in pursuit.

But the next thing Howard saw was the crippled galleass *San Lorenzo* creeping along very close inshore, with its hundreds of convicts pulling for Calais harbour. The sight was too much for him. Like Drake the week before, he could not resist a prize. He turned aside from the charge, and the whole of his squadron followed him.

By the standard of later naval morals, it was an indefensible act, with the battle of a lifetime ahead and the fate of England clearly to be decided. It was not even common sense: but if anyone thought ill of him then, nobody dared to say so. The galleass, seeing the pursuit, turned even closer inshore and ran aground on the beach; and as the tide ran out it heeled towards the land, until its seaward guns were tilted up and useless.

A galleass drew less water than a normal ship, and Howard could not approach it: that beach shelves gently, and a mile off shore there is a shallow patch that nobody would care to cross on a falling tide. So he sent his longboat, and other boats packed with enthusiastic volunteers. There was a musketry fight, and on both sides a good many men were killed. It only stopped when Don Hugo de Moncada, the commander of the squadron who had disagreed with the duke in the Channel, fell dead with a musket ball between the eyes. Then the crew, the soldiers and convicts abandoned ship and swam or waded ashore. The English swarmed up her sides and took everything worth taking they could carry. While the looting was going on, some Frenchmen came on board with a message from the governor. They found the only English officer who spoke French. The sailors, their message said, were welcome to the booty, but the ship was the governor's because it was in his waters. That might have been agreed, but some Englishmen, drunk with plunder, scrambled ashore and began to rob the citizens of Calais who were standing on the beach as spectators. Thereupon, the governor fired some shots from the guns in his fort, and the English beat a retreat.

The whole diversion was pointless. Even if Howard had left her alone, and even if she had got in to Calais harbour and made a new rudder, the *San Lorenzo* could not possibly have rejoined the armada. As it was, the Spaniards could not refloat her, nor could the French, nor could he. She lay there off Calais until she rotted away. He got no prize, and the whole of his squadron missed the first half of the battle.

So it was Drake, not Howard, who led the charge; and the duke in the *San Martin*, trying to protect his fleet, took the first shock of it. Both of them held their fire until they were very close.

Then the *Revenge* let fly with her bow guns, wore and fired her broadside. The *San Martin* fired back. Before she could reload, Drake's squadron came in astern of him, at least half a dozen of the queen's ships, and each repeated his maneuver – the same maneuver Howard had used off Portland.

Very close astern, even perhaps alongside, Hawkyns joined the attack in the *Victory*, with the *Mary Rose*, the *Dreadnought* and the *Swallow*. Four other galleons were coming up to join the duke: Oquendo in the *Santa Ana*, the *San Marcos* of the duke's own squadron of Portuguese ships, and a little later the *San Mateo*, also of his squadron, and the *San Juan*, the flagship of Don Diego Flores, who was with the duke as his adviser. Drake and his squadron passed on to the eastward, leaving this little group to be dealt with by the mass of ships coming in astern. Presumably he had seen the main body of the armada and was on his way to attack it; but Frobisher, who saw him go and did not understand what he was doing, was furious with him again: 'He came bragging up at the first indeed,' he said afterwards in a rage, 'and gave them his prow and his broadside; and then kept his luff and was glad that he was gone again, like a cowardly knave or traitor – I rest doubtful, but the one I will swear.'

In fact, whatever Drake was up to – and one assumes it was something intelligent – the fight grew round the group of galleons, and they became the nucleus of the battle. By nine o'clock, when Wynter came up in the *Vanguard*, a good many more Spaniards had beaten up with the help of the ebbing tide to join the duke in his rearguard action. Wynter had not seen them before at close quarters, and he remarked on their formation: 'Their admiral and vice-admiral, they went in the midst, and the greatest number of them; and there went on each side, in the wings, their galleasses, armados of Portugal, and other good ships, in the whole to the number of sixteen in a wing, which did seem to be of their principal shipping.'

That seems to mean he counted at least thirty-two, but by Spanish accounts they were fewer: at most the duke mentions thirty. Wynter may have been wrong about the galleasses: the Spaniards never mentioned them in the whole of the day. But he was right in thinking this was their principal shipping. Nearly all the Spaniards present were the first-class galleons, including the whole of the squadrons of Portugal and Seville. And they had regained a diminished version of their battle formation, which was no small achievement. Wynter wrote: 'My fortune was to make choice to charge their starboard wing without shooting of any ordnance until we came within six score [paces] of them, and some of our ships did follow me. The said wing found themselves, as it did appear, to be so charged, as by making of haste to run into the body of their fleet, four of them did entangle themselves one aboard the other.'

It was instinctive for the English to attack the windward end of the Spanish formation, and without much doubt it was there that the Spanish disaster began; for this fight was fundamentally different from all the fights in the Channel. English shots were now making holes in the Spanish hulls.

The first in serious trouble was the Portuguese galleon *San Felipe*, cut off and surrounded by English ships (one account says seventeen of them) which pounded her with gunshot, broke her rudder and foremast, holed her hull and before long succeeded in killing two hundred men. The *San Mateo* went to her rescue, and was also shot to the verge of destruction. One moment the range was so short that an Englishman jumped aboard her, heaven knows why, and was instantly slaughtered. Both ships were rescued by Recalde, but not for long: they were surrounded again, with two others. The duke heard small-arms fire, which signified a desperate defence, but could not see what was happening through the gunsmoke, though he himself climbed up to the fighting top to look. The flagship *San Martin* already had so many shot-holes between wind and water that her pumps were overwhelmed, and her rigging was badly cut up; but he managed to put her about to help the others, and most of the English assailants turned on him.

There is no time scale in the Spanish story: it is early in his own account that the duke says all his ships were so much damaged that they could hardly offer any more resistance, and that most of them had not a shot in their lockers. And in all the events that seem to have happened late in the day, the story is of defence with muskets and arquebuses. It becomes a tale of desperate attempts by damaged ships to rescue others even worse, with the duke in the *San Martin* and Recalde in the *San Juan* always in the forefront of these attempted rescues. The *San Felipe* tried a defiant stand. She

was full of holes, her upper deck and both her pumps and most of
her rigging were destroyed, five of her guns were dismounted and
another had been spiked by a mutinous Italian gunner; and her
commander Don Francisco de Toledo, grappling-hooks at the
ready, shouted to the English to come to close quarters. In reply,
they summoned him to surrender. An Englishman, standing in the
maintop with his sword and buckler, shouted, 'You are good
soldiers. Surrender on fair terms.' 'But the only answer he got,'
says the Spanish account, 'was a gunshot which brought him
down in sight of everyone . . . The enemy then retired, while our
men shouted out to them that they were cowards, and with rude
words reproached them for their lack of spirit and dared them to
return to the fight, calling them Protestant hens' – just as modern
children might shout 'chicken'. Later, however, the *San Felipe* was
seen to be sinking. An urca which had turned up from somewhere
came alongside and took off her survivors. But her captain said the
urca was also sinking. Don Francisco said if he had to die, he
would rather do it on his own ship, and he and the captain jumped
back to the *San Felipe*. The urca remained afloat, but the *San Felipe*
drifted off towards the coast of Flanders, manned only by her
general and her captain, with their dead, and fifteen or twenty men
still living.

The *San Mateo* was also in a hopeless state, and the duke sent
pinnaces to take off her crew. But her commander refused to leave
her. The duke sent her a pilot and a diver: divers were used to stop
underwater leaks. But she drifted astern and disappeared that
night. Both these ships finished up aground somewhere east of
Nieuport, were captured and refloated by the Dutch and finally
sank near Flushing.

A third ship sank that evening, in full view of the rest. This
was the *Maria Juan* of Recalde's squadron. Her disaster was
sudden. When she signalled for help she had lost her mizzen mast
and rudder and her crew was seen to have taken to the spars and
rigging. The duke sent boats, but only one boatload of men was
saved before she went down with two hundred and seventy-five
men still aboard, many of whom no doubt were already dead or
helplessly wounded. By their own accounts, six hundred Spanish
were killed that day, and eight hundred badly wounded.

*

English accounts of the battle were meagre in the extreme, and gave no clue to the numberless incidents and changing fortunes of those nine hours of close combat. The *Relation* dismissed it in a single paragraph, mentioning a dozen captains but saying only that they 'gave them a sharp fight' or 'behaved themselves valiantly'. At one moment it seemed on the verge of something more descriptive, but the effort petered out in bathos: 'Mr Edward Fenton in the *Mary Rose* and a galleon encountered each other, the one standing to the eastward and the other to the westward, so close as they could conveniently one pass by another, wherein the captain and company did very well.' Howard in his *Brief Abstract*, the first official report of events, gave sixteen lines to the attack on the galleass but only six to the battle. That very night, he wrote breathlessly to Walsingham, 'Their force is wonderful great and strong; yet we pluck their feathers by little and little.'

Drake wrote, 'God hath given us so good a day in forcing the enemy so far to leeward as I hope in God the Prince of Parma and the Duke of Sidonia shall not shake hands this few days.' And soon after, when he reluctantly sent his prisoner Don Pedro de Valdes ashore as a present to the queen, 'With the grace of God, if we live, I doubt it not but ere it be long so to handle the matter with the Duke of Sidonia as he shall wish himself at St Mary Port among his orange trees.' He could never have dreamed that the duke had wished himself there from the very beginning.

Thomas Fenner also wrote to Walsingham, and Seymour to the queen, but added nothing new. It seems that none of them knew they had won an important victory, much less the final one, and by the time they knew it everyone knew the story by word of mouth, and no eye-witness bothered much about writing it down. They did not exaggerate the damage they had done, as people after battles so often do; on the contrary, they understated it. They knew they had put two galleons out of action, but that was all, and it was not very much against a fleet of over a hundred ships. They did not suspect another dozen galleons were in danger of sinking, much less that the armada had given up hope of ever winning. So in their eyes their most important achievement was as Drake had said: they had driven the armada to leeward of Parma's base, and unless the wind changed it would have a struggle to get back again.

What brought the battle to an end was a short sudden squall of wind and heavy rain. The English broke off the fight to shorten sail. It must have come as a relief to them: very soon, they would have had to break off for lack of shot. But for the Spaniards there was no relief. It became a battle to keep themselves afloat and save themselves from the sandbanks to leeward.

It was a rough night, and a night of horror in the armada, the first of many. The men of the galleons had bravely faced their death against a human enemy: they seem to have found it harder to keep up their courage against the inhuman menace of the shoals. No doubt they were shocked and exhausted by nine hours of battle that had gone so badly for them; shocked also by the ghastly aftermath, the wreckage and the blood, the wounded groaning or screaming for help, and practically nobody with the skill to help them, the corpses to be thrown overboard with what little ceremony the priests could mutter. The duke's flagship herself had forty dead and an untold number crippled by their wounds. Her captain said she was hit by a hundred and seven heavy shot, many below the waterline. One fifty-pound shot was said to have gone right through both sides of her. She was making a lot of water, but nobody had the strength to do much to repair her that night, not even to stop the shot-holes with the tow and sheets of lead they carried for plugging leaks. They only manned the pumps and prayed to live till dawn.

In the long run their position was as grim as it could have been. Perhaps after voyaging so far the armada was a little better to windward than it had been when it had left Lisbon. But still it could not make good a course that was better than 90° off the wind. Therefore, once it was caught on a lee shore it could not get off, even if the shore were straight; and the shore of the Netherlands is not straight, it curves gently for two hundred miles up to the Friesian Islands. If the wind stayed where it was, nearly north on the modern compass, they were perfectly certain to hit that shore somewhere; and almost all of it was held by their enemies. In peace, they would have anchored and waited for the wind to change, but after the fireship disaster nobody spoke again of anchoring.

But their fear was more immediate. They knew they were

already in among the notorious Flemish banks where Wagenhaer warned all shipping not to go, and the wind was taking them farther and farther in. Leadsmen were calling seven, six, five fathoms; and at that depth a galleon's keel was stirring the sandy bottom. All that night and next morning, every man in every ship waited from moment to moment for the grinding shock that would be the prelude of shipwreck and death by drowning.

When the dawn came the wind moderated a little, but remained in the same direction. The duke was still to windward of his fleet, still expecting to defend it against a new attack. Only seven ships had stayed with him all night: Recalde in the *San Juan*, de Leyva in the *Rata Encoronada*, the galleon *San Marcos* and another named *San Juan*, and now the three remaining galleasses. Daylight revealed the English a mile and a half away up wind, and the rest of the armada far to leeward. The English bore down on him, and he came to the wind to signify that he accepted fight. So did the other galleons, and the galleasses took station ahead. It was a gesture, if an empty one: 'Nearly all our trustworthy ships,' the duke wrote, 'were unfit to resist an attack, both because of the damage the gunfire had done and because of their lack of shot.' But the English drew off again. Some Spaniards thought God had seen fit to blind them; others that the English knew the armada was running aground, and were content to wait and see it happen. But no Englishman says so. Their feint was an equally empty gesture. They drew off because they had not enough ammunition to start again. Each side was unable to fight, but neither knew for certain that the other was.

About this moment, Oquendo came up in the *Santa Ana*, and there was a shouted conversation between him and the duke. Several witnesses, or rumour-mongers, report it, but the reports do not agree how insulting it was. Calderon, who admired the duke, says he shouted, 'Senor Oquendo, what shall we do? We are lost.' Translated, this sounds like panic, but the duke was not apt to panic. Calderon certainly did not hear the shouts, and the duke may have meant it as a reasonable request for Oquendo's opinion and advice. Oquendo, Calderon says, shouted back, 'Ask Diego Flores. I am going to fight, and die like a man. Send me some more shot.' 'Ask Diego Flores' was sarcasm; the soldiers, and many old seamen, blamed him, as the duke's nautical adviser, for every disaster. Other reports suggest Oquendo was very much more offensive to the duke, and that his sailors shouted to the duke's to throw Diego Flores overboard. The shouting-match undoubtedly happened – so many people say so – but one can only take it as a sign that tension and emotions were running high, as well they might have been; for it was in this dawn that the Spanish commanders had to admit to themselves that they were beaten. In such moments, many commanders in history have said they would prefer an honourable death to disgraceful defeat. If one may judge by his diary the duke was as anxious as anyone to fight. But how they could do it, with the English still, as ever, to windward, neither Oquendo nor anyone else explained.

Captain Alonzo Vanegas of the *San Martin* wrote a vivid description of what happened on the poop of the flagship that morning, with the enemy close to windward, the shoals to leeward and the leadsmen calling seven fathoms. 'The duke was advised that if he wanted to escape with his life he would have to surrender. It was impossible to avoid being driven aground. He replied that he trusted in God and His Blessed Mother to bring him to a port of safety: he would not question the faith of his ancestors. People appealed to his conscience not to allow so many souls to be lost by shipwreck, but he would not listen to such advice and told them to speak no more of the matter. He summoned the pilots, among whom were an Englishman and a Fleming, the rest being Spanish, Basque or Portuguese. He discussed with them whether it would be possible to reach Hamburg or the Norwegian coast, or to attack some other harbour to save part of the fleet. They all replied that they would make every effort, but were doubtful of success unless God helped them with a miracle, and shifted the wind so that they could get out to the open sea. The duke ordered three shots to be fired to summon our fleet to rejoin him. Soundings were taken again, and the flagship was found to be now in six fathoms. It could be seen that the wind was blowing her down on the Zeeland shoals, which stick out three leagues into the sea. But on the other flank was the enemy fleet. It seemed to everyone that we could neither save the ships nor re-form the fleet to renew the attack on the enemy. We were expecting to perish at any moment. The duke was not convinced by these opinions, which showed such lack of courage;

and Don Francisco de Bovadillo was of one mind with him in saying everyone must trust that God would deliver them.'

The duke's was the only ship that had a Flemish pilot: there had evidently been two, but he had sent the other to the *San Mateo*, which was already ashore. He might have been better off without him, or the Englishman; they are not reported to have done anything but prophesy doom, and say that nothing could be done, except by God, to save a single ship. Probably they did not know where they were, and did not want to admit it. After a day and a night of constantly changing courses and speeds in a strong tidal stream, their dead reckoning would have been useless. The only other way they could find their position was by bearings of landmarks, and by then they were almost certainly out of sight of the low-lying shore.

The rest of the ships had nothing better than Wagenhaer's charts, if they had anything half as good. His chart of this bit of coast shows roughly the position of the worst of the sandbanks, and his rutter gives their bearing and distance from landmarks on shore. The bearings are reasonably accurate, but nobody could judge the distances, except by eye. However, the depths he gives correspond remarkably well with the depths on a modern chart. Most of the banks have three fathoms over them at low water, and at high water the spring tide adds another three. The biggest ships could have scraped across them at half tide, and certainly did. But here and there, unmarked and far from land, there are small patches even shallower, down to two fathoms or one – like the outer banks off Dunkirk, of which Wagenhaer wrote: 'There are also two or three dangerous banks, north west and north west by west from Dunkirk, the first lieth from the shore two Dutch miles and the other three. The middest is called Polder-van-dijckt: But that which is called Ruting is most dangerous for that it lieth in the fair way and in the very entry of the Channel. Either of them hath two fathom at low water, which you must warily pass by.' Given that they started seven miles off Gravelines, the galleons and perhaps the whole armada must have passed very close to both of these, not warily but by the purest chance; except at the top of the tide the biggest ships would have struck on either. At one time – it may have been then – the flagship lagged astern of the rest because she was sailing with an anchor down. It was not that the duke intended to anchor, it was somebody's idea – and not a bad one – to hang an anchor a trifle deeper than the keel, hoping it would bring her up before she grounded.

What Wagenhaer does not show, and none of them knew, is that most of the banks are long and very narrow, and lie more or less parallel with the shore with deep channels between them. They were sailing parallel with the shore – it was the only thing they could do – so there was always room for luck, or as they would have said, for the guidance of God. When they were in a channel there was a chance they would stay in it; and when they passed over a bank and their leads showed only a few feet under the keels, there was a chance they would soon be across it in deep water on the other side. Even the *San Felipe* and the *San Mateo*, which drifted out of control at right angles across the whole series of banks, did not go aground until they brought up on the shore. The immediate peril was not entirely hopeless, as the Flemish pilot said; but heaven knows it was bad enough. To be a captain caught in a place like that, without any accurate chart, in an onshore wind and a heavy sea, is a nightmare as horrible as any a seaman can imagine. But perhaps it was even worse for the soldiers, who heard the leadsmen's cries but knew nothing else, except that their captain and all the other captains had lost their way.

Some time early that morning the whole of the fleet must have crossed the Wielingen, the entrance to the River Schelde, where there was a clear run downwind to comparative safety. Wagenhaer described the way in, but his directions were excessively complicated and they depended (like the entry to Spithead) on seeing landmarks and having the local knowledge to recognize them: 'When Wotkerke is one with Blankenberge and St Catalina shuts into Ostend, you are then before the mouth of the Wielingen: but when the steeple of Ostend is one with St Catherines then you run upon the shallow called Trix, which always turneth about in manner of a whirlpool by reason of the violent meeting of sundry currents and tides . . .' Nobody in the armada seems to have thought of trying it, except perhaps the remaining Flemish pilot, and he was not in the van where he might conceivably have led the fleet, but was bringing up the rear.

The duke and his officers confessed themselves and prepared

to die as Christians, and no doubt many more of that devout band did the same throughout the fleet. Others continued to pray for deliverance. The English waited up wind. 'It was the most awful day in the world,' one Spaniard wrote. 'Everyone was in utter despair, and stood waiting for death.'

The wind changed very suddenly: in the afternoon, it backed to south west. They stood out to the open sea, and for all their terror not a single ship had grounded. Afterwards there was talk of a miracle, but not at the time. All winds were God's, and they accepted without any hesitation that it was God's deliberate intention to blow them off the banks. They were grateful, yet if one may judge by the few surviving comments, they accepted it as their right, as if they still confided they were voyaging in His cause and were only surprised that He had put them in their perilous position. The duke wrote simply, as a single sentence in his narrative, 'We were saved by the wind, which shifted by God's mercy to the south west.' And Calderon: 'God succoured us in our distress, as He always does, and changed the wind in our favour.' No formal thanksgiving is recorded.

Nobody who wrote about the battle at the time offered any answer to the questions which remain a puzzle now. Why were the effects of the English gunnery so suddenly and dramatically different? And why did the English emerge with no serious damage at all? For as Hawkyns wrote, 'Our ships, God be thanked, have received little hurt.' The contrast is almost unbelievable: the Spanish admitting six hundred killed and eight hundred wounded in this battle alone, and the English not a hundred in the whole campaign; all the leading Spanish galleons shot through and through and desperately striving to stop their leaks, and not one English ship obliged to put in to harbour for repairs.

It is clear, of course, that the English had learned their lesson at last and closed to very short range, even jumping distance. One has to believe Sir William Wynter when he wrote to Walsingham, 'I deliver it unto Your Honour upon the credit of a poor gentleman, that out of my ship there was shot five hundred of demi-cannon, culverin and demi-culverin; and when I was furthest off in discharging any of the pieces, I was not out of shot

of their harquebus, and most times within speech one of another.'
Yet off Portland, and again off the Isle of Wight, they had already
claimed to be within half-musket shot, or fifty paces; and the
alleged five hundred shot at the Spanish flagship then had done no
more than break a stay and a flagstaff.

The only possible answer would seem to be that there was a
critical range at which an English shot would penetrate the hull of
a galleon. It was very short indeed, a matter of yards; and for the
first time, after all their experiments, they had dared to come inside
it. This may explain why the English shooting suddenly became
effective: but it does not explain why the Spanish shooting did not.
It was not a question of aim; the Spanish gunnery may have been
bad, but at that sort of range not many shots could have missed.
Nor could it have been entirely a question of rate of fire. The
English could admittedly load and fire more quickly than the
Spaniards, and that would have meant the Spaniards would do less
damage. But the fact was that they did practically none.

It is true that Ubaldino says, in his second and longer
narrative, that Drake's ship was 'pierced through by several shot
of all sizes which were flying everywhere between the two fleets,
seeming as thick as arquebuses usually are'. But clearly these went
through the upper works which, unlike the hulls, were lightly
built, easily damaged and easily repaired. 'His cabin,' he adds, 'was
twice pierced by shot and there was an occasion on which two
gentlemen, who towards evening had retired to rest a little after
the battle, and one of them lying upon the bed, when it was broken
to pieces under him by a saker ball, without his taking the least
hurt. And shortly afterwards the Earl of Northumberland, who
had come to fight as a volunteer, and Sir Charles Blount were
resting on the same bed in the same place when it was again hit by a
ball of demi-culverin which passed through the cabin from one
side to the other without doing any harm other than scrape the
foot, taking off the toes of one who was there with them.'

It is an interesting picture, of the two gentlemen scrambling
out of the shambles of their bed and the unfortunate unnamed
man, probably a mere servant, hopping about and holding his
toes; and the story was almost certainly told to Ubaldino by Drake.
But the cabin would have been in the aftercastle, which any
random shot could penetrate.

There is more reliable evidence that no serious damage was done. Within a few weeks of the battle, all the queen's ships were surveyed under the supervision of Peter Pett and Matthew Baker, the two leading shipwrights of the age. It was a very thorough survey which reported every bit of rotten wood and every rope part-worn. The reports were signed by Pett and Baker and by the boatswain of each ship, most of whom could not write their name but had to make their mark. A few ships had masts that were damaged in battle, and most of them had lost their boats or had them split; but otherwise the scars of battle were negligible. In particular, not a single ship reported a shot-hole in her hull. The English shot had been going through and the Spanish shot had not.

There are many places in this history where one has to make a guess, as well-informed as possible; and at this point the most plausible guess lies in the supply of ammunition. By the end of the battle, both sides had shot off all they had, or very nearly all. In the early stages, the Spaniards were certainly using artillery, and in the later stages they were not. But a ship does not suddenly run out of shot; it does not blaze away until the very last is gone. There must be a period when the shortage is growing acute and the gunners are warned not to waste a shot until they have a perfect target. The Spaniards may have reached this stage very early in the battle, or even before it began. They may have fought all day with this threat hanging over them: that unless the English ran out before they did, they would be utterly destroyed.

Yet in each ship the moment when they ceased to fire may have come suddenly and unexpectedly, because shots which penetrated the gundecks were appallingly destructive of life and morale: not so much the shots themselves as the splinters of wood that flew in all directions. Some deserters who came ashore in Zeeland, in a boat with their shirts as sails, had a graphic phrase: 'They did see, through the portholes, an Italian ship all full of blood, which yet maintained the fight.' Nobody in the armada had been warned to expect a scene of carnage on the gundecks: it was not what they had been trained for. Indeed, such a thing had never happened before to any fleet. It may be that the gun crews, astonished at such an awful experience, stumbling over their dead and horrified by their wounded, were disorganized and demoralized as soon as the

English shot began to come through, and stopped firing before their own shot was exhausted.

Yet even this does not explain why there was not a single shot-hole in a single English hull. A final possible explanation has been offered within the last few years by skin divers working on the armada's wrecks. They have brought up guns and gunshot of every size, for it was only the fighting galleons, of course, that had run out of shot. These confirm the historical fact that Spain and Portugal were very backward in foundry work in the sixteenth century. The king's guns were all cast in Italy, the Netherlands or England. (The queen had forbidden the export of guns, but in 1587 illegal merchants smuggled a large number out to Naples.) Most of the iron shot, however, was cast in Spain and Portugal; almost half of it, indeed, had been cast in the few weeks after the duke arrived to take command in Lisbon. Analysis shows it was very badly made. The iron itself was full of impurities and had an excess of carbon and ferric oxide. Also, every shot had concentric rings which showed it had been quenched while it was still red-hot. Both these faults would have made it very brittle: much more so than the English shot, which was cast with experienced care in the Sussex forests.

Many armada commanders pointed out with pride that all their powder was the fine-grained sort used for muskets. That sort produced a quicker and higher pressure in the gun than the coarser serpentine powder the English used: in other words, a sharper and harder blow on the shot and the gun. It may well be that most of the Spanish shot broke into small bits, either at the shock of firing or the shock of impact on the enemy hull. That would have been invisible to the gunners.

The diving revealed other things too. Several of the guns that have been retrieved had burst. Every gun, of course, was proof-tested when it was made, but that was normally done with coarse-grained powder in them. It may have been a mistake to use the stronger fine-grained powder. A gun that burst on a gun-deck would have been devastating, not only to the gun-crews but to the ship itself, tending to blow out the caulking and start the planks, or lift the deck above with its concussion. Also, some guns were mounted not on naval carriages with four small wheels, but on army carriages with two enormous wheels. These must have been very difficult and dangerous to handle on board a ship at sea, unless they were immovably lashed to the ship's structure; and if they were, their recoil would again have probably strained the hull and made it leaky.

No report says the Spaniards tested their guns after they were installed in the ships. No doubt the galleons, which had always had guns, had often fired them. But the guns in the merchant ships were fitted in Lisbon. There might possibly have been a range in the river where they could fire them, but nobody says so; and if they had done it at sea – no easy exercise in a fleet of that size – the duke would surely have told the king in one of his letters. Yet in some of these ships, much weaker in construction than the galleons, they had put the biggest of all naval guns, the fifty-pounder cannon. There is plenty of evidence that after the battle many of the merchant ships were strained and leaking, and not only through the shot-holes the English made. It seems likely the Spaniards damaged their own ships by firing guns that burst, or guns that were too big, or guns on unsuitable mountings, in ships that were not built to carry them.

All this is more or less hypothetical, but it gives some pointers to the reasons why the English won, although the Spaniards fought with unimpeachable courage. First perhaps was the nimbleness of the English ships, the fact that the ships were commanded by sailors, not soldiers, and their skill in handling them. Next, the chance of the onshore wind. But the final and decisive fact was that English shot, at the very shortest range, could penetrate a hull and Spanish shot could not; and the probable cause of that, unknown to the Spaniards, was that their shot was badly cast and brittle, and some of their guns too big for the strength of their ships.

14

'Stormy Seas Unknown To Us'

On 7th August, the day of the fireships, the king in the Escorial was writing yet another letter to the duke, full of admonition and advice. He wished to impress on him, he said, the importance of entering the Thames and making himself safe in it. This would compel the enemy to maintain two armies, one on each side of the river; if they did, their forces would be divided, and if they did not the road to London would be open on the unprotected side. 'It will have the effect, moreover,' he added, 'of preventing disorder, and will cause desirable competition among the soldiers . . . As you will understand how anxious I am until I heard from you, pray send me almost hourly intelligence of events.'

By then, however, it was a week since the duke had been able to write to the king, and it was a fortnight before he was able to write again. The king's letter, of course, never reached him; nor did another the king wrote on the 18th, to congratulate him on a great victory reported in the Channel. But by then the first of a stream of horsemen were on the long road to Madrid bearing news, some of which was true but most of which was false.

The king's son, the Prince of Ascoli, who had been the first to bring the news of the battle ashore to Parma, wrote a letter three days after he landed. The importance of this young man, at least in his own eyes, may be judged from the fact that he took thirty-nine servants with him in the armada, more than anyone else except the duke. Now he had the unenviable job of explaining to his father why he had left the fleet. The letter is almost illegible and seems almost tearful, as if he was sure his father would accuse him of desertion. But his story seems pathetically incompetent and true. He had been one of the trusted men the duke had sent round the armada in boats on Sunday evening to warn every ship to be ready for fireships. Before he had finished his round, the fireships came and the flagship disappeared in the darkness. At dawn he found he was amongst the English fleet, which was charging down on his own. He met a larger Spanish boat that had been on the same mission, and he transferred to that, but he was chased by the English boats that had been attacking the galleass. He could not make headway against the ebbing tide, and witnessed the battle from astern of both the fleets. That night when the wind increased he had to run before it, lost and alone except for his sailors, who would not do anything he ordered. In the next dawn he sighted Calais again, but was too far to leeward to make it, and Dunkirk was the first port he came to. He had begged Parma, he said, to let him go out again to rejoin his ship, but Parma refused – and rightly, one may think, because nobody knew by then where the armada had gone. 'I am very unhappy to miss whatever may happen to the armada,' the poor young prince concluded, 'but as God has ordained otherwise, it cannot be helped, and my only wish is to be somewhere I can serve Your Majesty and do my duty in a manner worthy of my birth.'

Don Jorge Manrique also sent his sober report of what had happened so far, and Parma sent the most remarkable of all his letters. It was very long indeed. The first third of it repeated that he had been ready, and would have gone out as soon as the weather was perfect and the enemy had disappeared, and it described his meeting with Don Jorge. Then, and only then, it reported the fireships, the battle, the loss of the galleass and the *San Felipe*, and the disappearance of the armada to the north.

'What happened after that is unknown, except that the English continued to follow them with very fast vessels, manned by good and experienced sailors.' The final third was a mass of pious expressions: 'No one can be more grieved than I am. I will only say therefore that this must come from the hand of the Lord, who knows well what He does, and can redress it all, rewarding Your Majesty with many victories and the full fruition of your desires, in His own good time. We should therefore give him thanks for all things. Above all it is of the utmost importance that Your Majesty should be careful of your health.' It ended with a repetition that everything had been ready, 'if only the weather had been fair and the sea clear of enemies'; and last of all, an urgent request for money. Parma was still taking every possible care to explain that what had happened was no fault of his.

But these letters to the king were sent first to Mendoza, the ambassador in Paris, and forwarded by him to the Escorial. They took four or five days from Dunkirk to Paris and another nine from Paris to Madrid: and by the time Mendoza received the first of them he had already sent reports from other sources to the king. Mendoza had always been credulous: during that month of August he excelled himself in wishful thinking. Reports came in from fishermen, from agents and double agents, from diplomats, from unknown men who said they had come from England, from an Irish boy of very suspicious origins; and if they were favourable Mendoza believed them all, whether they were second-hand or third-hand or even more remote in origin.

His first report came by way of Rouen from his spies in Dieppe and Le Havre, who had spoken to French fishermen who said they had witnessed a battle on 2nd August in which the armada had gained the wind and sunk fifteen of the enemy's ships, including the flagship. Mendoza reported this victory as if there was no possible doubt about it, and it was on this that the king sent his letter of congratulation to the duke.

Two days later another report came from Calais, also by way of Rouen. It told a story that was mainly true; Mendoza's men must have heard it from men in the armada who came ashore while they were anchored there. But it added in a postscript that in the fight off Gravelines the Spaniards had captured Drake with many ships, sunk others and disabled fifteen which had taken refuge in Harwich.

Next came Parma's letter announcing that the armada was off Calais and Don Jorge Manrique's, closely followed by a report from the French ambassador in London that the English had lost seven ships off the Isle of Wight, among them three of the biggest the queen possessed. 'Don Jorge says nothing of this,' the king scribbled in the margin. 'Perhaps he did not see them.' Another report from Rouen said a man had just arrived from London, who said the English had lost heavily and were very sad because Drake had been wounded in the legs by a cannon ball.

About 16th August Mendoza rode to Chartres, where the King of France had his court, to request him to order the

Governor of Calais to hand over the stranded galleass to Parma. While he was away there was a pause in the flood of letters. When he came back he said he had suffered a lot on the journey; bad horses, old age and hot sun had combined to give him the worst time he had ever had in his life.

On the strength of the encouraging news, Count de Olivares in Rome tried again to extract the million ducats the pope had promised when Spanish soldiers had landed in England. He and a cardinal addressed the pope 'in terms that would have moved any other heart, but the pope only shrugged his shoulders, for when it comes to getting money out of him it is like squeezing his life-blood, and our efforts failed'. And after another attempt a fortnight later: 'When the subject [of money] is broached to him the only effect is that the moment my back is turned he babbles the most ridiculous nonsense, things that would not be said by a two-year-old. He has no sort of charity, kindliness or consideration, and everyone attributes his behaviour to the repulsion and chagrin he feels as the hour approaches for him to drag this money from his heart.'

Of course, he never paid the million ducats. It is undeniably tragic to think of the king rejoicing in victory weeks after his armada had been beaten and his project had been abandoned. But towards the end of the month he was growing suspicious of Mendoza's euphoric reports, mainly because Don Jorge Manrique's careful account did not mention any of the crushing victories. On the next that Mendoza sent him he wrote in the margin, 'I fear this will turn out like the first news he sent.'

Yet even after the armada had disappeared from the coast of Flanders, the stories of victory kept coming in, and Mendoza kept sending them on to the king. They grew in fantasy and scope. Mendoza had two men in Rouen, and they both wrote to him at the end of the month. 'I have not sent news of the armada,' one of them said, 'as the rumours have been so various and I like to send trustworthy intelligence. Statements, however, are now current in many quarters, Calais, Dieppe, Holland etc., and it is considered certain that the armada has fought the English and dealt them a mortal blow, sending many of their ships to the bottom and capturing more.'

And the other: 'I am positively assured that the English have lost over forty ships in an encounter which they could not avoid, at Newcastle in Scotland. They could not do as they had always done before, run for refuge into an English port. Our armada therefore attacked them so stoutly that we sank twenty of their ships and captured twenty-six in perfectly good condition. The rest of the English fleet, seeing only ruin before them, escaped with great damage, and their ships are now all in bits and without crews.'

Both these men said the armada was safe in Scotland, one in Newcastle (which of course is in England) and the other 'in a port or river which I believe is called Tirfle, or something that sounds like that'. But on the same day Mendoza's man in Calais told him, 'The armada is at a very fertile Norwegian island, where they will find an abundance of victuals without resistance.'

The armada had vanished into waters where even Mendoza's network of spies could not pretend they had any sources of knowledge, and on 1st September his claims of victories came to an end. By then, a pinnace was well on its way down the west coast of Ireland, bringing the king the diary the duke had written, and a letter from him which told the awful truth.

The day after the change of wind both commanders-in-chief had held councils of war. The duke's was attended by Recalde, de Leyva, several pilots and captains and the chief purser Calderon, besides Diego Flores and Bovadillo, who were already with him in the flagship. Oquendo does not seem to have been present. Perhaps he was still too angry. The meeting took the usual form. The duke mentioned the damage the armada had suffered, the lack of shot (all the principal ships had asked him for more), and the fact that Parma had not sent any word about coming out; and he asked the council's opinion whether they should go back to the Channel or make for home by way of the North Sea. There was only one feasible answer, because the wind, God's wind, had settled in the south west and was blowing strongly. Unless it changed to north east and stayed there, which in the normal course of nature was most unlikely, they could not possibly go back the way they had come. So they could afford the gesture of saying they were willing. They resolved unanimously to put back if the weather allowed it, and if not to 'obey the wind' and set the northerly course for Spain. The next time he could write to the king, the duke expressed his own opinion: 'The armada was so completely crippled and scattered that it seemed my first duty to Your Majesty was to save it, even at the risk of a very long voyage in high latitudes.' Calderon, in his report, said two captains asked him what the route would be by the northern passage to Spain. It seems surprising that sea-captains would ask a purser a question like that; but he was an educated man, and may have known better than they did. He told them it would be very laborious, round England, Scotland, and Ireland, seven hundred and fifty leagues through stormy seas unknown to them. Seven hundred and fifty Spanish leagues were 2625 nautical miles. He was not far wrong.

That same day another tragedy happened astern of the armada. The Spaniards were not aware of it, and it was only reported by Howard: 'One of the enemy's great ships was espied to be in great distress by the captain of Her Majesty's ship called the *Hope*; who being in speech of yielding unto the said captain, before they could agree on certain conditions, sank presently before their eyes.' It was a week before anyone in the armada reported another ship was missing.

The English council was a happier affair than the Spaniards', though none of its members believed the battles were over. Howard assembled more of his captains than usual, but Sir William Wynter was not there because he had been hurt by the recoil of a gun. Nor was Frobisher for reasons unexplained, but perhaps because he was not on speaking terms with Drake. The meeting was rather marred by Lord Henry Seymour, who was angry because Howard told him to stay behind and guard the Straits against Parma while the rest of the fleet followed the armada. Seymour wrote to the queen that he obeyed much against his will, and more forcefully to Walsingham: 'I find my Lord jealous and loth to have me take part of the honour of the rest that is to win.' Howard himself was annoyed by a catechism that had come from the queen's council. It demanded returns of the number and tonnage of the ships he had, the numbers of soldiers and mariners, the victuals and powder and shot, where the powder and shot had come from, and the losses of ships and men in both fleets in all the battles since Plymouth. Most irritating of all, it enquired why none of the Spanish ships had been boarded. The document is dated 'the last of July'. But Howard had certainly read it before the meeting. Coming at that particular moment, it was a classic of bureaucracy, and it showed the queen in council had still not understood the elements of her admirals' tactical plans. Howard refused to answer, 'which, by reason of the uncertainty of the service, no man can do'. He merely requested more food, more powder and shot, without delay, because 'we know not whither we may be driven to follow the Spanish fleet'. However, his council put a resolution in writing, and all of them signed it: '1st August, 1588. We whose names are hereunder written have determined and agreed in council to follow and pursue the Spanish fleet until we have cleared our own coast and brought the Frith [the Firth of Forth] west of us; and then to return back again, as well to re-victual our ships, which stand in extreme scarcity, as also to guard and defend our own coast at home; with further protestation that, if our wants of victuals and munition were supplied, we would pursue them to the furthest that they durst have gone. C. Howard. T. Howard. Fra. Drake. John Hawkyns. Thomas Fenner. George Coumbreland. Edmonde Sheffeylde. Edw. Hoby.'

On Wednesday the 10th, the armada was under full sail with a fresh south westerly wind and a heavy sea. The duke saw the English overhauling his rearguard, and that the rearguard under Recalde was short of ships; so he struck his topsails to wait for them, and fired a signal of three guns for the rest of the armada also to shorten sail. Before the English caught up, the rearguard had been re-formed with the flagship, the galleasses and a dozen other galleons; and the English also shortened sail and fell astern again.

This rearguard sparring led to a gruesome event in the armada which has never been fully explained. Two ships, the galleon *San Pedro* and the urca *Santa Barbara*, were seen to have disregarded the signal to shorten sail. They were several miles ahead of the fleet. Frigates were sent to catch them up and bring their captains back to the flagship, where both of them were told they had been condemned to be hanged.

Much the longest account of what happened was written by the captain of the *San Pedro*, whose name was Francisco de Cuellar. He protested furiously. After ten days without sleep, he said, he had gone to bed, and one of his officers, without his permission, had sailed ahead so that he could heave to for repairs, especially to stop some hidden shot-holes which were still letting in a lot of water. Cuellar swore he had done his duty all through the fighting: his accusers could ask his crew, and if one of his three hundred and fifty men said he had done anything wrong, they could hack him to pieces. And there is no reason to doubt he had done well; the *San Pedro* was one of the squadron of Seville, which had supported the duke throughout. However, to leave station and sail ahead was a technical offence, forbidden in the standing orders the duke had issued in Lisbon, and in the threat of hanging he had made on the way up-Channel. Most of the ships must have done it at one time or another, but both captains were sent to the ship of the Judge Advocate General, who was the man to carry out the sentence.

The Judge Advocate, Martin de Aranda, listened to Cuellar's impassioned defence, and wrote to the duke to say he would not carry out the sentence on him unless he had a written order signed by the duke himself. In reply the duke annulled the sentence. But no such plea was made for the other captain, Don Cristobal de Avila. Cuellar says his urca was far ahead of the *San Pedro*, and perhaps there were other accusations against him. That same day he was hanged from the yardarm of a frigate, and the hanging body was paraded round the fleet.

The duke has been held responsible for this barbarity, and of course he was, in so far as a commander-in-chief is responsible for everything that happens in his fleet. But in the letter Cuellar wrote afterwards, he said emphatically that the duke had nothing to do with it. It was Bovadillo, the senior army general, who made the accusations and sentenced both men to death. The duke heard nothing about it until he received the Judge Advocate's letter, because he had withdrawn to his cabin in a mood of melancholy and did not wish anyone to speak to him. Cuellar said he was melancholy because he had just heard of the fate of the *San Mateo* and *San Felipe*. But he had plenty of reasons to feel like that, and also to be utterly exhausted; and it may be that like Cuellar himself he had fallen asleep at last. At any rate, Cuellar insists he did not know what Bovadillo was doing in his name.

These two accusations were probably only a part of something much wider. Calderon, who was keeping well out of it all in his own ship, wrote in his diary the story that was going round the fleet: 'The duke on this day ordered Don Cristobal de Avila to be hanged, and condemned to the galleys other ships' captains, as well as reducing some army officers. It is said this was because on the day of the battle they allowed themselves to drift out of the fight.'

It stands to reason that the armada was seething with recrimination. It had been ingloriously beaten in battle, and on this day for the first time it was admittedly and ignominiously running away. Everyone was bitterly disappointed and ashamed. In particular, the army generals, without any doubt, were furious with the sea-captains, an inferior race at best, who in their eyes had caused the disaster because they had failed to put their ships alongside a single enemy, and so had never given the army a chance to fight. The duke, who was neither an army nor a naval man, had the sense to see that this was the fault of the ships, not of the captains or sailors. But the army was out for revenge. The centre of the fury between the army and the seamen would have been the two advisers, Bovadillo and Diego Flores, and Diego Flores was already in disgrace.

There are two possibilities. Perhaps in the face of a ferocious quarrel between the advisers the duke's authority had broken down at last, and he had felt unable to face it and shut himself in his cabin to escape it. Or perhaps he had really fallen into an exhausted sleep, after saying nobody was to disturb him, and Bovadillo had taken the opportunity to make the charges and demand the sentences in his name. The latter is more likely, because when the duke emerged later in the day and received the Judge Advocate's letter, he at least had the strength of mind to countermand Cuellar's death sentence – though Cuellar was deprived of his command and remained in the Judge Advocate's ship. Probably by then Don Cristobal was dead, for the execution was carried out at once, without any formal trial.

The duke may have been too mild a man, and too inexperienced, to make a good commander-in-chief: he said so himself. But he was remarkably consistent. He had done his best to carry out the hateful duty the king had put on him; but the king had not ordered him to judge his fellow-officers, and he never did so. The most notable thing about his diary and letters is that they do not contain a word of criticism of anyone. On this occasion, he carefully avoided putting his own opinion in writing. Ten days later, as soon as he had a chance, he sent a pinnace ahead which carried his diary to the king, by hand of a man called Don Baltazar de Zuniga. It was a frank and comprehensive document. But after describing the rearguard action that day he had written a significant sentence: 'What was done in these circumstances in our armada will be related by Don Baltazar.' It was pretty clear he was ashamed of the whole affair. But it was up to the king to judge, if he wished, when the armada came back to Spain. By then, however, the disaster was immeasurably worse, and dissension had been forgotten.

A vendetta against sea-captains was a bad beginning for the voyage home. The voyage was a tremendous undertaking. Those seas were not only unknown to the Spaniards – scarcely anyone knew them, except deep-sea fishermen and the native Irish in their leather boats. Occasionally German ships came up the Irish Channel and round the north of Scotland on their way from Lisbon to the Baltic ports, but very seldom round the west and north of Ireland. More seldom still had anyone tried it from east to west, against the prevailing wind; and no large fleet had ever been that way, not even in Viking times. Wagenhaer's charts extended up the east coast of Scotland, growing vaguer the farther north they went; but no sea-chart existed of the north and west of Ireland except the small-scale general chart in Wagenhaer's atlas, which extended from the Canaries to the Baltic. Some armada ships may have had the map of Ireland from the atlas of Abraham Ortelius of Antwerp, who had been appointed some years before as geographer to the King of Spain; but that was only a land map, and its outline of the coast had hardly any resemblance to reality. The only man of authority in the armada who is known to have been in Ireland was Recalde, and he had only seen the south west tip of it.

So the duke, with all the advisers he could muster, resolved to keep away from Ireland, and after passing the northern islands of Scotland to make the whole voyage out of sight of land. It was a job for ocean navigation, not the coastal pilotage the armada had used so far, and most of the pilots were not much good at that. Calderon says he took a French friend of his who was a pilot to the flagship. He does not say what his qualifications were, but the duke must have thought he was better than the others: he offered him two thousand ducats if he could conduct the armada home to Spain.

It may have been that Frenchman who helped him to draft the sailing orders he issued while the armada was progressing up the North Sea. Copies of the orders were issued to all the ships, and afterwards the English found one of them in Ireland. The orders were very brief: 'The first course to be held is north north east, until you reach $61\frac{1}{2}°$. After that, you will take great care not to be driven on the coast of Ireland, for fear of the harm that may come to you there. Leaving the islands and rounding the cape in $61\frac{1}{2}°$ [this referred to the northern point of Shetland] you will run west south west until you reach $58°$; then south west to the height of $53°$; and then south south west, heading for Cape Finisterre, and so find your way to Corunna or Ferol, or any other port on the coast of Galicia.'

The last of these courses was a mistake, probably in the original translation into English – for only an English copy has been found. It should be south east.

Otherwise, the orders were standard practice for a voyage like that, in the centuries when latitude could be observed and longitude could not. If a ship sailed due west, her pilot would have only dead reckoning to tell him how much westing she had made. But if she could hold a steady diagonal course, he could reckon how many degrees of longitude she had made for each degree of latitude. Wagenhaer's atlas had tables for working it out. The route the duke gave was quite specific, and took the armada clear of everything.

But his worst worry was not navigation, it was food and water. They thought they had left Corunna with eighty or ninety days' supply. Since then, they had been at sea for twenty-one days, and from such enquiries as the duke could make the Corunna estimate looked far too optimistic. At the best guess the voyage ahead might take a month, and to make the food and drink last so long he had to put everyone, of every rank, on a starvation ration right away: half a pound of biscuit, a pint of water and half a pint of wine a day. To save water, which was the worst worry of all, they threw overboard the horses and mules they had brought for the land artillery. One wonders why they did not eat them. A merchant ship that crossed the armada's track reported the sea full of animals, still swimming.

The duke himself, with his overbearing conscience, probably stuck strictly to the diet he had ordered for everyone else. All the way, between worry and seasickness, he had not been able to eat much more. But Calderon came on board again, this time with a revelation. Pursers through the centuries have always been known as shrewd men of business, if not rogues; and Calderon had hidden in his own ship, the urca *San Sebastian*, a large supply of what he called hospital delicacies, which he had meant to sell. Among them were fifty-pound sacks of rice. He offered a sack to the duke, for the sick and wounded in the flagship, 'which present,' he said, 'was greatly esteemed. The duke begged him to do the same for all the ships that had been in action.' So Calderon continued to hand out his fifty-pound sacks and other unspecified luxuries: and presumably not only to the sick, but to anyone who would pay a purser's ransom.

The English followed the armada closely for four days, until it was in 55°, which is the latitude of Newcastle. By then, they estimated it was a hundred miles off the coast, and it showed no signs of making for Scotland, which everyone had expected. So they left it there, intending to go to Scotland themselves, to enter the Firth of Forth for water and whatever food they could get, and to put the Earl of Cumberland ashore to tell the King of Scots what was happening and persuade him to join the defence if the armada tried to land. They left two pinnaces to shadow the armada up to the Orkney and Shetland Islands, or if they altered course by a change of wind, to come back with a warning. When they were half-way to land, the wind did change – to the north west, which might have brought the armada back to the south.

Thomas Fenner was the best letter-writer of Howard's council: he could produce the most beautiful Elizabethan English, even at sea in a storm, and he sent a letter to Walsingham about the plans and speculations of the English fleet: 'Counsel therefore taken,' he wrote of that change of wind, 'it was thought meet to take the benefit thereof for our reliefs of powder, shot and victual, and so to bear with all possible speed to the North Foreland [i.e.

the southern shore of the Thames]; so that if the enemy should
return, we might be beforehand furnished of some of our wants,
the readier thereby to offend them.

'I will deliver Your Honour mine opinion, wherein I beseech
your pardon if it fall out otherwise. I verily believe [that only]
great extremity shall force them to behold England in sight again.
By all that I can gather, they are weakened of eight of their best
sorts of shipping, which contained many men; as also many wasted
in sickness and slaughter. Their masts and sails much spoiled; their
pinnaces and boats, many cast off and wasted; wherein they shall
find great wants when they come to land and water, which they
must do shortly or die; and where or how, my knowledge cannot
imagine . . . The wind as it is at north west, they have no place to
go withal, but for the Scaw in Denmark, which were an hard
adventure as the season of the year approacheth. If the wind by
chance suffer them, I verily believe they will pass about Scotland
and Ireland to draw themselves home; wherein, the season of the
year considered, with the long course they have to run and their
sundry distresses, and – of necessity – the spending of time by
watering, winter will so come on as it will be to their great ruin.'

Fenner wrote this perceptive letter, which diagnosed exactly
the armada's troubles (even its need for water) during his voyage
south, and it had a postscript: within two hours after it was
written, the wind changed again and a very great storm arose from
the south west. It blew for two days. The English were 'forced to
ride out in the sea the extremity thereof . . . Mine opinion is they
are by this time so distressed, being so far thrust off, as many of
them will never see Spain again; which is only the work of God, to
chastise their malicious practices.'

In fact, the Spanish accounts of that storm were much less
lurid than they had been in the Bay of Biscay. Perhaps they were
getting accustomed to heavy weather, and more able to deal with
it; and of course they were running before it, not trying to beat
against it. Calderon recorded squalls, rain and fog with rough seas.
Ships could not be distinguished from each other, he said, and for
four days the fleet was scattered in separate groups. A man in the
galleass *Zuniga* reported sighting the coast of Norway to
starboard, and two days later the coast of Scotland to port. If they
had ever thought of landing in either, nobody mentioned it.

A priest on board the flagship provided a glimpse of the duke on one of those stormy nights, and also a glimpse of human charity, which is rare in the story. The duke was standing alone on the poop, where he had stood most of the way since Plymouth, under the light of the stern lanterns he carried as commander-in-chief, staring out at the dark and wild sea. It is tempting to wonder what he was thinking: perhaps of failure, or perhaps of home. It was very cold, and he was wearing only a short cloak over his ordinary clothes. He had started the voyage with two warm cloaks, but he had given one to the priest, who had joined the ship ill-provided; and now he had spread the other over a boy who was lying wounded in his cabin.

They did not go right up to 61° north, the latitude to clear the north of Shetland. On the 19th the weather moderated, and for a while the wind shifted to the north east. The change came at just the right moment. Shetland had been sighted ahead, and down wind was the Fair Isle channel, between the Shetland and Orkney Islands. They sailed successfully through. Ten days from the sands of Dunkirk to the Fair Isle channel: it is six hundred miles, say seven hundred if they really sighted Norway. With a wind astern which was never less than a brisk breeze and some of the time was a gale, they were still only making two and a half to three knots. None of them had been careened all summer, and the barnacles and weeds were growing thick.

Mendoza reported the armada's passing of Fair Isle. It was something of a triumph of espionage to get any news at all from the Orkney Islands to Paris, except that it did not reach him before the first of the armada had reached Spain. Scottish fishermen, returning to Edinburgh, told the story to a man who brought it overland through England. The Spaniards, they said, had taken all the dried fish the fishermen had, and paid a good price for it. They had also taken some pilots and ships' masters. English boats which were fishing there had been captured and their crews put in irons. The weather was so fine (this was Mendoza's optimism again) that the armada would soon be home.

It did stay fine for another couple of days. In those days, the duke finished his diary with the words, 'We have now set our course with a north east wind for Spain.' It was then he sent it, with a letter, by the hand of Don Baltazar de Zuniga to the king.

The letter expressed the same kind of holy condolence other people had offered: 'I have instructed Don Baltazar to submit to Your Majesty other cases in which our Lord has seen fit to dispose matters differently from that which had been expected; and as this enterprise had been so fervently commended to Him, the result will doubtless be of the greatest advantage to His service, and that of Your Majesty. I hope during Your Majesty's time yet to see your holy plans completely successful, to the greater glory of Almighty God.'

But he did nothing to minimize the tragedy. There were three thousand sick on board – and sick of course meant incapacitated – besides the wounded, who were also numerous. Everything was in such a state that a great deal of help would be needed as soon as the fleet reached Corunna. He had written to the Archbishop of Santiago and the bishops in Galicia, asking them to be ready to serve the sick. In the letters, as usual, there is not a word of criticism of anyone: neither of Parma, nor of his own advisers, nor of the sea-captains, nor their crews. Nor is there any of the self-criticism he had expressed so often at the beginning. It reads as if disaster had strengthened him, as if he knew at last that the task had been impossible, that he had done his best and no one could have succeeded; and that the further intervention of God had not been merited.

Don Baltazar's pinnace stood off with these letters, to the king and the bishops, on 21st August. On that same day, the galleass *Zuniga* reported sighting the northern point of Ireland. That only showed how fatally vague their sense of geography could be. The northern point of Ireland is four hundred and fifty miles from Fair Isle, which they had passed two days before, and to reach it a ship would have to alter course round the Hebrides. What they saw, if anything, would have been Cape Wrath in Scotland, or one of the outlying skerries.

It was the day after that when the wind went round and headed them from the south. The armada perforce had to stand away to the north west, at right angles to the course the duke had ordered; and it was then and there, in the wild seas somewhere off Cape Wrath, that it began to break up.

15

Wrecks

n immense amount of work has been done to solve the many problems of the armada's wrecks. There are plenty of contemporary documents, but they present insoluble puzzles: people who reported wrecks, whether they were English, Irish or Scottish, seldom knew the names of the ships they had seen, and if they heard them from the mouths of Spanish sailors they usually got them wrong – apart from the fact that so many Spanish ships had similar or identical names. Some ships foundered in the open sea, unseen by anyone, and some struck coasts that were uninhabited. The research has gained impetus in the last decade or so from new techniques of diving and underwater archaeology, and it will certainly continue in the future. More is being discovered all the time.

But some wrecks were described in fearsome detail by witnesses or survivors, and from those one can form some impression of the voyage as a human experience. 'God send,' one survivor wrote, 'that the reader may be able to imagine some small part of what it was like, for after all there is a great gulf between those who suffer and those who observe suffering from afar.'

To begin with, one may try to imagine life on board at its best when the prospect of death was not immediate. The ships, when they entered the Atlantic, were already stinking with sewage, creeping with vermin and riddled with disease. They contained no provision whatever for human comfort. As September began, it grew ever colder and wetter. Between rain and spray and the reeking damp of the lower decks, no man, either day or night, can ever have had dry clothes. When the Atlantic voyage began, the duke had said, three thousand men were already sick – and that meant seriously sick – from one or another of the usual ship diseases, the scurvy and what the English called fevers and fluxes. At least another thousand were lying badly wounded, unless indeed they had already died of their wounds. Something like one in five were therefore helpless, and needing what little help they could get from the other four – and this at the beginning of six weeks in the north Atlantic with winter coming on, six weeks with nothing to eat except half a pound of hard tack a day. Added to all this was the endless physical strain of sailing ships in very heavy seas, and the endless labour: for the sailors, of working aloft and trying to make repairs, for the soldiers of manning the pumps – work which grew harder as the men grew weaker, until some of the ships ran aground in Spanish harbours because there was nobody left with the strength to drop an anchor or furl a sail, and survivors, home at last, lay down and died.

Reading all their reports, the main impression is that most, if not all the ships, were lost and did not know where they were. Driven here and there by changing storms and squalls, they had no possible means of guessing their longitude, and with skies overcast they seldom had a chance to observe their latitude. Under stress of weather and in the darkness they separated into groups which kept dissolving and then coalescing again as other ships were sighted. Some ships, for week after week, were alone. Whenever the wind allowed them, they did their best to head to the southward, but most of the time the wind was south west and none but the galleons could make any headway homeward.

The next impression is that many of them were slowly breaking up, either because they were already strained by gunfire, or simply because they were too weakly built for equinoctial storms in the north Atlantic. In this, there was a great difference between the galleons on one hand, which were built for gunnery and for the Atlantic, and the urcas and Mediterranean merchant-men on the other, which were built for coastal trade. Of the Portuguese galleons of the duke's own squadron, only one was wrecked – apart from the two that were driven ashore in battle; likewise only one of the ten Spanish galleons of Castile. But of twenty-four urcas, fifteen were wrecked or disappeared, and of the ten Mediterranean ships in the squadron of Levant, only two survived.

The wreckage of one of the Mediterranean ships shows exactly why this happened. She was the *San Juan de la Rosa*, she hit a rock and sank off the Blasket Islands in the extreme south west of

Ireland, and the wreck has been found and excavated. Her Spanish tonnage was 945, and she had started the voyage with twenty-six guns, two hundred and thirty-three soldiers and sixty-four sailors. But her outer planking was only three inches thick, her keelson was ten inches by eight, and her largest frames at their strongest point were twelve inches by eight, with a smaller frame between each pair of big ones. These are extremely light scantlings for a ship of such a size. Yet she was carrying the largest of all cannon balls, fifty-pounders, which required guns that weighed three tons apiece. It is impossible to believe she was strong enough to fire those guns with safety, and if she tried she must have strained her hull and started leaks before she left the Channel. Nor was she strong enough to beat against Atlantic seas. She was built to carry cargo in the Mediterranean, and although the Mediterranean can be rough it never has the huge seas of the north Atlantic in a storm. Moreover, Mediterranean trade was more or less seasonal: and even if a trading ship was caught out in a storm, she would never have to beat against it, but could always run to a harbour to leeward and wait for the wind to change. The *San Juan de la Rosa* was already on the verge of sinking before she entered Blasket Sound; and the reason why she hit a rock was that she had only one anchor left, and dragged it. That was the work of the Calais fireships.

Probably these Mediterranean ships were also over-masted for Atlantic weather and had rigging which was too light, like the hulls. The *San Juan* was the ship that had lost her mainmast off Corunna. The divers in the 1960s found the temporary box, still in place, which had been built around the foot of the mast on that occasion to keep the stone ballast out of the way. Broken rigging, and masts which whipped about as the ships rolled to the Atlantic waves and swell, would have hastened the break-up of those fragile hulls.

The breaking up of a wooden ship was a terrifying experience. It was slow, but once it had started it grew inexorably worse. It would start with the whole hull flexing under the impact of waves, so that adjacent planks were moving minutely against each other. That would cause the caulking to work its way out. There is a phrase for it: a ship is said to spew her oakum. The next stage would be for the trenails to loosen – the wooden pegs that fastened the planks to the frames. Finally, the clenched iron bolts that held the plank ends might also loosen, or else the iron nails that fastened the plank ends to the stern and stem. At that stage, nothing could be done, except man the pumps, day and night, and set human chains with buckets to bail the water out.

These then are the reasons why so many armada ships were wrecked – according to the latest researches, twenty-six in Ireland, two or three in Scotland, one in England and two in France, besides those that disappeared, supposed to have foundered at sea. First, they were lost, and most of them could not sail at all to windward, so that when they suddenly sighted a coast ahead they became embayed and could not get off again. Second, many were breaking up through battle damage and the stress of sea, and saw their only hope of survival in getting ashore, no matter where. And third, the crews of some were dying of hunger and thirst and sought land for food and water; and of those many came to anchor and then were driven ashore because they had left their principal anchors off Calais.

The first group that lagged behind comprised three urcas and one of the biggest Mediterranean ships: the *Gran Grifon*, flagship of the squadron of urcas, the *Castillo Negro*, the *Barca de Amburg*, and the *Trinidad Valencera* of 1100 tons, which came from Venice. They lost the rest of the fleet as soon as the wind turned against them, somewhere north west of Scotland about the 23rd of August. For weeks, they beat against head winds as best they could, and one by one all four of them beat themselves to destruction. On 1st September the *Barca de Amburg* fired a gun in distress: she was sinking. The *Gran Grifon* and *Trinidad* took off her three hundred and fifty men and then watched her go down. On the night of the 3rd, the remaining three lost sight of each other. The *Castillo Negro* was never seen or heard of again: she must have gone down in the open ocean with all her men. A fortnight later the *Trinidad*, also on the point of sinking, ran herself on a reef on the coast of Donegal; most of her men got ashore, to face further tribulation and slaughter. The *Gran Grifon* was alone.

She was one of the ships that carried a careful diarist, so her story is known in detail. Nobody knows who the writer was. He might have been Don Gomez de Medina, commander of the squadron of urcas, who was aboard; but he did not write like a commander, or like a sailor, more like an outsider, which makes one suspect he was a priest.

The *Gran Grifon* was not a big ship – 650 Spanish tons – but she must have been stronger than the others. She came from the ancient German Hanseatic city of Rostock, and the griffin was Rostock's heraldic emblem, so her name suggests she was the pride of the city's fleet. She had lagged astern of the fleet off the Isle of Wight and had been attacked by several English ships, one of which was probably Drake's *Revenge*. Recalde on that occasion had dropped astern to rescue her, but not before she had taken a battering. The damage was not recorded, but she was said to have had seventy casualties, a much higher number than any other ship in the Channel fights. In spite of that, she survived until 7th September before the fate of the others overtook her too: her seams opened up.

It happened very suddenly in a stormy night. By next day, the diarist said some planks were gaping a hand's breadth apart. That is a figure of speech that other people used in other ships; but anyhow, she was in such a bad state that she could only keep afloat with the wind and sea astern. She had to sail whichever way the wind blew her.

They ran north east for three days, and sighted an island that might have been St Kilda off the Outer Hebrides. Then the wind went round and blew them back south west: in three days more, they were well down the coast of Ireland. It changed again, and took them back to the latitude of St Kilda. 'The wind was so strong and the sea so wild, throwing the ship about, that the men were all exhausted and could not keep down the water that came through our gaping seams . . . By God's mercy, in the next two days the weather moderated, so that we could patch up some of the leaks with hides and planks.'

In that break in the weather, they probably had some hope of going back to Rostock. One or two of the Baltic urcas may have succeeded in reaching home, after arguments between the soldiers and sailors – for the soldiers, in command and in the majority, were mostly Spanish, while the sailors and their captains were mainly the original German crews. But the *Gran Grifon* failed. 'We ran until 23rd September, when the wind turned against us again and we decided to go back and try to reach Scotland. Again, the weather became so bad that our poor repairs were all undone, and we had to keep both pumps always going to keep the water down. We decided to make for the first land we saw, even if we had to run the ship aground.'

On the night of the 26th they were back among the Orkney Islands, which they had passed almost six weeks before. This time, they were lost in the islands on a pitch dark night, only relieved by a few gleams of moonlight, or perhaps the aurora borealis, which revealed breakers on rocky shores all around. 'Truly our one thought was that our lives were ended, and each of us reconciled himself to God as well as he could, and prepared for the long journey of death. To force the ship any more would only have ended it and our lives the sooner, so we gave up trying. The poor soldiers too, who had worked incessantly at the pumps and buckets, lost heart and let the water rise . . . At last, when we thought all hope was gone except through God and His holy Mother, who never fail those who call upon them, we sighted an island ahead of us. It was Fair Isle, and we anchored in a sheltered spot we found, this day of our great peril, 27th September 1588.'

Fair Isle is only three miles long. They had rounded the southern tip of it and found a bay called Swartz Geo. Island tradition has always said they tried to beach the ship next morning in the bay, but she was swept away by the tide and wedged herself head first into a narrow cleft in the cliffs which is called Stroms Hellier: the crew, it is said, escaped by climbing along the yard-arms and jumping on to a ledge of the cliff. Indeed the ledge is still there, and so is the ship: her few remains were found by divers in 1970.

This was the most successful of the shipwrecks. All the men got ashore, three hundred of them, and they saved their most valued possessions. They far outnumbered the islanders. Only seventeen crofting families lived there. They were people of Norse origin who had lived under Scottish rule for only a century, and still resented it. Apart from that they knew nothing of world politics or war, and had no particular antipathy for Spaniards, if indeed they had ever heard of the race; when they saw the Spaniards coming across the hills, it is said they thought it was the heavenly host and the Day of Judgement had come. The diarist calls them dirty savages, neither Christian nor altogether heretic.

In the circumstances, both Spaniards and islanders seem to have behaved remarkably well. But the weather continued so bad it was a month before a boat could be sent to the mainland of Shetland to beg for a ship to take the Spaniards off; and it was the middle of November before the ship arrived. By then, the Spaniards had eaten the island bare – the cattle, sheep and ponies (which they paid for) and whatever fish and seabirds they could catch. The islanders are said to have hidden their breeding stock. By then also, fifty of the Spaniards had died, mostly, the diarist said, of hunger, but also, one would suppose, of the shipboard diseases. They were buried at the south end of the island at a spot which is still called the Spainnarts Graves.

In November the survivors were taken to Shetland, and in December to Scotland, where they landed at Anstruther and the local minister wrote that there were thirteen score, 'for the most part young beardless men, silly, trauchled and hungered, to whom kail, porridge and fish were given'. Thence they were shipped to Edinburgh, where they were feted by the Catholic faction which for years had been begging King Philip for troops against the English.

They lived there for no less than eight months, while more and more fellow-refugees came in from other adventures, six hundred in all, of whom four hundred were said to be serviceable and the rest sick, lame and miserable. A year after the battle they were shipped for France and home.

There is a tradition in Shetland that another unknown armada ship was wrecked there, and the tradition is strengthened by a marginal note by Lord Burghley on a list of 29th September 1588, which says two ships were lost in Shetland. Its men, the tradition says, were imprisoned for safety's sake on a very small islet called Kirkholm, not far from the village of Scalloway, the ancient capital. The *Gran Grifon*'s crew were said to have built themselves huts on the mainland of Shetland, as indeed they must, for there was no other shelter for so many men. Those huts have disappeared under the plough. But Kirkholm has never been ploughed, and there one may still see a long row of very small huts, although the islet is much too small for normal habitation. In the middle of them, slightly bigger than the rest, is one with a rounded end like the apse of a church. They might be Spanish relics, or might be even older, the cells of monks from the era of St Columba; or they might have been both, old cells which the Spaniards used. Nobody yet has excavated them.

The much larger number of men who suffered shipwreck in Ireland met a different and more terrible fate in a country whose own affairs were in chronic turbulence. Ireland had already been under English rule for four centuries. Most Irish lived in as primitive a manner as the Fair Islanders, but they still had the remnants of their ancient laws, their artistic tradition and their organization of clans under local chiefs. On this the English perpetually tried to impose their own laws and their own system of government, and the clashes between the two kept the country in a state of sullen discord, some chiefs allied with the rulers, some in hateful opposition, and many more or less at war with each other. The English were only successful because the Irish by temperament were unable to co-operate and organize against them.

In 1588 the country was more peaceful than usual, although it was only the peace of exhaustion. A few years before Queen Elizabeth had put down a rebellion, and the cruelties of the campaign had been followed by famine. It was said 'The lowing of a cow or the voice of a ploughman could scarcely be heard from Cashel to the farthest point of Kerry.' The survivors, unable to walk, crawled out of the woods and glens 'like anatomies of death; they did eat the dead carrion and each other'. Ireland was so weakened that it could be ruled by a force that seems astonishingly small. That year the English had fewer than two thousand regular troops, very badly equipped, in addition to Irish irregulars, scattered in small garrisons over the whole country.

This meagre force was controlled from Dublin by Sir William Fitzwilliam, the Lord Deputy or Governor. Connacht, the western part of the country, was ruled from Galway by Sir Richard Bingham who was known, for his extreme cruelty, as the Flail of Connacht. Fitzwilliam was an elderly man – he was over sixty – and he was in his second term of office: he had been Lord Deputy from 1571 to 1575. Both these men were confident of their ability to rule and had only one thing to fear: that King Philip would organize an invasion of Ireland and Spanish troops would provide the military discipline and leadership the native Irish lacked.

From time to time ever since, in the complicated relations of Irish and English, both sides have blamed the other for what they did to the shipwrecked men in 1588. In fact neither side behaved well by any standards, but to cite their deeds in modern political arguments is absurd. One might say the English had no right to be there at all, except the right of conquest; but after admitting that, the most one should do is try to see the events through everybody's eyes, Irish, English and Spanish, and deduce the factual reasons why they behaved as they did.

Fitzwilliam had been at his post only three weeks when it happened. On 18th September Bingham wrote to him to report the sighting of strange ships: 'Whether they be of the dispersed fleet which are fled from the supposed overthrow in the Narrow Seas, or new forces come from Spain directly, no man is able to advise otherwise than by guess, which doth rather show their coming from Spain.' For some time this guess remained; but wherever the ships came from it appeared to Fitzwilliam and Bingham to be a planned invasion, as well it might have been: invasion of Ireland had often been discussed in Spain, and King Philip had proposed it as the armada's secondary plan. When news began to come in of thousands of Spaniards ashore, the rulers resolved to annihilate them: England and Spain were at war, there was no way of keeping thousands of prisoners, and there seemed a serious danger of a planned rebellion. It was some weeks before it was clear that the Spaniards had come as fugitives, not invaders. Then some junior officers recommended mercy, but Fitzwilliam had had a fright and would not change his orders. He executed the very last of the frightened harmless men and boys he could lay his hands on, and only spared a very few rich men who promised valuable ransom. If a nationalistic defence of the English is needed, it is worth pointing out that Spaniards who landed in England, where people were less afraid of them, were treated as prisoners of war and sent home in safety; and when the Scottish ships taking Spaniards home down the North Sea were forced to shelter in English ports, the queen sent orders to let them go again.

As for the Irish, their behaviour varied, depending somewhat on the characters of their local chiefs. Usually, the first to meet the Spaniards were humble peasants and were overawed; they did nothing, except sell them food, like the Fair Islanders. In one place, Clare Island, the local chief ordered the slaughter of fifty or sixty Spaniards. In another, where the Irish were numerous, they discovered three shiploads of Spaniards struggling through the surf and set upon them, stripped them of all they had, clubbed them if they resisted and left them naked to die in the cold of the autumn nights. But after that orgy the same people treated wandering naked men with rough kindness; and one must say in their defence that they were extremely poor, the Spaniards' clothes and jewels represented unimaginable wealth, and shipwrecks and shipwrecked mariners were often regarded as riches from heaven all over the coasts of Europe. Bishops often helped their fellow-Catholics, but Irishmen in English pay were most ruthless of all: one of these, named Melaghlin McCabb, won a place in history by claiming to have killed eighty Spaniards with an axe. A few of the chiefs risked their lives and lands by refusing to surrender Spaniards to the English, but this was more an act of defiance of the English than an act of charity; and a few also, mainly among the clans of Scottish descent in Ulster, actively helped them to escape.

Although one can thus find excuses, both for the Irish and English, the fact remains that some six thousand Spaniards met the most miserable deaths in Ireland or off its shores.

A grim and typical fate befell the crew of the *Trinidad Valencera*, which had lost the *Gran Grifon* in the dark and, on the point of sinking, ran on a reef in Donegal, just outside the mouth of Lough Foyle. The story was told by Don Alonso de Luzon, the ship's commander, and another officer under English interrogation, and by two soldiers who escaped to Scotland and thence to France. So it is not without prejudice; but the accounts from these different sources confirm each other pretty well.

When the ship crashed on the reef Don Alonso was the first to land, with five others in the only boat, which was broken. They were armed with their rapiers. They met four or five savage people, as he called them, who seemed to make them welcome; but before long another twenty appeared, and succeeded in making off with a bag of a thousand silver coins and a gold embroidered cloak.

Four hundred and fifty men were in the ship, because she had taken an extra hundred off the sinking urca. They hired another boat from the local people, paying handsomely for it, and in the next couple of days boatloads of men were brought off, and some swam ashore. But then the ship broke her back and went to pieces, and a good many left on board were drowned. Perhaps they were the sick and wounded. The savages sold ponies to eat, and some butter. None of the story tellers revealed their thoughts on that desolate beach so far from home, the camp fires, the half-cooked horse meat, the stormy days and bitter winds at night, the bodies of their companions in the surf.

At length Don Alonso heard of a Catholic bishop called Cornelius who lived in a castle not far away (it was near Derry), and he organized his men and marched them there, sending a messenger ahead to ask the bishop for his help and advice. The bishop sent a message back that they could come to the castle and make a show of attacking it, to deceive the English; then it would be surrendered. But in sight of the castle, the Spaniards met a force of cavalry and infantry which carried the banner of the queen.

This force was not nearly so strong as the Spaniards thought it was; in fact, they outnumbered it two to one. Nor was it mostly English. It was commanded by an Irish major named Kelly in English pay, with two English captains, and most of the men were Irish mercenaries. Both the forces halted on either side of a bog.

Then followed two days of skirmishes and parleys, which were shouted across the bog. Kelly asked what they wanted in the queen's dominions. Don Alonso said they were shipwrecked and only wanted a ship to take them home, which they would pay for. Kelly said that was impossible, they must surrender as prisoners of war. He threatened that three thousand troops were coming to cut their throats, but promised if they surrendered to take them safely to Dublin, whence the governor would send them to the queen. For two nights and a day Don Alonso refused; but his men were starving, and at last he accepted the promise, with the added provision that each man should keep the best suit of clothes he had. The Spaniards laid down their arms and Kelly's men took them away; and then attacked the defenceless Spaniards, robbed them of everything they possessed and left them naked. When Don Alonso protested, Kelly said it had been done by the soldiery without his orders; and no doubt it was true they were an undisciplined gang.

Nobody said what language they used for their parleys. Perhaps Don Alonso had an interpreter who struggled with Kelly's dialect, or perhaps they used ecclesiastical Latin. Either way, there was plenty of scope not only for trickery but for real misunderstanding. But nothing could excuse what happened next day. Kelly's men formed a square and put the Spanish officers and priests inside it. Then the rest of them attacked the naked soldiers with arquebuses from one side and cavalry from the other. 'They killed over three hundred with lances and bullets,' the survivors said. 'A hundred and fifty managed to escape across a bog, most of them wounded, and took refuge in the castle, where Bishop Cornelius received them and sent a hundred or so by boat to Scotland.' The worst wounded stayed in the castle, where many died. Those who recovered were sent from one friendly house to another until they reached the care of a chief named Sorley Boy McDonnell of Dunluce Castle on the coast, who had sworn to protect the Catholic faith and all who held it, against the governor, the queen and all England. He sent them in two boats across to Scotland.

Numbers of men are always vague in such reports, but the numbers of these refugees diminished tragically, even after they escaped from Ireland. Over a hundred were said to have escaped. A month later, fifty were reported in Scotland, 'poor and miserable'. Twenty Spaniards and sixteen Italians were counted in Edinburgh. When they arrived in France, at Le Havre on the day after Christmas, there were thirty-two; and they still had a long way to go.

After the massacre, the officers, priests and gentlemen, naked or almost naked, were marched a hundred miles to Drogheda, which was an English headquarters. They had been spared because they were supposed to have a ransom value, but several died on the way of hunger and exhaustion, including Don Alonso's younger brother. The rest, Don Alonso among them, were interrogated in Drogheda by two English officers interpreted by David Gwynne, the man who claimed he had taken command of the galleys. It must have been a final blow to whatever pride the gentlemen retained to find themselves at the mercy of an ex-convict with a fanatical grudge against Spain.

In spite of whatever Kelly promised, only Don Alonso and one other officer survived the interrogation and the ghastly vengeance of Fitzwilliam. Soon after, however, Gwynne got his deserts. He was found to have stolen gold chains and money from the captives and – which was thought to be worse – to have claimed he had evidence that Walsingham was in the pay of Spain; and he was sent back to England with a letter from Fitzwilliam to the queen's council that said he was a lewd and undutiful villain.

It was a tragic but muddled story, full of unanswered questions, like most of the things that happened in Ireland. Was the massacre committed by unruly soldiery, or was it ordered, as the Spaniards believed, by the Irish Earl of Tyrone, who led the queen's forces in Ulster? Did Kelly deliberately lie, to trick Don Alonso into surrender? Or were his words misunderstood, shouted in dialect across a windy bog? Or had he never been told, as a junior officer out with his troop in the wilds, of the governor's vindictive policy? And did Don Alonso give up too easily, or had he already suffered more than he could stand? The only important people who come out of it with unquestionable honour are Bishop Cornelius and Sorley Boy McDonnell, who for whatever reason stood by their faith.

Another even greater tragedy came to its climax in sight of Sorley Boy's castle of Dunluce; but in this one there was nobody to blame.

Most of the ships had got much farther to the westward than the *Trinidad Valencera*. Calderon, flogging against the weather in the vice-flagship of the urcas, wrote: 'From 24th August to 4th September we sailed without knowing where we were, through constant fogs and storms. As this urca could not beat to windward we had to keep well out at sea, and we could not find the main body of the armada until the 4th when we sighted it.' And on the 3rd, the duke managed to get off another letter to the king, written in 58° north, which is the latitude of the isolated speck of Rockall, and very well clear of Ireland. 'On four separate nights we have had heavy gales with strong head winds, thick fog and rain. This has made seventeen ships separate from the rest of us, with Don Alonso de Leyva, Juan Martinez de Recalde, and other important people. By God's mercy, yesterday at noon, the wind shifted to the west, somewhat more in our favour. We have counted ninety-five sail during the day . . . I pray that God in his mercy will grant us fine weather so that the armada may soon be in port; for we are so short of provisions that if, for our sins, we are long delayed, we shall all be irretrievably lost. There are now a great number of sick, and many die. Pray consider the distress of this armada after such a terrible voyage, and the urgent need for prompt measures of relief.'

But later he wrote that the weather grew worse, and only sixty ships were in company. 'These followed me until the 18th, when a severe storm overtook us and we all expected to perish. I was then left with only eleven ships.' The duke himself was very ill by then with the fever and flux, but he did not say so.

It seems the bulk of the armada held together and followed the duke as far as the Rockall Bank, where they were in soundings which may have given them some idea of their position. Then in increasing numbers they began to fall back towards Ireland. It was not entirely because they could not sail to windward: Calderon proved that even an urca could make it, if it was strong enough, by taking advantage of every shift of wind. Most of them headed for Ireland on purpose, in spite of the orders the duke had given, either because their ships were breaking up or because their crews were dying of hunger and thirst and disease. As the duke had observed, the admiral of the fleet, Recalde, and de Leyva, the deputy commander, were among the first to go. Both of them turned up in Ireland, for both reasons: their ships were damaged and their crews were dying.

What happened when they sighted the coast was entirely a matter of luck, and all the odds were against them. Wagenhaer's chart was too small to be any practical use, and the map of Ortelius showed the west coast of Ireland as almost a straight line, running due north and south by the sixteenth-century compass. In particular it scarcely hinted at the existence of the great promontory of Mayo and Connemara, which projects fifty miles to the west of the line it imagined, and culminates in the cliffs of Erris Head and Achill Head. At least ten ships came in to the north of this, entered various parts of Donegal Bay and could not beat out again round the headlands they had not known were there.

De Leyva in the *Rata Encoronada* made his landfall on the promontory itself, between Erris Head and Achill Head, and he ran into Blacksod Bay, which lies to the north of Achill Island. He was in company with another Mediterranean ship, the *Duquesa Santa Ana*. They found their way in so unerringly that one suspects one of them, probably the *Duquesa*, had somebody on board who had been there before. But the bay has two arms. The northern one leads to an anchorage called Elly Bay, which is one of the safest places on the whole of the coast. The *Duquesa* anchored there. But the *Rata* entered the southern arm, which is exposed to the westerly wind, and dropped her one remaining anchor opposite a castle called Doona.

No Spaniard could have imagined such a desolate scene. The ruins of the castle are still there on the low-lying shore, forlorn and remote from the world. In summer they are beautiful, but in September the salt winds howl around and through them and the seas break at their foot. Across the bay are the mountains of Achill Island, but inland behind the castle is the biggest peat-bog in the whole of Ireland, miles and miles of sodden level land, impossible for a stranger to cross. When the anchor went down on 21st September 1588, there was no sign of life in the castle or on the shore. De Leyva sent fifteen men in his only boat to prospect for fresh water and food. The rest saw them pull up the boat on the beach, enter the castle, come out again, hold a discussion and then march off towards the bog. They were never seen again. He waited all day, and then sent swimmers ashore, supported by casks, to retrieve the boat.

The *Rata* was a very crowded ship. She had left Corunna with three hundred and thirty-five soldiers and eight-four sailors, which was rather more than the normal complement. But de Leyva's glamour and popularity had attracted a much larger number of young gentleman adventurers than most. There were about sixty of them, and all of them brought servants: de Leyva himself had thirty-six, several others had a dozen or so, and all had one at least. So there must have been at least six hundred men in a ship of only 800 tons. Gentlemen took much more space than anyone else, and the congestion of the lower classes must have been awful. In spite of it, she had taken a very active part in all the Channel fighting, and was one of the few that stood by the duke all through the Battle of Gravelines. Her hull was probably weakened by the firing of her own guns, and certainly by the English shot and the stress of sea, and she had lost her principal anchors to the fireships. In the tide and wind of the following night she began to drag, and at dawn she grounded on the shelving shore.

There was no immediate danger, but the ship was immovable. The whole company got ashore, even the sick and wounded. They took over the empty castle and fortified themselves, and then according to Spanish custom they burned their ship.

De Leyva may have been a courtier, but he was also a great commander, never at a loss. Two days after the wreck, he set off with all the men to march round the whole of Blacksod Bay to join the *Duquesa Santa Ana*. It is only about twenty-five miles, but even today it would be a difficult walk, along the shores, round all the boggy inlets and across the rivers; and finding a way without a map might have doubled the distance. But they arrived, and de Leyva took command of both companies, about a thousand men, out on the barren peninsula which separates Blacksod Bay from the open sea.

This was exactly the situation the English governors feared: a Spanish force, well armed and well led, in an almost inaccessible part of Ireland. Indeed, if de Leyva had wished it, and had made an alliance with the nearest of the Irish chiefs, he could have taken over the whole north west of the country and held it indefinitely. But the Spaniards' only thought was to get away again and back to Spain as quickly as they could.

So they patched up the *Duquesa*, which was damaged like all the rest, and packed all the men aboard and put to sea again. But they did not think she was fit to sail to Spain, so they went north, to try to reach Scotland.

There is only a single eye-witness account of what happened next, from an Irishman on board who was interrogated by the English. 'By a contrary wind,' he said, 'they were driven back on M'Sweeney ne Doe's country to a place called Lough Erris, where falling to anchor, there fell a great storm, which brake in sunder all their cables and struck them upon ground.' M'Sweeney ne Doe's country was the north west of Donegal, and Lough Erris was a rocky bay which is now called Loughros More. De Leyva, he added, 'before he came to land was hurt in the leg by the capstan of the ship in such sort that he was neither able to go nor ride'. That sounds as if it was the pawl of the capstan that broke, not the cables, and that one of the flailing capstan bars hit de Leyva's leg and probably broke it. But again, he got his huge crew ashore and they fortified themselves, this time on an island in a lough, which had a castle that was already ruined then; and again, they brought ashore their small arms and powder, their clothes and armour and money, and the private treasures that every gentleman carried.

The Elizabethan English sneered at Spanish gentlemen for their foppish manners, but they were tough below the surface, and these terrible circumstances, the double shipwreck, brought out the genuine gallantry in them, and especially in de Leyva. They would not give up. The alarm of the English grew, for the M'Sweeneys were a warlike clan. Bingham wrote to Fitzwilliam that he expected a general revolt and foresaw that the Spanish and Irish together would march on the headquarters at Sligo, which were commanded by his brother. De Leyva had indeed come to terms with the M'Sweeneys, but only for the supply of food. From them he heard there were three other Spanish ships in the harbour of Killybegs, on the north shore of Donegal Bay and twenty miles south across the mountains from Loughros More. He gave the order to march there: he had to be carried in a litter.

There had been three ships: now there was only one, because two had been wrecked beyond repair. The survivor was the galleass *Girona*; her crew was trying to patch her with planks from the others. Her rudder was also broken yet again. Something like sixteen hundred men assembled in the village. The *Girona* could not possibly take them all. But some were Irish, who were willing to stay, and some, the sick and wounded and dying, could not bring themselves to face the sea again and chose to take a chance of life where they were. At last three hundred or so were weeded out, and thirteen hundred were crammed on board the galleass. On 26th October, the repairs were as complete as they could be, and she sailed.

It was a forlorn endeavour, now nearing mid-winter, in a dreadfully overloaded and weakened ship. They set a course again for Scotland, rounding the northern point of Ireland with a south west wind. But off the northern coast the fatal wind, the wind of God which so often had blown against them, went round to the north, increased to a gale, and blew them towards the shore. The ship began to break up again, the rudder was lost, the seas were too high for the oarsmen to use their oars. Close to Dunluce Castle in the middle of the night she hit a reef, and in a few minutes she was smashed to pieces. All the thirteen hundred men except nine were drowned: with them de Leyva himself, the commanders and captains of three other ships, and gentlemen from most of the noblest families of Spain.

In 1968 the site of this disaster was discovered by the Belgian diver Robert Sténuit. The ship has vanished, pounded to tiny fragments by four centuries of storms. He found nothing of wood or of iron, except an anchor and some gunshot: only bronze, gold, silver, lead and copper artefacts had survived, sheltered in the crevices of boulders. He salvaged two bronze guns, some nautical instruments, twelve hundred coins, parts of silver dinner services; and, most poignant of all, many of the jewels, medallions, rings and gold chains that all rich Spaniards wore, which lay where they had fallen from the drowned bodies of de Leyva's gentlemen. A few could be identified, like the ring inscribed with the name of Madame de Champagney and the date 1524: her grandson Don Tomas de Granvela died in the wreck at the age of twenty-two. The most evocative relic of tragedy was a lover's golden ring embossed with a hand and a heart and engraved with the words *No tengo mas que dar te* – 'I have no more to give thee.'

16

Escapes

The most astonishing escape, from shipwreck, the English and the Irish, was that of Captain Francisco de Cuellar, the man who had been sentenced to death in the North Sea and then reprieved by the duke. The letter he wrote to a friend in October 1589 ('to amuse yourself somewhat after dinner,' he said) was the longest of all the personal stories of the armada, and it was first published in English in 1897.

Cuellar was still in the ship of the Judge Advocate, who had been ordered to hang him and refused: she was probably the Mediterranean *Lavia*, vice-flagship of the squadron of Levant. She came in to Donegal Bay, in company with two other ships, and like so many others she found herself embayed: she could not beat out again round Erris Head. All three of them anchored off a sandy beach called Streedagh Strand, a few miles from the town of Sligo where Bingham had one of his headquarters.

Streedagh remains today exactly as it was four hundred years ago, except that it is now a popular place for picnics at summer weekends: a long curve of fine white sand, with dunes and a tidal marsh behind it, and at its eastern end a rock which (like many others in Ireland) is still called Carricknaspania, the Spaniard's rock. It is a shallow shelving shore, and in westerly gales tremendous breakers extend far out to seaward. Such a gale blew up when the ships had been there four days, and they shared the final fate of so many: their remaining anchors could not hold, and they dragged them till they were aground. All three, Cuellar reported, were smashed to bits within an hour. Their men stood very little chance of getting ashore through the surf, and it was said that more than a thousand drowned.

Cuellar, who could not swim, held on till the last possible moment, clinging to the poop of his ship together with the Judge Advocate, while men were swept overboard and sank or clung to pieces of timber or barrels. 'The waves and the storm were very great,' he wrote; 'and on the other hand the land and the shore were full of enemies, who ran about dancing and jumping with delight at our misfortunes; and when any one of our people reached the beach, two hundred savages and other enemies fell on him and stripped him of what he had on until he was left in his naked skin.'

He saw the senior officer of the ships, Don Diego Enriquez, with three other grandees, put off in the ship's boat. It was decked, and they went below and had the hatch battened down on top of them. But so many others jumped aboard it that it overturned and was carried ashore bottom up. He also saw a hatch cover floating, and got on to it with the Judge Advocate. A wave washed the Judge off it and he sank, crying out and calling upon God; he was loaded with crown pieces which he had stitched in his clothes. Another piece of timber crushed Cuellar's legs, and then, without knowing how, he was thrown ashore. 'The enemies on the beach, who were stripping those who had reached it by swimming, did not touch me or approach me, seeing me with my legs and hands and trousers covered with blood. I crawled on, little by little, meeting many Spaniards stripped to the skin, without any kind of clothing whatever, shivering with the cold, which was severe. I stopped for the night in a deserted place, and lay down in great pain on some rushes.'

He was joined by a naked young man who was so dazed he could not speak. Two men, one armed with an axe, came by, and unexpectedly cut some rushes and grass and covered them up; but the young man died in the night.

By the morning the English garrison from Sligo had arrived to take part in the looting. Cuellar dragged himself away, but not far; it hurt him to move and he did not know anywhere he could go. In the next three days, he witnessed all the ingredients of that awful scene. In an abbey he found twelve Spaniards hanging from the rafters. In the woods he met an old woman who lamented over him, and two Irishmen who stripped him of all his remaining clothes, and an Englishman who attacked him with a knife and cut a tendon in his leg, and a very beautiful girl who saved him from the Englishman, but told him she was a Christian and took his reliquary which was all he had left, and hung it round her own neck. 'She was as good a Christian as Mahomet,' he wrote; in the most desperate situation he retained an eye for a pretty girl and, in retrospect at least, a sense of humour.

The English troops, or Irish mercenaries, were capturing any Spaniards who seemed to be rich and killing the rest. The Irish were drunk with plunder, and caring little if they killed a man when they ripped off his clothes. But when they had taken all there was to take, and left a man without a shirt or shoes, they showed signs of relenting, and began to advise the naked wretches which way to go to avoid the English. It was the beautiful girl who rescued Cuellar, sending him some oatcakes and milk and a dressing for his wounds, and finally a boy, perhaps her younger brother, to guide him towards a friendly village. He wrapped himself in bracken and an old bit of matting he found and, bare-foot and lame, he began to stumble away from the shore towards the mountains.

One would not have given him a dog's chance – lost, lamed, naked, winter coming on, surrounded by two sets of warring enemies, thousands of miles from home, and knowing no language but Spanish and the Latin of the Church. But he must have been a friendly and attractive man, and probably handsome; he was resourceful too, and had an indestructible instinct for survival. Also, of course, he had faith in the power of prayer. 'I begged God most earnestly,' he wrote of that first trek towards the village, 'that He would take me to some place where I could die confessed and in His grace.'

It took him about a week to reach the village, and when he found it it was a disappointment. Its chief, Sir Brian O'Rourke, was away somewhere fighting the English, and the place was already overwhelmed by seventy starving Spaniards. However, somebody gave him an old blanket to wear, full of bugs, which he said somewhat improved matters. He wandered off again, and met on the road a priest in lay clothes, who spoke Latin and gave him a share of the food he was carrying. This was the first local man he had been able to talk to, except by signs. The priest directed him to a castle twenty miles away, which he said belonged to a savage gentleman who was a great enemy of the Queen of England. Before he found it, he met a wicked blacksmith, who lured him to his hut in a deserted valley and put him to work. 'He said I must stay there all my life,' Cuellar wrote, 'and he would teach me his trade. I did not know what to answer, and I did not try, in case he put me in the smithy fire. I worked with the bellows for more than a week, so as not to vex him and an accursed old woman he had for a wife.' It seems it did not occur to Cuellar that the blacksmith might have thought he was being kind.

'The whole story is ludicrous,' he wrote to his friend, 'but true, as I am a Christian, so I must go on to the end of it and to give you something to laugh at.'

The priest turned up again and rescued him. The castle was Rossclogher; the last of its ruins still stand on a very small island in Lough Melvin. Its chief was Dartry, of the McClancy clan. Cuellar had not come very far in all those weeks of wandering: as the crow flies, Rossclogher is only a dozen miles from Streedagh. But there he found a kind of sanctuary, and he stayed there three months, living, he said, as a real savage like his Irish hosts. Dartry had already collected ten other Spaniards, and was glad to keep them as trained soldiers to help in his perpetual skirmishes against the English and the rival chiefs. Cuellar always made the best of a bad job. 'The wife of my master,' he wrote, 'was beautiful in the extreme, and showed great kindness. One day we were sitting in the sun with some of her girl friends and relations, and they were asking me about Spain, and in the end someone suggested I should read their palms and tell their fortunes. So, giving thanks to God that things had not gone even worse for me than to play the gipsy among the savages, I began to look at the hands of each and tell them a hundred thousand absurdities, which pleased them so much that no Spaniard was in greater favour with them. By day and night, men and women pestered me to tell their fortunes, and I was always in such a crowd that I had to ask my master's permission to leave his castle. He would not give it me, but he gave orders that nobody should annoy me or give me trouble.'

Cuellar must have been learning the language fast, mostly from sympathetic girls. He naturally formed a very low opinion of the standard of life and civilization in Ireland, where he said there was no justice or right, and everyone did as he pleased. But he summed up the Irish behaviour very fairly. 'The savages liked us,' he said, 'because they knew we had come against the heretics; and without the help of those who looked after us, not one of us would have been left alive. So we felt goodwill towards them, although they had been the first to rob us and strip us to the skin and steal great riches from us in money and jewels.'

He soon had a chance to pay for Dartry's protection. Word came that the governor, Sir William Fitzwilliam himself, was advancing with seventeen hundred men, to round up the remaining Spaniards and punish anyone who had looked after them. Dartry decided he could not hold Rossclogher, and he retreated into the mountains with the whole of his clan. But Cuellar and the rest of the Spaniards said they would stay where they were and defend the castle whoever came against it. They armed themselves with some boatloads of stones, six muskets and six crossbows.

There are not many dates in Cuellar's story – no doubt he had long lost count of days – but Fitzwilliam's march from Dublin to the north and back again began on 4th November and ended the day before Christmas; so it must have been the end of November when he appeared at Rossclogher. Before he came there, he had ridden along the beach at Streedagh. Not long before that, he was told, twelve or thirteen hundred bodies had been lying there; what he saw was 'a great store of the timber of wrecked ships, being in mine opinion (having small skill or judgement therein) more than would have built five of the greatest ships that ever I saw, besides mighty great boats, cables and other cordage answerable thereto, and some masts for bigness and length, as in mine own judgement I never saw any two could make the like.'

Reporting to the queen's council, he wrote little about the clans of the far north west, because all of them disappeared to the mountains when they heard he was coming, and nothing at all about Rossclogher. He failed to take it.

At first sight it seems an unlikely tale that eleven men defended a castle against seventeen hundred. But in fact this castle was impregnable by the kind of force Fitzwilliam had. It was surrounded by deep water; the nearest shore was a bog, and what Dartry probably feared was a siege with too many mouths to feed. The English had cavalry and infantry, but no boats and no artillery; so the attack, to say the least, was half-hearted. They encamped a mile and a half away, and ostentatiously hanged two Spaniards they had already caught. They sent a trumpeter closer, to demand surrender and promise a safe conduct to Spain. Cuellar shouted to him to come closer still, pretending he could not understand what he was saying. But he never came close enough for the Spaniards to use their weapons. The desultory siege went on for seventeen days. Then there was a snowstorm, and the English gave it up and went away.

Dartry came back with his people in a mood of celebration, 'offering us whatever he possessed. He wanted to give me his sister in marriage. I thanked him very much, but asked instead for a guide to take me somewhere to get a boat to Scotland. He did not want to let me go, or any of the other Spaniards; he said the roads were unsafe, but he really wanted to keep us there as his guards. So much friendship did not seem good to me; so I decided secretly with four of the other Spaniards to leave one morning two hours before dawn, so that they could not catch us up on the road.'

Of the few Spaniards still at large in Ireland after Fitzwilliam's journey, most were probably in the same position, treated as honoured guests by warlike chiefs for their military skill, but also effectively in captivity. Eight years later, when invasion of Ireland was being discussed again in Spain, eight armada survivors still serving as soldiers for Irish chiefs petitioned the king for their wages.

Others perhaps found women who pitied them, and settled down content with humble lives as fishermen or herdsmen, or whatever trade they had known before they were soldiers. For centuries, there was a legend or tradition that the swarthy complexion of the western Irish was due to descent from survivors of the armada wrecks. No doubt the survivors were virile, and no doubt there were plenty of Irish girls who found them for a moment attractive and romantic, and a change from the rather boorish manners of their husbands. Reading between the lines of Cuellar's story, it is fairly obvious that he means to imply he did his best. But it seems unlikely there were enough survivors, or that they lasted long enough, to leave a permanent mark on the native race. The same thing is said about Fair Isle and there, where the Spaniards far outnumbered the island girls and stayed a month in peace, it is easier to believe.

Cuellar, however, had no intention of spending the rest of his life with savages. He knew now where he was going, and soon after Christmas he set off on a march that took him twenty days, up to the northern coast and then along it until he came to Sorley Boy's Castle of Dunluce. It was slow going, because one of the wounds in his legs opened up again. Limping along, he could not keep up with the other Spaniards, and they left him; and when he arrived it was a disappointment. The countryside was full of English soldiers, and the chief he was looking for – not Sorley Boy, but another called O'Cahan – had changed sides, joined the English and refused to see him.

Again, he was rescued by women. 'When they saw me alone and ill, they pitied me and took me away to their little huts on the mountain, and kept me there for more than a month in safety, and cured me so that my wound was healed.'

Like any classic of escape Cuellar's story reached a climax in a face-to-face encounter with the enemy. When O'Cahan was away, he ventured back to his village where, inevitably, he knew some very beautiful girls whom he visited from time to time 'for society and conversation'. One afternoon, two English soldiers also came to call. They asked if he was a Spaniard, and he said he was, one of the soldiers of Don Alonzo de Luzon: he had surrendered, but had not been able to leave the district because of his leg. They told him to wait. He would have to go to Dublin, and if he could not walk they would find him a horse. He said he was very willing, at which they were reassured and 'began to make fun with the girls'. He ran for it, and hid in some brambles, and met two boys who were herding cows. They took him up to the mountains again while the hue and cry in the village spread around the country. And at last he also met a bishop who was collecting Spaniards and able to find him a boat to go to Scotland.

That was another disappointment, after a stormy crossing. 'It was said the King of Scotland protected all the Spaniards who reached his kingdom, clothed them and gave them passages to Spain. But it was all untrue, he did no good to anyone, and never gave a dollar in charity. We suffered the greatest privations, and were left for six months as ill-clothed as when we arrived. For the King of Scotland is a nobody; he does not move a step, or eat a mouthful, that is not by order of the Queen of England.'

Another winter was coming before an appeal to Parma brought a ship from Flanders to collect the Spaniards at five ducats a head. Even then Cuellar's adventures were not over. His ship was attacked by the Dutch off Dunkirk and ran aground; and exactly a year from the first of his shipwrecks he suffered another. But his luck still held. Out of two hundred and seventy Spaniards he was one of three who survived, and he crawled ashore again wearing nothing but his shirt.

On 21st September, the day when de Leyva was driven ashore in Blacksod Bay, another ship sank at the far end of Ireland in a drama of storm and tide. This happened among the Blasket Islands at the end of the Dingle peninsula in the far south west, and it was an episode witnessed by many people ashore and afloat.

It began ten days before, when the galleon *San Juan Bautista*, vice-flagship of the squadron of Castile, sighted land where no land should have been. Her commander was Marco de Aramburu, and he kept a thorough narrative log. He had lost the main fleet somewhere off Rockall on 27th August. For three days more he had struggled westward, until he reckoned, from sun sights, soundings and dead reckoning, that he was in 58° north and well clear of Ireland. Then, more or less in accordance with the duke's instructions, he began to work to the southward, making use of every shift of wind. On 9th September, a sun sight put him in 54° north which is the latitude of Achill Head. From his dead reckoning, he still believed he was a hundred and twenty leagues, which is four hundred and twenty miles, to the west of Ireland. But at dawn on the 11th, islands were sighted ahead.

So the *San Juan Bautista* was not among the ships that made for Ireland on purpose, to seek for water or food. She had come there by a combination of errors of navigation. The headlands of Ireland were much farther west than they were shown on the charts, and even a good navigator, after weeks of strong and variable winds and heavy seas, could be hundreds of miles wrong in his longitude.

They beat out to the westward again, all day on the 11th and 12th. That night there was 'a most violent storm from the south, with a very wild sea and pitch darkness because of the heavy clouds'. It blew the ship back again. In the next two days, the wind again at west and north west, they had glimpses of two other ships. At dawn on the 15th, again there were two big islands ahead, and the mainland to starboard. 'The two other ships were beating to seaward, and we recognized them now as the flagship of Juan Martinez de Recalde and a frigate. We turned towards the flagship with the wind on our beam, for we were totally ignorant of this coast, and despaired of escaping it. The admiral cleared one of the islands, and then altered course straight towards a part of the mainland which he saw ahead of him, We followed to windward of him, presuming he had some knowledge of this landfall.'

There is no such record of how or why the admiral, Recalde, had come to be there. There had been no report of him since the north of Scotland, when Calderon, who knew the flagship was badly damaged, believed he saw him set course for the Faeroe Islands. Bingham said Recalde's was one of several ships that sheltered in the mouth of the Shannon; but one of the crew, who was captured and interrogated, said they had not seen any land before. The same man said Recalde was very ill, and had not left his bunk until the day the land was sighted.

But Aramburu was right in thinking the admiral knew this landfall. This was the one and only bit of the Irish coast he had seen before. In 1580 he had commanded a squadron of six Spanish ships which had landed a force of Italian mercenaries in Smerwick Harbour, not half a dozen miles away from the place where he now made land. The landing force had met the usual disaster, but Recalde had had ample time to study the coast.

It would be interesting to know if he had come there for the second time on purpose, because his crew was desperate for water, or if it was purely chance. He could deliberately have found the place, by sailing southward well offshore until he observed the right latitude, 52° north, and then sailing east until soundings warned him he was near. Or did his officer of the watch see land, like Aramburu, with horrified astonishment, and call the admiral from his bunk, and did the admiral say, with equal astonishment or feigned omniscience, 'Ah yes, I know exactly where we are'?

At any rate, he recognized Great Blasket Island, he knew that in the sound between the island and the mainland there was a feasible anchorage, and he knew that approaching from the north in a westerly or south westerly wind, there was one possible but perilous way in, a very narrow and crooked channel between Great Blasket and the lesser islands and reefs to the north of it.

Aramburu saw him turn towards what seemed a solid line of breakers. He followed, trusting, and the frigate followed him. The sound opened up, there were certainly some breathless minutes with white water close on every side, and then they were through and all three of them anchored in calm sea off the beach at the north east end of the island. It would be hard to find a more daring bit of seamanship in all the history of square-rigged ships.

The first thing they did was compare the anchors they had left after Calais. Aramburu had only one cable, and Recalde had lost his main one-and-a-half-ton anchor. Recalde sent Aramburu two cables and a small anchor with a broken stock, and Aramburu sent back a large anchor. Then Recalde sent eight seamen in a boat to the mainland to look for a source of water. They were a curious mixture of men, among them at least one Dutchman, one Basque, one Italian, two Portuguese and a Scotsman who had been taken from a fishing boat off Fair Isle. Perhaps he thought they would stand a better chance than Spaniards; but none of them was ever seen again. Many people had been watching from the cliff-tops, the news had reached the English garrison in the town of Dingle, and the sailors were seized as soon as they came ashore. They were interrogated, again by David Gwynne, and all told stories that reassured the English: that in the *San Juan* 'There are eighty soldiers and twenty of the mariners sick, and they do lie down and die daily, and the rest are very weak, and the Captain very sad and weak . . . There is left in this flagship but twenty-five pipes of wine and very little bread, and no water but what they brought out of Spain, which stinketh marvellously, and the [salt] meat they cannot eat, the drought is so great . . . The admiral's purpose is with the first wind to pass away for Spain.'

Their statements are tragic, when one recollects they were forced to speak under the cruellest compulsion, and as soon as they had told what little they knew they were taken out and hanged.

Next day, Recalde tried again to send a party ashore, fifty well-armed soldiers, but they did not land. 'They found only great rocks,' Aramburu wrote, 'with the sea pounding against them, and saw a hundred armed men marching along the cliffs, carrying a white standard with a red cross.' The English, or their Irish troops, had arrived, and thereafter they watched everything that happened in the sound, quite confident the Spaniards had neither the strength nor spirit to attack. Recalde gave up the attempt on the mainland, but laboriously got a little water in barrels from a spring on the top of a cliff on the island. Aramburu got none, because he had no boat.

On 21st September, when the ships had been there a week, a severe westerly gale blew up. This would seem to have been the same storm that the duke reported, some hundreds of miles to the south west, on the 18th, and the same that drove de Leyva ashore in Blacksod Bay and the three ships at Streedagh Strand – though the latter wreck is dated three days later. Legend has said the armada was wrecked by exceptional storms; but the Spaniards, of course, had never before seen the north Atlantic in September, while it suited the English to believe God had sent special winds to destroy their enemies, for it proved He was on their side. In fact, this storm of the 21st was the only one that caused any comment among the English who lived in the west of Ireland: one called it 'a most extreme wind and cruel storm, the like whereof hath not been seen or heard a long time'. It seems that what the Spaniards had met hitherto, what had strained their hulls and driven them in to the coast, was fairly normal equinoctial weather, and not at all the exceptional heaven-sent wind the legend has said.

In Blasket Sound that morning the gale came out of a blue sky, 'cloudless and with little rain', Aramburu said. To have seemed remarkable at that time of year, one would suppose it was at least force 10, and anyone who has seen the Atlantic seaboard in a wind like that can imagine the Sound: the salt spray from the outer shores blowing in clouds right across the thousand-foot peak of the island and far inland; the rocks and smaller islands hidden beneath the foam; even within the anchorage, the wind whipping the spindrift off the tops of the waves and taking it in swirling columns down to leeward. And the noise, the unchanging roar of the breakers far and near, and the shriek of the wind in the rigging. In such a storm the surface of air and sea is blurred, the senses are numb, and everything one has to do is an effort.

One thing even Recalde did not know, and indeed nobody knew until divers searched the sound in the 1970s, was that the whole of it is very bad holding ground, bare rock with a thin layer of sand on top. Recalde's ship was the first to begin to drag. She drifted down on Aramburu's. Recalde dropped a second anchor, but before it brought her up the ships collided, and Aramburu's stern lantern and mizzen rigging were smashed.

In the midst of it all, to everyone's amazement, another ship was sighted, coming in by the north east entrance. This was the Mediterranean *Santa Maria de la Rosa*, a bigger ship than either of the galleons. She fired a gun as she entered, as if to ask for help, and another farther in. All her sails were torn to bits except the foresail. She let go a single anchor, which Aramburu supposed was all she had.

The tide was rising, setting up north westward through the Sound at two knots, and the ships all lay to the wind with the tide beating against their sterns. The *Santa Maria* held her ground until two o'clock. Then the tide turned, and with the wind and tide together she dragged her anchor, dragged it across Aramburu's cables and took him also down to leeward. 'In an instant we could see she was going down, trying to hoist her foresail. Then she sank with all on board, not a man being saved, a most extraordinary and terrifying sight. We were dragging on her still, to our own perdition. But our Lord had willed us, in case of such a crisis, to fit a new stock to the anchor Juan Martinez had given us. We dropped the anchor, and it brought her head to wind; and we hauled in the other one, and found only the stock with half the shank, for the rest was broken away.'

Nobody had exchanged a word with the *Santa Maria*: she had appeared out of the storm, and two hours later vanished below the sea.

In fact, one man survived the wreck, an Italian boy named Giovanni, who was son of the ship's pilot. He was washed ashore 'naked on a board', and was immediately captured. In the next two days he was interrogated three times over. Dragging her anchor, he said, the ship had hit a rock in the middle of the sound. His father the pilot had cut the anchor cable. This, at the moment when Aramburu saw her try to hoist her only remaining sail, was a seamanlike thing to do: the breaking waves would have shown the rock was isolated, the anchor was holding her on it, and the only hope was to let her drift over it and beach her on the mainland. But a captain of soldiery, understanding nothing, killed the pilot. Some of the gentry tried to escape in the boat, but they could not undo the knot and the sinking ship dragged it down.

But what fascinated the English was the numbers of important people Giovanni said had been on board and were drowned; among them Oquendo and the Prince of Ascoli. Under pressure, he even described what the prince looked like and what he was wearing. He was quite wrong; neither the prince nor Oquendo had ever been on board, nor any of the other distinguished people he mentioned. Perhaps he was mistaken: a humble pilot's son would have had no contact with the grandees he saw around him. Or perhaps he had discerned that this was a thing the English were pleased to hear, and in his terror embroidered the stories more and more, hoping to prolong his life. But of course he failed. When they had extracted all he could tell they hanged him like the rest.

That same day, two other ships came in. One has never been identified with any certainty, and may have been a pinnace. The other was yet another *San Juan Bautista* (which of course means St John the Baptist): three *San Juans* were assembled in the Sound. This one was not a galleon but a West Indies merchantman; not a warship, but a ship at least designed and built for heavy weather and long voyages. But she had lost her mainmast, and her hull was so battered that her captain had given up all hope of reaching Spain. The day after he arrived, when the storm had subsided a bit, he put across in a boat to report to the admiral, and Recalde agreed to take off her crew and scuttle her. His own ship was not in a much better state, and he divided the soldiers between Aramburu and the pinnaces.

With over a hundred extra men to feed, Aramburu was anxious to get away. Recalde gave his permission, and in the morning of the 23rd he abandoned his anchor, which was fouled in the rocks, and set sail with an easterly breeze. He had another nightmarish voyage through the reefs, not now in a gale but in a breeze that kept dropping to calm and leaving him adrift on the tide. He was still at it when night fell, and the wind rose against him. 'In a dark and cloudy night we tried to get out to windward of the reefs, but the tide would not allow us; rather, it was carrying us to our destruction. We turned and tried again by an opening between the islands. The wind was freshening, and the sea was rough, with heavy clouds and violent squalls of rain. It pleased Our Lady, to whom we prayed, that we should find a way. We sailed all that night to the west, and by morning we were eight leagues from the land.'

Recalde waited a few days longer, to try to salvage the guns from the abandoned *Bautista*, which in the circumstances, and in his state of health, showed remarkable determination and energy. What happened to the *Bautista* is unknown. Recalde almost certainly set her on fire. Perhaps her anchor cable burned through and the burning remains of her drifted out of the Sound and sank in deep water.

Recalde and Aramburu both reached home, Aramburu to make a distinguished career at sea, and Recalde to die. Recalde was perhaps the greatest hero of the campaign on either side. At sixty-two he was too old for such an experience, and he had been a sick man before he started. Nevertheless, he was always wise, always loyal to the duke and to the king, and always in the forefront of every battle from Plymouth to Gravelines. Now as a final duty he brought his ship back to Corunna, and the remnants of her crew; and having done it, he lay down resigned to death. He died four days after he reached safety, it was said of shame and horror at the failure. People do not die of those emotions, but perhaps he felt such memories would make old age a burden, and was content to let exhaustion take its course.

17

Home

t the beginning of September, Drake still believed the
armada might come back, if only because it might be forced
back by contrary winds. In all, six weeks went by after it
disappeared to the north before the English in general were sure it
had gone for good, and a service of thanksgiving could be held in
St Paul's Cathedral. There was intense relief, of course, but not
much of the elation a positive victory would have brought.

In those six weeks the navy's senior officers, especially
Howard and Hawkyns, were struggling with the problems of sick
and destitute sailors, and angrily pleading for supplies to feed
them and money to pay them. They were not in a mood for self-
congratulation. Nor was the country especially grateful for what
the navy had done. Howard was criticized for the way he fought
the battle, and for failing to destroy the armada. The only things
that roused them again to indignant boastfulness were the stories
of Spanish victories that Mendoza spread. Howard wrote to the
ambassador in Paris to 'let Mendoza know that her Majesty's
rotten ships dare meet him with his master's sound ships, and in
buffeting with them, though they were three great ships to one of
us, yet we have shortened them some sixteen or seventeen,
whereof there is three of them a-fishing in the bottom of the seas,
God be thanked of all'.

And a broadsheet was published with the title 'A Pack of
Spanish Lies sent abroad into the world, translated out of the
original and now ripp'd up, unfolded, and by just examination
condemned, as containing false, corrupt and detestable wares,
worthy to be damn'd and burnt'. It said with truth that 'with all
their great terrible ostentation they did not, in all their sailing
round about England, so much as sink or take one ship, bark,
pinnace, or cockboat of ours, or even burn so much as one
sheepcote on this land'. With rather less truth, it described the

armada 'beaten and shuffled together from the Lizard to Calais, and from Calais chased out of sight of England and round about Scotland and Ireland'.

But that was journalism. At the time, to people who knew, it did not seem a famous victory, and it was not until long after that history made it one. Perhaps the well-known inscription on the medal the queen had cast came nearest to putting it in its proper light: *Flavit Jehovah et dissipati sunt* – God breathed and they are scattered. Or a verse from the song she wrote, which was sung before her in Fleet Street, probably at Temple Bar, when she made her progress through the city to a second more formal thanksgiving in St Paul's:

> My sowle assend to holy place
> Ascribe him strength and singe him prayse
> for he refrayneth Prynces spyrits
> And hath done wonders in my daies
> he made the wynds and waters rise
> To scatter all myne enemyes

In a battle under sail, the most important factor was always the wind. However brave and skilful the crews might be, however good the plans, a change of wind changed everything. If one believed, as everyone more or less believed in those days, that God observed human actions and decreed the wind, then clearly a battle at sea was directly subject to His will. From Lisbon to Corunna the wind had been against the armada. All the way from Corunna to Calais, excepting one brief storm, it had been exactly what the armada wanted. On the night of the fireships the same wind favoured the English. On the day of Gravelines, the onshore wind made the plight of the Spaniards worse, and when it changed and blew them off the sandbanks it also blew them for ever away from any chance of meeting Parma. Finally, the weather in the north Atlantic wrecked them, and in the legend that weather grew to a heaven-sent storm. So both sides could ascribe the result of the voyage to God's intervention. The English in victory would have been glad to claim superior human strength, but preferred to claim that God was on their side. For the Spaniards, it was easier to admit defeat at the hand of God than a human enemy.

*

Three days after the first service in St Paul's – on 21st September, the fateful day of storm when the *Santa Maria* went down and de Leyva suffered the first of his shipwrecks – the duke in the *San Martin* was in sight of Spain. Not that he probably saw it himself: he was very ill, and like Recalde had spent most of the final weeks in his cabin. By then, his ship was alone. His pilot thought they were off Corunna, but a boat came out and told them it was Santander and they were in danger of drifting ashore – for at this last moment, the weather had fallen calm. The duke fired guns to summon boats to tow the ship in. When they came, he had himself carried to land, and left Diego Flores to see the ship into port. He had been on board that ship four months and a half, and he wanted never to see her or the sea again.

On the 23rd he sent a letter to the king. Eight ships, he said, were already in Santander, five or six under Oquendo had run for Biscay ports, and six or seven more were said to be lying offshore; he hoped to God all the rest would come in one after another. As for himself, he had had the fever and flux for twenty-five days, and it had so weakened him that he could not face the multitude of urgent problems. 'The troubles and miseries we have suffered cannot be described to Your Majesty. They have been worse than have ever been seen in any voyage before. On board some of the ships that are in there has not been a drop of water to drink for a fortnight. On my own ship, a hundred and eighty men have died of sickness, three out of the four pilots succumbed, and all the rest of the people on board are ill, many of typhus and other infectious diseases. All the sixty men of my own household have either died or fallen sick, and only two remain able to serve me. God be praised for all He has ordained.

'Great as the miseries have been, we are now worse off than ever, for the men are all ill and the little biscuit and wine we have left will be finished in a week. We are therefore in a wretched state, and I implore Your Majesty to send some money quickly to buy necessities . . . Everything is in disorder, and must at once be put in competent hands, for I am in no condition to attend to business.'

As usual, however, he undervalued himself: he had already sent a special messenger to Corunna for the supplies he thought had been collected after the armada sailed, and had written to the Archbishop to beg for doctors and hospital staff.

On the same day he sent Bovadillo, the military adviser, to report to the king in the Escorial, taking another letter: 'I pray Your Majesty to give him credence about the expedition, for he was an eye-witness and will tell the truth. He will also bear witness to my own lack of health to serve Your Majesty here, for truly I have come back almost at my last gasp. I am in bed, unable to attend to anything, much as I wish to do so.'

In spite of the duke's trust, no doubt Bovadillo told the king a partisan story, from the army point of view, in which the sea-captains took an ignominious part; and that may have been why Diego Flores, the nautical adviser and Bovadillo's colleague in the flagship, was the only man the king imprisoned. But of course Bovadillo could not tell the whole story, for neither he nor the duke had yet heard of the disasters in Ireland, which indeed were still in progress.

For about three weeks after the duke came in to Santander, ships continued to creep in to the northern ports of Spain. All those which had followed his sailing orders made harbour, though many were on the point of sinking, and all were crammed with dead and dying men. Hope for the rest died slowly: it was a long time before people admitted to themselves no more were ever coming. To this day, nobody knows exactly how many were lost. Two lists were published at the time, probably in October: one of the ships that had returned and one of the ships that were missing. There were sixty-five in each list, sixty-five safe and sixty-five missing. Among the missing were said to be forty-one major ships, three of the galleasses, one galley and twenty pinnaces. But the lists were certainly not exact. Some ships appeared in both; even then, officials were confused because so many ships had the same name. A few listed as missing were in fact safe: the urca *David Chico*, for example, which had been dismasted a few days out of Lisbon, but had almost certainly found her way to port; and the galleass *Zuniga*, which had nearly reached home but then had been blown right back to the Channel and finished up in Le Havre, where she stayed at least a year under repair; and the urca *Falcon Mayor*, which was captured by the English, back at her normal trade, in the following year. Some of the twenty missing pinnaces had been sent off by the duke with messages and had never rejoined the fleet, but were safe in harbour somewhere. Finally, the list included one urca that sank in harbour after it reached Spain, and one galleon, Oquendo's flagship *Santa Ana*, which exploded and sank in Santander, still with a hundred men on board; and historians have never made up their minds whether to count these two as casualties or not.

Professor Garrett Mattingley in the 1950s concluded that the figure of sixty-five missing was far too high: he made it forty-four at most. But he included only ten ships 'lost around Ireland'; and more recent research in Ireland, notably by Mr Niall Fallon, has identified twenty-six ships, including some pinnaces, wrecked on the Irish coast or foundered near it. Adding sixteen to Professor Mattingley's list and subtracting three from the ancient Spanish list would make the numbers almost the same: sixty and sixty-two.

But exact numbers do not matter much. It is enough to say that more than a third, and probably nearly a half, of the one hundred and thirty ships that sailed never returned to Spain. A more important fact is that many, perhaps most, of those that did return were too badly damaged to be repaired, and had to be scrapped. It was not mainly battle damage, but sea damage. A shot-hole could always be repaired by replacing two or three planks and strengthening one or two frames inside them. But if tens of thousands of nails and trenails were loosened by the straining of a hull, nothing could be done for a wooden ship except take it to bits and use the best of its timbers to build another.

And more important still, of course, was the loss of life. This was a far higher proportion than the loss of ships, because even the ships that returned had buried so many men at sea. The duke's flagship, for example, was safe in Santander, but a hundred and eighty of her men were dead of sickness and forty of battle – just about half her company. Probably, of the thirty thousand or so who sailed, twenty thousand died: very roughly, fifteen hundred in battle, six thousand in shipwrecks, a thousand by murder, judicial or otherwise, and the rest from starvation and disease. Even in Spanish ports, they went on dying, weakened by hunger, dehydration and scurvy, a prey to the shipboard diseases, typhus, dysentry, influenza, pneumonia and untold sicknesses nobody could put a name to. Once these diseases had taken hold in a fleet, there was nothing much that anyone could do except wait for men to die or recover. The small Spanish coastal towns were over-whelmed, and probably reluctant to risk the diseases spreading ashore. A man appointed by the king on 10th October to take charge in Santander reported a thousand sick in that harbour alone. 'If they are brought ashore,' he wrote in despair, 'the hospital would be so overcrowded that infection would spread, and if they are left to sleep in the stench and wretchedness of the ships, the fit are bound to fall ill. It is impossible to attend to so many.'

The duke had written to the king as soon as he arrived, begging to be relieved of his command and the new responsibility he was too sick to assume. The king let him go. For all his faults, the king seldom withdrew his trust from a man he had bestowed it on, and he seemed to accept that the duke had done his best. Whether any man could have done better was beside the point, for the task had been impossible: the faults of the armada were technical, not human. The duke, without question, had been loyal, intelligent and brave, and had commanded his diffi-cult officers with discretion and grace. He left Santander on 10th October, to be carried in a horse litter the whole length of Spain to his home at San Lucar. There with his family he recovered; but it was said it was spring before he could ride round his estates again, and it is doubtful whether he ever recovered in spirit.

It was also said that on the journey he and his few remaining servants avoided towns and noble houses for fear of hostility. That is pure surmise; but it is true of course that Spaniards in their grief were looking for someone to blame, and to the ignorant the obvious man was the duke. His reputation in Spain remained low even when the armada was ancient history; Captain Duro, who collected the documents in 1884, still said the duke was weak and foolish, although the papers he published proved exactly the opposite. The senior army men blamed not the duke but Diego Flores, and captains and sailors in general; and everyone in the armada united in passionately blaming Parma.

This was the criticism most widely heard among people who knew the facts: so much so that in December Don Juan de Idiaquez, the king's secretary, had to write to Parma to ask for the real truth of the matter – in particular, at what date his army could have been ready to sail 'if the weather had been favourable and the armada had performed its task'.

Parma replied, he said, freely and frankly. 'Notwithstanding all that has been said, or may be said, by ignorant people, or those who maliciously raise doubts where none should exist . . . the boats might well have begun to get out that night and joined those from Nieuport next day.' He was referring to 8th August, the very day when he had so angrily said the very opposite to Don Jorge Manrique, insisting that the weather made it out of the question. In short, he now wrote a shameless lie. The rest of his letter revealed the things that were being said against him. 'There was no need to supply water to the boats, whatever some people may say, because no cooking was needed for such a short passage and there was plenty of beer to drink. Nor was there any need, as others imagine, to waste time in fitting artillery in the warships, as we counted on the support of the armada.' He admitted, however, that there were only twenty rafts for the cavalry, not enough to carry them all. Rafts to take horses across the Channel: these had not been mentioned in earlier papers, and they added another degree of fantasy to the preparations he claimed to have made.

If one still looks for human blame, Parma deserved it more than anyone: anyone, that is, except the king. Nobody in writing blamed the king: the king was above the blame of ordinary mortals. But they must have known in their own hearts, the senior men at least, that the primary fault was the king's. The duke in particular must have reflected, on that long and painful journey back to San Lucar, that the king had set him a task not only distasteful but impossible, lethal and disgraceful; that the king had been mistaken time and again in making his secret plans; that he had listened to nobody's advice; that he had given his orders in such a way that his commanders could never meet to discuss them; above all that he had wrongly believed his own aims were the aims of God, and that God would solve any problems with timely miracles.

Of the private thoughts and feelings of the king himself, as the terrible story reached him bit by bit from Ireland and the Spanish ports, nobody really knows anything. The very few people who saw him in those weeks agreed he received the growing story of disaster calmly, impassively, without any visible emotion, so that they wondered if he understood how huge the disaster had been. A surprising number of reports, addressed to the queen's council by the rulers of Ireland, found their way to the heaps of papers on his desk and were filed away in the royal archives with his trivial comments scribbled in their margins: even the tragic confession of the boy who survived the wreck in Blasket Sound, with its lists of distinguished people he believed to have drowned. 'He is wrong about many of these,' the king wrote on it. 'Perhaps he is wrong about the rest.' Did he feel, one wonders, the slightest twinge of pity for the boy alone in that alien land who had faced the hangman in his service?

One witness says he was more distressed by the death of de Leyva than anything else. Another attributes to him the comment, 'I sent them to fight against men, not storms.' That does not sound like him: he was not given to aphorisms. Nor did it make much sense, since they had signally failed in the fight against men. But it may give a clue to what was in his mind. Since he believed that the winds were sent by God, it could only have meant, if he really said it, that he accepted his servants had done their duty, but that God had decreed the armada should fail. Why God had so decided was not for him to ask.

The evidence, such as it is, all suggests he was struggling with this theological problem, which was beyond the power of brains far better than his. He had commended the armada to God and ordered it to sail in His name. To have expressed human pity, sorrow, remorse or anger at the outcome, or even to allow himself to feel them for a moment, would have been to question the wisdom of God.

His only public utterance was to countermand the prayers for victory which, on his orders, every church in Spain had been offering since the armada began. It is a document so confused that one can scarcely trace any logical thought in it. The prayers, he wrote, could end now that the ships had come home, 'some rather badly damaged by the long and troublesome voyage'. Instead, every church was to celebrate a mass of thanksgiving. 'It is our duty to thank God for all it has pleased Him to do. I have therefore returned Him thanks for the mercy He has shown us; for the violent storm that attacked the fleet might well have been expected to have a worse result. I attribute this favour to the devout and incessant prayers that have been offered. Although I cannot avoid feeling some regret for the damage to the ships and the sufferings of the people on board them [he put it in that order] I consider the prayers have done their work for the present and may now cease.'

He then ordered all clergy and other devout persons to continue, in their private prayers, to commend all his actions to God, 'so that it may please His Divine Majesty to direct them to that issue which will be most to His service, the exaltation of His church and the good and preservation of Christendom, which is my only object and desire'.

Among those actions was the planning of a new armada to do what the first had failed to do. Indeed, he despatched three more before he died in 1598. The first of them, for an invasion of Ireland, sailed at his insistence and against the advice of his admirals at the worst possible time of year, November 1596. It was wrecked by a storm before it left Spanish waters. The next, in 1597, was to land Spanish troops at Falmouth and occupy Cornwall. It came nearest of all to success, but was beaten back by a northerly gale a few miles short of its landing. The third, only six months before the death of the king, did one thing the great armada of 1588 might have done: it sailed up-Channel out of sight of the English coast, and so reached Calais undetected. But it was not intended for an invasion of England, only to reinforce the Spanish army, which still lay between France and the Netherlands.

There is no evidence that it ever entered the muddled mind of King Philip that he might be wrong in his interpretation of God's will, or that he changed his least opinion, or felt the slightest remorse at having sent twenty thousand men each to his private agony. He shut himself if anything more securely into the comforting seclusion of his rooms in the Escorial, seeing nobody, tottering from his bed to his desk and back to his bed again, poring over his papers, gazing through a window which overlooked the altar of his church, and spending long hours on his painful knees communing with his God. His creed had left no place for pity.

Sources

The principal source of Spanish letters and documents is *La Armada Invencible* by Cesáreo Fernandez Duro, Madrid 1885. This has never been translated in full, but a selection of the documents is in the *Calendar of State Papers Relating to English Affairs*, Vol. IV, edited by Martin A. S. Hume, 1899. Translations of a few other narratives, especially of the Irish adventures, are scattered around in journals, and Captain Cuellar's letter was first published in English in 1897. Eleven more of King Philip's letters were discovered at Greenwich by George Naish, and published with a translation from the Italian of Ubaldino's second narrative by the Navy Records Society in 1952. King Philip's correspondence with Parma may be found in the *History of the Netherlands* by J. L. Motley, 1860. Whether I have used the original Spanish or the old translations, I have put all the Spanish documents into modern English. There is no particular virtue in nineteenth-century English, or in using language that is falsely archaic.

But I have left the English documents in their original language, and followed the usual practice of modernizing the spelling. The main source of these is J. K. Laughton, *State Papers Relating to the Defeat of the Spanish Armada*, also published by the Navy Records Society in 1894. The first tactical analysis of the battles, with which I have dared to disagree, is in *Drake and the Tudor Navy* by Sir Julian Corbett, 1898. The most authoritative work on armada guns is by Michael Lewis, first published in the Mariner's Mirror in 1942-3.

The original documents about the Irish part of the story are summarized in the *Calendar of State Papers Relating to Ireland*, Vol. IV, edited by H. C. Hamilton, 1885. A good modern account is *The Armada in Ireland* by Niall Fallon, 1978. The searches for Spanish wrecks are described in *Treasures of the Armada* by Robert Sténuit, 1972, and *Full Fathom Five* by Colin Martin, 1975. The latter has an appendix by Sidney Wignall on the armada shot and guns.

Of course there are dozens of accounts of the armada written from the English point of view. I think Garrett Mattingley's *The Defeat of the Spanish Armada*, 1959, is outstanding, especially for the way it puts the armada episode in its historical setting.

I am very grateful to Gillian Temple for the difficult job of translating many sixteenth-century documents which, so far as I know, have never been put into English before; to Professors Christopher Lloyd and Geoffrey Best for casting scholarly eyes on my manuscript; to the Hydrographer of the Navy for information on the state of the tides in the Channel in August 1588; to the National Maritime Museum for their advice, and to the London Library for their incomparable service.

Index